Limited Classical Reprint Library

THE PROPHET JONAH.

BY THE REV.

SAMUEL CLIFT BURN,

AUTHOR OF "A HUMBLE COMPANION TO THE PILGRIM'S PROGRESS."

SECOND THOUSAND.

Foreword by
Dr. Cyril J. Barber

Klock & Klock Christian Publishers, Inc.
2527 GIRARD AVE. N.
MINNEAPOLIS, MINNESOTA 55411

Originally published by
Hodder and Stoughton,
London, 1880

ISBN: 0-86524-071-X

Printed by Klock & Klock in the U.S.A.
1981 Reprint

FOREWORD

Plautus, the Roman dramatist of the second century B.C., on one occasion passed the self-disclosing remark, "My tunic is nearer to me than my mantle."

This attitude is found often even in the best of people and may easily be applied to Jonah upon whom the mantle of prophet had fallen for, as is well known, when he was commissioned by God to go to Nineveh, his pride of race caused him instead to leave Samaria for Tarshish.

God's subsequent dealings with His disobedient prophet have been preserved for us in Jonah's *memoirs*–a work which has been subjected to analysis as well as commentary ever since its first appearance.

But what relevance does this ancient record have for you and me? What can we possibly hope to gain by reviewing events which transpired more than two-and-a-half millennia ago?

Of the many expository studies on the Book of Jonah which have been written in the post-Reformation era, few have come down to us. One of the most satisfactory was provided a century ago by Samuel Clift Burn, pastor of the South Parade Chapel, Tenby, England. With insight into the prophet's motivation as well as understanding of his spiritual odyssey, Burn has laid bare the essence of Jonah's frustrations in eighteen expository addresses. In these discourses he combines historical data with personal realism, and biblical symbolism with theological accuracy. He is never tedious, and readers will find each exposition to be timely and relevant, uplifting and edifying

In addition, Burn does not shy away from difficulties in interpretation or fine grammatical distinctions, but incorporates these into each study without being either dry or pedantic. The result is a masterly blend of thoroughness and practicality.

For the preacher, therefore, as well as the informed lay person, Burn's delightful work on *The Prophet Jonah* promises personal satisfaction as well as spiritual edification.

Cyril J. Barber, D.Lit.
Author, *The Minister's Library*

PREFACE.

THE Author has been induced to issue these Lectures in their present form by a regard to the following circumstances.

He has been repeatedly, and somewhat urgently, requested to publish them by certain of those who heard him deliver them on consecutive Sunday evenings from the pulpit of South Parade Chapel during the former part of the present year. Naturally glad to comply with such a request, his pleasure will be much enhanced by any intelligence which may hereafter intimate that some of his readers are as deeply interested in the Lectures as all his hearers appear to have been.

The Author's congregation having undertaken to erect a more commodious place of worship than the one in which he now officiates, he conceived the idea of aiding the Building Fund by the sale of this work, and has been enabled by the kindness of friends to place the first thousand copies at the disposal of the Building Committee.

He would, however, have shrunk from its publication, had he not been very greatly encouraged by the reception accorded to a previous work. The generously appreciative terms in which his *Humble*

Companion to the Pilgrim's Progress was noticed by the reviewers, and by many of its readers who privately communicated to him the impression it had produced on their minds, enables him to entertain some little hope that his present venture will not expose him to the charge of outrageous and insufferable presumption.

It appears to him, moreover, that there are not even yet too many printed expositions of the Book of Jonah. The most fascinating work of the kind with which he is acquainted is that of the late lamented Dr. Raleigh. The most erudite and exegetically helpful is that of Dr. Pusey; to which, indeed, the former is manifestly much indebted. Dean Smith has some valuable remarks on the subject in his *Prophecy a Preparation for Christ*, and Dr. Smith's *Dictionary of the Bible* contains more than one article upon it which cannot be overlooked. Henry Melvill's Sermon, *The Greater than Jonas*, Dr. Peddie's *Practical Exposition of the Book of Jonah*, and Dr. Kitto's remarks on the subject in his *Daily Bible Illustrations*, are the only other works upon it which the Author remembers to have seen. King on *Jonah*, Fairbairn's *Jonah*, Blackburn's *Nineveh, its Rise and Fall*, and Tweedie's *Man by Nature and Grace; or, Lessons from the Book of Jonah*, are doubtless very useful to those who have access to them.

TENBY, *October*, 1880.

CONTENTS.

PAGE

I.
MEMORABILIA 1

II.
FULFILLED PROPHECY 18

III.
THE WANDERING DOVE 36

IV.
THE VOYAGE 51

V.
CATECHISED BY THE CREW 70

VI.
OVERBOARD 84

VII.
CONVERSION OF THE CREW 100

VIII.
IN THE SEA 117

IX.
THE GREAT FISH 133

X.
THE PREACHING OF JONAH IN NINEVEH 150

PAGE

XI.

REPENTANCE, HUMAN AND DIVINE 167

XII.

THE PROPHET'S DISPLEASURE 182

XIII.

THE BOOTH 198

XIV.

THE GOURD 215

XV.

THE WORM 229

XVI.

THE EAST WIND 247

XVII.

JEHOVAH'S APPEAL TO JONAH 264

XVIII.

CHRIST'S REFERENCE TO JONAH 285

I.

MEMORABILIA.

"He restored the coast of Israel from the entering of Hamath unto the sea of the plain, according to the word of the Lord God of Israel, which He spake by the hand of His servant Jonah, the son of Amittai, the prophet, which was of Gath-hepher."—2 KINGS xiv. 25.

SUCH is the earliest mention of the prophet Jonah. The book which bears his name was indeed written long before this second book of Kings, but this latter book nevertheless records many things which took place before Jonah was sent to Nineveh. The prediction to which the text refers was uttered by the prophet before he went thither. Chronologists have not as yet demonstrated this, but it is implied in the language of our Divine Lord respecting "the sign of the prophet Jonas." The resurrection of Christ, like that of Jonah, was after He had exercised His ministry in Israel, and before He addressed Himself to the Gentiles. It is proper, therefore, that we bestow attention upon this passage before we proceed to the book of Jonah itself. We have before us the testimony of the inspired penman who compiled this book of Kings. Some think the compiler was Jeremiah, and others Ezra; but in either case, or in any, his chronicle was cited by our Lord as an

authentic and canonical scripture.[1] The particular
prediction mentioned in the text will engage our
attention in the next lecture. At present we shall
find it sufficient to consider the particulars here furnished respecting the name, the parentage, the place
of residence, the office, and the personal character of
this remarkable man.

I.

His name was Jonah, and Jonah was the Hebrew
word for dove. It was doubtless an appropriate
name, but its propriety as an appellation for the
illustrious person who bore it may not be at once
apparent. You have read the book of Jonah, and
are probably of opinion that there was nothing par-
ticularly gentle and loving about the man it describes.
He was much too harsh and stern to be considered
dove-like. But a man may be dove-like in some
respects though not in others, and thus it was with
Jonah.

A dove is a messenger, and doves have been
employed as messengers from very early times in
the service of men. Thus the patriarch Noah sent
forth a dove from the ark when no other messenger
could have done his errand. The greatest of all
God's messengers was that " Messenger of the
Covenant" on Whom was seen " the Spirit of God
descending like a dove," while a Voice from heaven
proclaimed, "This is My beloved Son, in Whom I
am well pleased ! " Jonah was a type of Christ,
inasmuch as he was a messenger in God's service,
and inspired by that Holy Spirit of God Who was

[1] Luke iv. 27.

more fully present in Christ Himself. The Spirit of
the Divine Messenger was in Jonah, and therefore
he was appropriately named.

But this remark is no more applicable to him than
to many another servant of the Most High. It is
applicable to all the prophets, and also to the Apostles.
True; but a dove is not only a messenger: it is a
mourner. At all events, it has a mournful voice.
"I did mourn as a dove," said King Hezekiah; and
the prophet Isaiah, speaking on behalf of the penitent
Jews, exclaimed, "We . . . mourn sore like doves."
There is a prediction relative to the doom of Nineveh,
which was uttered by a later prophet than Jonah, and
in which the sentence occurs, "Huzzab shall be led
away captive, she shall be brought up, and her maids
shall lead her as with the voice of doves, tabering
upon their breasts."[1] Maidens in attendance upon a
captive mistress, and moaning at her misfortunes,
are described as employing the voice of doves. Now,
the voice of Jonah was a mournful voice. Not only
as a Divine messenger was he a type of Christ, but
as a mournful messenger. Our Lord was a Man of
Sorrows and acquainted with grief; and Jonah is
chiefly remarkable for the mournful mission to Nineveh which God entrusted to him, and the distress he
experienced in connection with it. It was a dove-
like voice which proclaimed in the great Gentile city,
"Yet forty days, and Nineveh shall be overthrown!"
It was a very dove-like voice which afterwards found
its way into the ear of the Most High: "I pray
Thee, O Lord, was not this my saying when I was
yet in my country? Therefore I fled before Thee

[1] Isa. xxxviii. 14, and lix. 11; Nah. ii. 7.

unto Tarshish : for I knew that Thou art a gracious
God, and merciful, slow to anger, and of great kindness, and repentest Thee of the evil.   Therefore
now, O Lord, take, I beseech Thee, my life from me;
for it is better for me to die than to live."

Jonah, then, was a mournful messenger of the
Most High, and as such appropriately named.   There
is some reason to believe that his name was cherished
with affectionate reverence by the descendants of
those Ninevites who were brought to repentance and
saved from destruction by that most mournful proclamation which he made in their city.   "It is
supposed that the dove was placed upon the standards
of the Assyrians and Babylonians in honour of Semi-
ramis," says a modern writer; but may we not
suppose that it was placed on them in commemora-
tion of Jonah's mission to Nineveh and its happy
consequences?   It is known that doves were sacred
in the estimation of those who dwelt in Assyria and
thereabouts long after the time of Jonah—sacred to
Venus, perhaps; but who shall say that the sanctity
attaching to them did not originate in the mission of
the prophet to the great city ? [1]

There may be one of God's Jonahs present; not,
indeed, an inspired messenger of the Almighty, but
one to whom some mournful mission in His service
has been manifestly entrusted, and who experiences
much consequent distress.   Be of good cheer, my

[1] See Article " Dove " in Smith's " Dictionary of the Bible."   The
idea of the writer of the article that the word יָנָה , *yanah*, in Jer. xxv.
38, may be translated " dove," rather than " oppressor," and is an
allusion to the dove upon the Assyrian standards, must be dismissed,
as this word occurs in the Pentateuch and other parts of Scripture,
where no such allusion can be supposed.

brother! "They that sow in tears shall reap in joy. He that goeth forth and weepeth, bearing precious seed, shall doubtless come again with rejoicing, bringing his sheaves with him." You and I are exhorted to live in the constant contemplation of One "greater than Jonah," who, for the joy that was set before Him, endured the cross, despising the shame."

II.

We learn something from the text respecting the parentage of Jonah. He was the son of Amittai. The Scriptures furnish us with no information respecting the prophet's mother, and record no more about his father than his name.

It appears that the Jews were not content with the scanty information thus supplied with regard to Jonah's parentage, and that a tradition grew up among them in connection with the subject to which it may be as well to refer. In 1 Kings xviith we have the story of that widow of Zarephath in whose house Elijah found shelter and sustenance during the prolonged drought which afflicted Israel and the adjacent countries in his time. In the next chapter we have an account of Obadiah, who, though occupying high office in the service of Ahab, remained faithful to the Lord God of Israel, and befriended His persecuted servants at great risk and expense to himself. In 2 Kings ixth we read of a youthful prophet who was commissioned by Elisha to anoint Jehu king over Israel, and actually did so. Now, the tradition to which I refer connects these persons with each other in a remarkable manner. It says that the widow of

Zarephath became the wife of Obadiah, and that this youthful prophet was their son. It says, moreover, that Obadiah was surnamed Amittai, a word which expresses the idea of truth or fidelity, as an acknowledgment of his faithfulness in the service of Jehovah during the persecution of His prophets and worshippers. It says, finally, that their son was that Jonah who was afterwards sent to Nineveh. In a future lecture we shall have occasion to remark the untrustworthiness of such traditions as in strong contrast with the reliable testimony of Scripture history. At present it may suffice to say that this particular tradition is supported by no particle of evidence, and has no serious claim upon our attention. All that we know of Jonah's parentage is that he was the son of Amittai.[1]

But this is worth knowing, for it shows us that the prophet mentioned in the text was really the same person as the prophet sent to Nineveh. There might easily have been two men named Jonah; but it is not to be supposed, in the absence of any evidence to that effect, that there were two men who were both named Jonah, both sons of Amittai, and both prophets of Jehovah. Two of our Lord's apostles were named Simon, and two were named Judas, and two James; but the one Simon was the son of Jonas, and the other was Simon the Zealot; the one Judas was the son of Alphæus, and the other was Judas Iscariot; the one James was the son of Zebedee, and the other of Alphæus. There was, however, only one Jonah, and he was the son of Amittai.

[1] The earliest account of this tradition is, I believe, supplied by Jerome.

The case stands thus : the man of whom I speak was the illustrious son of an obscure father. A man is not bound to remain on the same level as that which his father occupied before him. He may easily descend from it, but he may also rise above it. There are young people who are greatly encouraged to live noble and Christian lives by the circumstance that their parents were illustrious among the servants of God, and that their praise is in all the Churches of the locality in which they lived. On the other hand, there are young people who have no such encouragement. Neither father nor mother, neither parent nor grandparent, has left them the legacy of a good example. If remoter ancestors were servants of Christ, their fame as such has not survived them. But let not such young people be discouraged. Children may do better than their parents as surely as they may do worse, and as surely as Jonah was more distinguished in God's service than Amittai.

There are Christian parents who may entertain this idea with advantage. They have themselves done less than they might have done in the service of God, and look back on their defective procedure with intense regret. If they could only begin life again, ah what a noble life they would live! That is, however, impossible; but have they not children? and is it impossible to train them for a nobler career in connection with the Church of Christ than their own has been? I venture to think that many an Amittai has been prompted by his penitent conscious- ness of personal failure to train a Jonah for the accomplishment of what he himself has left undone.

III.

Another thing we learn from the text is the place of Jonah's residence. He was of Gath-hepher. He may have been born there, but this is not certain; and it is still less certain that he was buried there, although his tomb, or what was shown as such, long remained in its neighbourhood. All that we know is that Jonah belonged to Gath-hepher, as we say. It was his place of residence, and this is a very interesting circumstance because Gath-hepher was in Galilee.

At the close of John viith is an account of the manner in which the Pharisees spoke of Christ. One of themselves ventured to speak a word on His behalf. Nicodemus, with a candour which appears to have been characteristic of the man, demanded, "Doth our law judge any man before it hear him and know what he doeth? They answered and said unto him, Art thou also of Galilee? Search and look, for out of Galilee ariseth no prophet." How could these men say this? Did they mean that their Scriptures contained no history of any prophet who had arisen out of Galilee, or that they contained no prediction of any prophet that should so arise?

It is possible that the latter was their meaning. In that case they must have overlooked, purposely or otherwise, certain Old Testament predictions to which the evangelist Matthew refers. "He came and dwelt in a city called Nazareth : that it might be fulfilled which was spoken by the prophets, He shall be called a Nazarene." "And leaving Nazareth, He came and dwelt in Capernaum, which is upon the sea-coast, in the borders of Zabulon and Nephthalim :

that it might be fulfilled which was spoken by Esaias
the prophet, saying, The land of Zabulon and the
land of Nephthalim, by the way of the sea, beyond
Jordan, Galilee of the Gentiles; the people which
sat in darkness saw great light; and to them which
sat in the region and shadow of death light is sprung
up."[1] If, then, the Pharisees meant to say that there
was no prediction in the Old Testament that any
prophet should arise out of Galilee, it is obvious that
their testimony on this subject was in exact opposition
to that of the evangelist, and that they were more
ignorant than he (unless their ignorance was affected)
of the prophetic portions of Holy Writ.

But it is probable that these men intended rather
to affirm that no prophet had arisen out of Galilee.[2]
They spoke in heat and haste, no doubt, but they
spoke with a characteristic perversity. They must
have known that Jonah was of Gath-hepher, and
could yet assert that no prophet had arisen out of
Galilee. We know that they searched the Scriptures,
for Christ Himself admitted that;[3] but we know also
that they missed or misunderstood much that is contained in them. The explanation of this is furnished
by the Apostle Paul when he says that their minds
were blinded. In other words, they were prejudiced
readers of the Scriptures, finding in them only what
they wanted to find, and failing to find, or failing

---

[1] The former passage is quoted from some Scripture which has not
come down to us, but it must have been accessible to Matthew's
contemporaries. The latter is from Isa. ix. 1, 2.

[2] Some MSS. have ἐγήγερται, *hath arisen.*

[3] John v. 39, where we should read, " Ye search the Scriptures,"
etc.

to remember, what was distasteful to themselves. Hence it was that, when Christ appeared, they could not, or would not, see that He answered to the prophetic accounts of Him which were in their possession, and so rejected Him to their ruin.

There are many among ourselves who resemble the Pharisees in this respect more closely than they suspect. There are things in the Bible which are plain enough to other people, but are not plain to them. They pick out certain portions of the sacred volume which can be plausibly interpreted as in favour of their peculiar tenets when separated from the rest, and then boast of their scriptural creed on the ground that they can give chapter and verse for the articles of which it is composed. On the other hand, they cannot or will not see many things which are revealed in the Word of God, and are not impressed by them even when they are pointed out. Do they not, then, observe good faith in connection with this matter? To a certain extent they may do so. They are not perhaps conscious of any want of good faith, and yet it is certain that they are themselves to blame in large measure for the prejudice which prevents them from perceiving more clearly and fully what God says to them in the Scriptures of truth. May we not be numbered with such persons, but rather with those who have a right to say, "We all, with open face, beholding as in a glass the glory of the Lord, are changed into the same image from glory to glory, as by the Spirit of the Lord."

IV.

Coming back to the text, we observe that mention is made in it of the office which Jonah sustained. He is spoken of as "the Prophet."[1] He was not merely a prophet, but the prophet of Jehovah for the time being. It must be remembered that Israel was a Theocracy; and that, although God had allowed His people to have an earthly king, Saul and David and Solomon, the two Jeroboams, and the other occupants of the earthly throne, were rather viceroys than sovereigns. It was their business to execute the law which God had given to His chosen people for their guidance under ordinary circumstances, and also those particular directions which He issued from time to time as applicable to circumstances of another kind. Such particular directions were more frequently than not conveyed through the medium of some prophet, and there was usually some one person who had a certain primacy among the prophets which rendered him a very important personage in all affairs of state as well as of religion. Such a primacy pertained to Samuel, to Nathan, to Abijah, to Elijah and Elisha, and to Jonah. Samuel was in one sense a subject of Saul, and Nathan of David, and Abijah of the first Jeroboam, and Elijah of Ahab; but when the "burden"[2] of the Lord was upon them, the prophets were superior to the princes. The prophets

---

[1] הַנָּבִיא. The prophet was one whose spirit was apt to be stirred within him by a Divine inspiration until it bubbled up and boiled over in the speech or action he was commissioned to employ.

[2] מַשָּׂא, *massa*, a sentence, decree, decision, or burden, *i.e.*, load of responsibility.

I have just named actually sentenced the several princes named in connection with them to the various penalties they had incurred by their misuse of power and disobedience to the Divine King. Nor was the jurisdiction of the prophet limited to the land or people of Israel. The later prophets, at all events, were, in some instances, commissioned to address themselves to Gentiles as well as Jews in the exercise of their peculiar functions. It was to the prophet Jeremiah that Jehovah said, "See, I have this day set thee over the nations and over the kingdoms, to root out, and to pull down, and to destroy, and to throw down, to build and to plant." The first great prophet who was commissioned to address himself to the Gentiles, as he and his predecessors had long been used to address themselves to their own country-men, was the one mentioned in the text. Moses, indeed, had long before confronted Pharaoh in the manner described by himself; but the ministry of Moses must be regarded as an earnest of that which was afterwards exercised by the entire prophetic order.

Consider, then, the dignity of the office sustained by Jonah. The prophet of Jehovah, he was in direct communication with the Most High, and it was his prerogative to speak with an authority to princes and peoples which none might gainsay. He was liable to impulses which might in some instances be unwel-come to himself, but which he was unable successfully to resist, and which were of such a character as to ensure his own moral elevation and shape his official procedure in conformity with his high vocation. As to any opposition he might encounter from kings or

mobs, he might well be indifferent to it. The word
of the Lord entrusted to him was both true and pertinent, and was certain to be fulfilled in due time.
If he perished at the hands of those who resented
its publication, so much the worse for them, and so
much the better for himself. There was an ordinance
of the Most High in force from age to age, which
men could only violate at their peril,—" Touch not
Mine anointed, and do My prophets no harm!"
Talk about " the divinity which doth hedge a king"!
The greatest of the kings who reigned in Jonah's
time was the king of Nineveh, but in Nineveh itself
the prophet was more reverenced than he. The
very name of that Assyrian potentate is lost, and
may never be recovered; but the name of Jonah the
Prophet shall be preserved to all generations.

V.

It remains to say a few words respecting the personal character of this great man. He is described
in the text as the " servant "[1] of the Lord God of
Israel; and this expression might be regarded, if it
occurred by itself, as descriptive either of his office
or his personal character. It does not occur by
itself, however, and we have already had occasion to
notice the official appellation applied to him. In
reference to his office he is described as " the prophet;" in reference to his personal character he is
described as the " servant " of the Lord.

There are some who have read the book of Jonah

---

[1] עֶבֶד, *ebed*, a servant, slave, or agent; a word which is very
frequently employed in the Scriptures, and is sometimes applied with
peculiar emphasis to the most illustrious servants of the Lord.

without deriving from it any favourable impression
of the prophet's character. They have found it
almost impossible to suppose that one who said and
did the things attributed to Jonah could have been a
truly pious man. I am anxious that we should enter
on the study of that book with a prejudice in the
prophet's favour, for we shall find as we proceed with
the narrative thus supplied ample evidence that he
really was, as the memoir before us at this moment
says, a servant of the Lord.

It is the more needful to urge this by reason of the
circumstance that a prophet was not necessarily a
good man. Balaam was a true prophet, and yet a
bad man, and there were others of whom we read in
the Scriptures to whom the same remark may apply.
But it does not apply to Jonah. With all his faults,
and they were sufficiently serious, he was a true
servant of the Lord God of Israel. There are two
things which should not be overlooked in any commentary upon Jonah's character.

1. One is that his fidelity to the Most High was
displayed at a time when it was neither fashionable
nor popular nor safe to be His servant. Things were
getting worse and worse in Israel, notwithstanding the
ministry of Elijah, Elisha, and himself. As the two
former prophets served the Lord at the risk of their
lives, and were repeatedly rescued from death by
Divine interposition on their behalf, so in all probability was it with their successor. At all events, we
find that the condition of Jonah's contemporaries
was more deplorable than that of their fathers in the
time of Elijah and Elisha; and the terms of God's
covenant with Israel were such as to assure us that

this resulted from their religious deterioration. If the piety of the two former prophets was all the more remarkable because of its exceptional character, so was it with that of Jonah. We should be thankful that we are not called to serve God in circumstances like those in which he was placed, but that the lines are fallen to us in pleasant places in this respect. Nevertheless, the service of God is never so easy as some may desire. Christ does indeed say that His yoke is easy and His burden light; but however easy the yoke may be, it is still a yoke; and however light the burden may be, it is still a burden. "Easy" and "light" are relative terms, and they have relation not only to what is carried, but also to the strength of those who carry it. It is the strength which Christ supplies to those who learn of Him which renders His yoke easy and His burden light to them. The yoke was not so easy in Jonah's time as in ours, and the burden was not so light then as now. Yet Jonah was a true servant of the Lord God of Israel, and as such was one of those whose example we are enjoined to copy, and "who through faith and patience inherit the promises."

2. The other thing to be observed with regard to Jonah's personal character is that we know nothing of his faults except what he has himself related. He is the author as well as the subject of the book which bears his name. This is the opinion of those whose opinion in respect of such matters is most worthy of regard. Its place in the Hebrew Canon is evidence that the Canonist believed its author to be some person of Jonah's prophetic status. There is internal evidence even to a careful English reader that Jonah

alone could have written it, and such evidence is more abundantly supplied by the original text. The circumstance that the prophet writes of himself in the third person is by no means peculiar to his style. To say nothing of the many celebrated profane writers who have done so, I may remind you of some of the sacred penmen who have employed this method. Amos, Isaiah, Jeremiah, Daniel, and Haggai did so among the prophets, and John and Paul among the apostles ; not, indeed, invariably, but to such an extent as makes it by no means remarkable that Jonah wrote of himself as he might have written of another person. Now, when a good man writes of himself, he is apt to relate his shortcomings with a severity which another good man would be less likely to manifest in writing of him. John Bunyan was probably the only good man who would have described John Bunyan as the chief of sinners. Jonah was perhaps the only good man who would have described Jonah's faults as they are described in the book which bears his name. The story could doubtless have been told quite as truthfully in terms adapted to convey a more favourable idea of the prophet's character to the superficial reader. But it was not Jonah's object to make his readers think well of himself. He desired to make them think well of God, and in proportion as this becomes plain to us shall we think well of the prophet after all.

It should not be enough, however, to think well of the prophet. There should be some attempt to copy his example in this respect. We should be less sensitive in relation to our own reputation, and more desirous of promoting the Divine glory, than it may be feared that many of us are. In the long run, it will be found that those who have most earnestly sought the glory of God have found the highest honour for themselves. Remember that "before honour is humility;" for "whosoever shall exalt himself shall be abased, and he that shall humble himself shall be exalted."

II.

FULFILLED PROPHECY.

"He restored the coast of Israel from the entering of Hamath unto the sea of the plain, according to the word of the Lord God of Israel, which He spake by the hand of his servant Jonah, the son of Amittai, the prophet, which was of Gath-hepher."—2 KINGS xiv. 25.

AS we read this sentence we perceive that it relates to men who were remarkable for the points in which they both resembled and differed from each other. Jonah was eminent among the servants of God, while Jeroboam was notorious for his wickedness; but both were Israelites, both were occupants of high office in the theocracy, both were ardent patriots, both rendered important service to their country, and both were concerned with the same prediction. It is to this last point that our attention will be chiefly directed, though, as we proceed, the others will not be overlooked. The prediction with which these two men were concerned was, of course, the one to which allusion is made in the text. It was uttered by Jonah and fulfilled by Jeroboam, though only in a subordinate fashion; for it was "the word of the Lord God of Israel, which HE spake by the hand of His servant Jonah," and the people of Israel were indeed insensible of His goodness if they were unaware that "HE saved them by the hand of Jeroboam the son of Joash " when it was accomplished. The prediction and its fulfilment were alike Divine, and to these two things the present lecture will be devoted.

I.

The prediction was one of many such utterances which proceeded from the prophets of Jehovah. They were enabled to foretell coming events, not by means of any calculations of their own, but by means of the Divine revelations vouchsafed to them ; and exercised this power in relation to the remote as well as the immediate future. This is a subject in which we have all reason to be intensely interested, but we must confine our attention at present to such considerations as are suggested by this notice of the particular prediction attributed to Jonah.

1. The purport of this prediction was that the coast of Israel should be restored from the entering of Hamath unto the Sea of the Plain. There was little apparent prospect of any such restoration when Jonah predicted it. In the time of Jeroboam's grandfather, Jehoahaz, "the anger of the Lord was kindled against Israel, and He delivered them into the hand of Hazael, king of Syria."[1] At the prayer of Jehoahaz, the Syrian monarch was prevented from effecting the absolute ruin of Israel, but it remained in a deplorable condition till Joash, the son of Jehoahaz and father of Jeroboam, was on the throne. To him the dying prophet Elisha gave the assurance that he should smite Syria thrice ;[2] and accordingly we read that Joash, or "Jehoash, the son of Jehoahaz,

[1] 2 Kings xiii. 3. [2] 2 Kings xiii. 19.

took again out of the hand of Benhadad, the son of
Hazael, the cities which he had taken out of the hand
of Jehoahaz his father by war. Three times did Joash
beat him, and recovered the cities of Israel."[1] Joash
was succeeded by Jeroboam, and Elisha by Jonah;
and Jonah was enabled to predict that Jeroboam
would be more successful than his father in waging
war with the Syrian oppressors of Israel. Notwithstanding the miserable condition to which those
oppressors had reduced them (" for the Lord saw the
affliction of Israel, that it was very bitter; for there
was not any shut up, nor any left, nor any helper for
Israel "), Jonah was commissioned to predict that
the coast of Israel should be restored from the entering
of Hamath unto the Sea of the Plain.

To understand this, it is necessary to bear in mind
that when the kingdom of Israel was in its most
flourishing condition, Solomon had reigned from the
river unto the end of the earth; in other words, from
the Euphrates to the Mediterranean. Within those
limits, but beyond the limits of Palestine proper, is
the Valley of the Orontes, watered by the river thus
named. This valley was known as Hamath, and the
" entering of Hamath " was a town so placed as to
be, in a military sense, the key to the entire district.
To predict, therefore, that the coast of Israel should
be restored from the entering of Hamath unto the
Sea of the Plain was to predict that much of the
territory which had been wrested from Israel by the
Syrians before the first Jeroboam had mounted the
throne should be restored to it by the second king of
that name. The Sea of the Plain was the volume of

[1] 2 Kings xiii. 25.

water which is otherwise known as the Salt Sea and
the Dead Sea.

2. The publication of this prediction is described
in terms which have a claim of their own upon our
attention. The prediction is referred to as "the
word of the Lord God of Israel, which He spake by
the hand of His servant Jonah."

It is possible that this is merely a Hebraism, in
which *hand* is put for mouth, on much the same
principle as that which underlies an idiom of our
own ; for do we not speak of an author's *works* when
we mean his *words?* In 1 Kings xivth we have an
account of a prediction uttered by the prophet Ahijah,
and of its fulfilment Ahijah told the wife of Jeroboam I. in so many words, "When thy feet enter
into the city the child shall die, and all Israel shall
mourn for him." Accordingly, it is narrated that,
"when she came to the threshold of the door, the
child died; and they buried him, and all Israel
mourned for him, according to the word of the Lord,
which He spake by the hand of His servant Ahijah
the prophet." Here, then, is an instance in which
God spake by the mouth of a prophet, and is yet said
to have spoken by that prophet's hand. It is therefore possible that the prediction noticed in the text
was spoken by the mouth of Jonah, notwithstanding
this mention of the prophet's hand.

But it may have been otherwise. The prediction
in this case may have been written as well as spoken,
or it may have been written only. It would then
have been the word of the Lord which He spake
literally by the hand of His servant Jonah. At all
events, the Lord has thus spoken by the hand of

many an inspired man, and among such persons
Jonah has a noteworthy place. He is the first of
that series of author-prophets whose writings constitute the concluding section of the Old Testament
scriptures. If those writings were chronologically
arranged, the Book of Jonah would begin where that
of Isaiah does actually begin in our version of the
Bible. It is a blessed circumstance that the Most
High has been pleased to speak by the hands of prophets and apostles and other inspired men, not merely
to their own countrymen and contemporaries, but
also to ourselves and to all mankind; for the Scriptures thus produced are able to make us wise unto
salvation through faith which is in Christ Jesus.
Nor has God only spoken by the hands of inspired
writers. There are many literary compositions which
have been produced in modern times, and through
which God has spoken to myriads of men, women,
and children. He has thus spoken to you, doubtless,
whom I now address in His Name; but it does not
follow that you are the better for the words which
have been traced by the hands of His servants. You
ma be worse rather than better as the result of your
reading. It depends upon the spirit in which you
have read the works to which I refer, and the spirit
in which you remember them. It is not improbable,
let me add, that God has spoken to some of you by
the hands of beloved friends, who wrote to you personally from distant places in terms which evinced
their deep interest in your spiritual welfare, and
whose letters were among the most valuable of the
many means of grace which have been employed for
your benefit. What about the appeals thus addressed

to you, and the counsels thus conveyed?   Very likely
you could put your hand upon one of these letters at
any time, inasmuch as you have fondly preserved it
in memory of the writer.   Very likely you have
recently perused it again.   Does it still retain its
heart-stirring potency?   Does it still move you to
penitence, to prayer, to purposes which point to
self-improvement, and to the performance of hitherto
neglected duty?   In that case, God has indeed
spoken to you by the hand which penned that pious
letter; and thus also has He spoken to many another
human being from time to time.

There may be yet another explanation of the curious
expression before us.   The prophets had sometimes
to dramatise their predictions.   You will see at once
what I mean as soon as you have turned to the fourth
and fifth chapters of Ezekiel.   There is only time at
present to read a portion of one of those chapters.
The first few verses of the fifth chapter direct a
dramatised prediction.   " Son of man, take thee a
sharp knife, take thee a barber's razor, and cause it
to pass upon thine head and upon thy beard : then
take thee balances to weigh, and divide the hair.
Thou shalt burn with fire a third part in the midst of
the city, when the days of the siege are fulfilled ; and
thou shalt take a third part and smite about it with a
knife; and a third part thou shalt scatter in the wind;
and I will draw out a sword after them.   Thou shalt
also take thereof a few in number, and bind them in
thy skirts.   Then take of them again, and cast them
into the midst of the fire, and burn them in the fire ;
for thereof shall a fire come forth into all the house
of Israel."   The remainder of the chapter is explana-

tory of the procedure thus directed; and, when the prophet did as he was commanded, the word of the Lord was spoken by the hand of His servant Ezekiel. God still speaks to mankind by the hands of His servants. It is true that those who serve Him in these days are not inspired in the same way as Ezekiel and Jonah, but He still speaks by their deeds and their gifts. The truth to which God calls the attention of mankind is largely illustrated by the deeds of some of His servants. They are deeds which imply faith and patience, courage and self-control, on the part of those who perform them. They are deeds which may or may not obtain applause and reward from men, but which can only be performed by those of whom the world is not worthy. They are deeds which may or may not demand the exercise of superior intelligence, but which can only be expected from those who are wise unto salvation. They are deeds which may or may not be imitated by those who witness them, but which must awaken the admiration of all dispassionate observers. As often as such deeds are performed God speaks by the hands of those who do them to all who may become aware of them. So is it also when His servants give what it is in their power to bestow for the good of others. It may be money or money's worth, in larger or smaller measure, or it may be that which only costs them a little trouble to confer. But whether it be a cup of cold water only which is given for Christ's sake to one of His fainting disciples, or the widow's contribution of two mites to the cause of God, or the dispensing of the manifold and munificent charity to which some of our wealthier brethren have been prompted, every such gift may be regarded as the word of the Lord by the hand of the person who bestows it. Oh the eloquence which belongs to such deeds and gifts as those to which I now refer! The rhetoric which rushes from the mouth of the most brilliant pulpit orator in the world is far less eloquent than they; and it should be the desire of our hearts that the word of the Lord may be spoken by our hands in this most impressive manner.

3. The purpose which this prediction was intended to serve was probably that which it was apparently *adapted* to effect.

For one thing, it was clearly adapted to encourage the people of Israel. They might well have resigned themselves to despair if no such encouraging word of the Lord had been addressed to them. You remember how it was with their first earthly king. Saul said to Samuel, " I am sore distressed; for the Philistines make war against me, and God is departed from me, and answereth me no more, neither by the hand of prophets nor by dreams."[1] Soon afterwards Saul committed suicide; and the despair which he experienced might have been the portion of the entire people of Israel in Jonah's time if they, like Saul, had received no encouragement from the God of their fathers. But they did receive encouragement from Him, for this word of the Lord was spoken among them by the hand of His servant.

This prediction was also adapted to cheer the heart of the prophet himself. It may as well be said at once that the account which is given of Jonah in the book

---

[1] 1 Sam. xxviii. 15. Observe the expression to which the marginal note calls attention, " By the hand of prophets." בְּיַד הַנְּבִיאִים.

which bears his name, is much more intelligible on the hypothesis that a passionate patriotism was one of his characteristics, than it could be otherwise. On this hypothesis also we can perceive how cheering to Jonah would be the commission to utter the prediction noticed in the text. The prophet would probably [1] pass from city to city, and village to village, repeating the Divine assurance that the border of the kingdom was to be re-extended to a line which would reach from the entering of Hamath unto the Sea of the Plain. What has been called the accent of conviction would be in his words ; but it is not enough to say that. Peter the Hermit, in calling upon the princes and peoples he addressed to go on Crusade, spoke doubtless with the impressiveness which that accent ensures. But there was no such bubbling up of God-communicated emotion in the heart of the hermit as that which boiled in the breast of the prophet. As the words of Jonah rang along the valleys and re-echoed among the hills of his native land, as he poured his passionate speech into the ears of its princes and warriors, and as he observed the kindling enthusiasm of all classes and conditions of his countrymen in relation to the subject of his discourse, we may be certain that his spirit thrilled with patriotic gladness. Moreover, with the joy thus occasioned would mingle a measure of pious hope. The people of Israel had been threatened repeatedly in the Name of the Lord, and the threats addressed to them had been largely fulfilled. But they had not repented, and it might be that promises would do more to bring them to repentance than threats.

---

[1] But see what is said in a former part of this lecture, p. 21.

Commissioned as he was to try the experiment, Jonah might well be animated by a cheerful hope, as he set about it, that he might be the honoured instrument to effect that spiritual reformation for which his illustrious predecessors, Elijah and Elisha, had laboured in vain.   He was disappointed, as we know; but of the bitterness of the disappointment which awaited him he had no experience at the time of which I speak.   In mercy to him the Lord would not reveal to the prophet his own future experience ; and for the time being, therefore, Jonah was able to serve the Lord with gladness.   As God dealt with His servant of old in this particular, so is He apt to deal with His servants now.   They know that ultimately their joy will be full, but they do not know what disappointments and failures and other troubles await them in the immediate future ; and it is well for them that such is the case.   " Sufficient unto the day is the evil thereof," and there should be no gloomy foreboding with respect to it on the part of those of God's servants who are now prospering in His ways.

II.

The fulfilment of this prediction must now engage our attention.   It was fulfilled very speedily.   There are some predictions which were uttered by the prophets, and have not been fulfilled yet.   But this one was doubtless fulfilled during the life of the prophet who uttered it.   Jonah and Jeroboam were contemporary with each other, and I cannot entertain a doubt that the prophet had the satisfaction of witnessing the accomplishment of his prediction by the hand of

the monarch. I can understand the book of Jonah
better on this supposition than a contrary one,[1] and I
confidently anticipate that chronologists will sooner
or later confirm it.

1. The fulfilment of this prediction was effected by
the agency of a wicked man. Jeroboam II. resembled
Jeroboam I. in several particulars. He was, like his
namesake and predecessor, a mighty man of valour,
a victorious commander, a prosperous prince, and a
flagrant wrongdoer. " He did evil in the sight of the
Lord : he departed not from all the sins of Jeroboam
the son of Nebat, who made Israel to sin." Yet of
this bad man it is said that " he restored the coast
of Israel from the entering of Hamath unto the Sea
of the Plain, according to the word of the Lord God
of Israel, which He spake by the hand of His servant
Jonah."

Do we wonder that such a work should have been
entrusted to such a man ? There was nothing exceptional about the arrangement in that respect. It is
not an uncommon circumstance for God to employ a
wicked man in His own service. He employed Balaam
and Caiaphas to give utterance to prophecy, Jehu to
put an end to the abominations which Jezebel had
introduced into the court and kingdom of Israel, and
Jeroboam to restore the coast of Israel in accordance
with His own word.

Such men are not always conscious that they are
carrying out the Divine plans. Those I have now
named were aware that they were doing so, but there
are many wicked men whose iniquitous proceedings
are divinely overruled for good, as they have been

---

[1] See p. 1.

divinely anticipated, without any idea on their own part that such is the case. A notable instance of this kind of thing will readily recur to you. Speaking of his Master to the men who had murdered Him, the Apostle Peter said, "Him, being delivered by the determinate counsel and foreknowledge of God, ye have taken, and by wicked hands have crucified and slain." [1] Thus the most stupendous crime which has been committed since the foundation of the world was anticipated by its Supreme Ruler, as it has been overruled by Him for the advantage of mankind, the salvation of His people, and the glory of His own most holy Name. Yet those who committed that crime had no idea that it had been thus anticipated, and would be thus overruled. Their ignorance in relation to it was only exceeded by their guilt.

Even when wicked men are conscious that God is employing them in the furtherance of His plans, they are not always reclaimed from their wickedness thereby. Jeroboam knew that the restoration which he effected was according to the word of the Lord, and he ought to have been won by the knowledge to a life of grateful devotion to Him. It was not so, however, for "he departed not from all the sins of Jeroboam the son of Nebat, who made Israel to sin." Judas Iscariot was an apostle of Christ, and ought to have found it morally impossible to betray his Master after the experience he had had as such. The truth is, that employment in the service of God is to the person conscious of being thus employed a means of grace; and, like any other means of grace, it will

[1] Acts ii. 23.

result in spiritual gain or loss, according to the spirit
in which it is accepted. There are some among ourselves who are preachers, teachers, Church officers,
and agents of various societies which are maintained
for the work of the Christian ministry in the broadest
sense of that expression. These men know that they
are engaged in God's service, and the inevitable alternative is that they will be numbered with the best
or the worst, the noblest or the basest, members of
the human race. " I speak as to wise men ; judge ye
what I say."

2. The fulfilment of this prediction vindicated
Jehovah's faithfulness to His covenant engagements
with Israel. He was determined to show that if the
children of Israel were involved in ruin, it was not
because He had forsaken them, but because they
had forsaken Him. Thus, while they were actually in
rebellion against Him, He interposed on their behalf,
and enabled Jeroboam to restore their coast from the
entering of Hamath unto the Sea of the Plain. This
was wondrous mercy on His part, but it is clearly
explained. " The Lord was gracious unto them, and
had compassion on them, and had respect unto them,
because of His covenant with Abraham, Isaac, and
Jacob, and would not destroy them, neither cast He
them from His presence as yet."[1] Jehovah was the
same God in the time of Jonah and Jeroboam as in
the time of Abraham, Isaac, and Jacob; and He is
the same God still. " With Him is no variableness,
neither shadow of turning." He is as merciful as
ever, and as faithful to His engagements as ever.
Reflect, then, on those Divine engagements which

---

[1] 2 Kings xiii. 23.

are made known to us in the Scriptures, and consider
how you are likely to be affected by them.

Some of them relate to sinners as such, and may
be regarded as summarised in words once spoken by
the Lord to the prophet Ezekiel, " When I say unto
the wicked, Thou shalt surely die; if he turn from
his sin and do that which is lawful and right; if the
wicked restore the pledge, give again that he had
robbed, walk in the statutes of life without committing
iniquity, he shall surely live ; he shall not die. None
of his sins that he hath committed shall be mentioned unto him : he hath done that which is lawful
and right ; he shall surely live." [1]

Some of God's engagements relate to His own
saints. He promises to console them in time of
trouble ; to endow them with those virtues or graces,
both active and passive, which belong to sanctified
humanity; and to exalt them to a condition of
celestial and consummate blessedness when the discipline of the present life has become a thing of the
past.

Some of God's engagements relate to the Church
in its collective capacity. We must not dwell upon
them now, but the time will surely come when the
true Joshua shall say to the true Israel, "Ye know
in all your hearts and in all your souls that not one
thing hath failed of all the good things which the
Lord your God spake concerning you ; all are come
to pass unto you, and not one thing hath failed
thereof." [2]

3. The fulfilment of this prediction prepared the
way for Jonah's great mission to Nineveh. God

---

[1] Ezek. xxxiii. 14-16.   [2] Josh. xxiii. 14.

intended that the prophet should go to that great
heathen city with a merciful warning from Himself.
He intended also that Jonah's proclamation of the
word entrusted to him should appear credible to the
Ninevites.   If Jonah were first to predict the restoration of the coast of Israel by the hand of Jeroboam,
and that prediction were fulfilled, the circumstance
would be noised among the nations to such an extent
as to secure attention to the prophet's message to
the Ninevites on his arrival in their city.   That was
God's plan, though Jonah himself was as yet ignorant of it ; and God has so arranged matters as to
render all the warnings and promises and announce-
ments He has addressed to mankind similarly credible.   The doubt and disbelief which so many now
acknowledge with respect to the Word of God will
not be easily justified hereafter, or rather will not be
justified at all.   The grand theme of the Scriptures
is Christ, and " he that believeth on Him is not condemned : but he that believeth not is condemned
already, because he hath not believed in the name
of the only-begotten Son of God." [1]

4. The fulfilment of this prediction afforded an
illustration of the spiritual reformation which has to
be repeated from age to age.   Jeroboam was the King
of Israel, and he restored the coast of Israel. So does
the King of the spiritual Israel restore its coast from
time to time.   The Israel of God is the Church of
Christ, and the King of God's Israel is Christ Himself.   The coast of Israel was the boundary beyond
which dwelt the uncircumcised and the unclean.
But that boundary was frequently overrun by the

---

[1] John iii. 18.

heathen, and portions of the land which God had
given to His chosen people were wrested from them.
The Syrians had invaded and despoiled the land of
Israel in Jonah's time, but Jeroboam restored its
coast in accordance with the prophet's prediction.
There are spiritual processes in operation which are
obviously analogous to these. There is a boundary
between the Church and the World, but it is not
always maintained in its integrity by the people of
God. Does any one ask concerning the nature of
this boundary?

It is partly doctrinal, and it is necessary to insist
on this circumstance. The Creed of the Church
properly consists of those truths which God has
revealed to His people in the Scriptures. What if
some of these truths be lost sight of by them? What
if some of them be rejected in favour of specious
errors and falsehoods such as have so often been
adopted by the professed people of God? In that
case the coast of Israel needs to be restored, and the
King of Israel is the only One who can effect its
restoration.

The boundary between the Church and the World
is partly disciplinary. There are certain divinely
instituted offices and ordinances which are properly
peculiar to the Church, and these should be despised
by none of its members. But what if they are
despised? What if others are substituted for them
which God has not sanctioned? In that unhappy
and too frequent case the coast of Israel needs to
be restored by its King.

The boundary between the Church and the World
is, however, chiefly moral and spiritual. The Chris-

tian who behaves as such conducts himself towards
God and men in a manner which distinguishes him
from the worldling, and at the same time attests his
own superiority.   The Church is composed of Christians ; of those who are the light of the world and
the salt of the earth.   But if the light be darkness
and the salt have lost its savour, if there be the form
of godliness without its power, if it be largely overrun
by worldliness in its more refined or coarser develop-
ments, then is there urgent need that the coast of
Israel should be restored by its anointed King.

The Scriptures teach us to anticipate " the times
of the restitution of all things ; "[1] and we are sure
therefore that, as Jeroboam restored the coast of the
Israel in which he reigned, the Divine King shall
restore to the Israel of God all that distinguishes it
from the rest of our race.   But in the meantime it
behoves all who are Israelites indeed to acquit themselves as such.   Jeroboam did not, it is clear, restore
the coast of Israel without repeated conflict with its
foes.   Many of his subjects who followed him to battle
experienced severe trials in doing so.   They had to
leave their homes, their fields, their accustomed
avocations, and all that was most precious to them.
They had to endure the hardships of the march and
of the camp.   They had to submit to a burdensome
taxation.   They had to expose themselves to the
sword of the enemy ; and, in so doing, many of them
were wounded, and many slain.   But they were
animated to the last by the assurance which Jonah's
prediction conveyed to them that their exertions,
endurance, and exposure would result in the restora-

[1] Acts iii. 21.

tion of their coast. So has it been, my brethren, with many of our fellow Christians. They have loyally surrendered their substance to promote their Master's cause. They have toiled and fought and bled and died in His service. They have been carried from the field of conflict, to which we are now called as their successors. Pick up, then, those fallen banners! Secure those empty chariots! Blow a cheerful blast again from those now silent trumpets! Take unto you the whole armour of God, and fight the good fight of faith, in cheerful anticipation of the times when the restitution of all things shall take place and every word of promise shall be fulfilled, and the armies of triumphant Israel shall rend the air with a cry of grateful acknowledgment, " Thanks be to God which giveth us the victory through our Lord Jesus Christ! "[1]

[1] Cor. xv. 57.

III.

THE WANDERING DOVE.

" Now the word of the Lord came unto Jonah the son of Amittai, saying, Arise, go to Nineveh, that great city, and cry against it, for their wickedness has come up before Me. But Jonah rose up to flee unto Tarshish from the presence of the Lord."—JONAH i. 1-3.

MUCH has been said about the way in which this Book of Jonah commences. The first word in it is not really " Now," but " And." "And the word of the Lord came unto Jonah." There is nothing peculiar to this particular Book in its commencing with this conjunction. The second, third, and fourth Books of Moses commence in the same way. So do the Books of Joshua and the Judges, of Samuel and the Kings. So does the Book of Ezekiel, and so do other Books of the Old Testament. There is a reason for this, of course, and it has been suggested that the continuity of Scripture is thus and purposely attested. " The Scripture cannot be broken," and its sixty-six several books, written by different men, in different languages and at different times, are so connected with each other as to really form One Book of which the Author is God Himself. Thus the " And " with which the Book of Jonah begins is the link which connects it with the earlier Scriptures; and not only connects itself with them, but also the entire series

of writings produced by those author-prophets of
whom Jonah was the first.

This is an ingenious idea, but must not be insisted
upon too strongly.   The word, or rather letter, on
which it is supposed to rest not only occurs at the
commencement of the Book, but at the commencement of many a sentence in the Book where no such
idea can be supposed to find expression.   Every verse
in this chapter, with the exception of the second,
which begins in the middle of a sentence, commences
in the same way.   Where our version has "Now,"
"But," "Then," "So," "Nevertheless," or "Wherefore," a free rendering has been employed for the sake
of euphony instead of the more literal "And."   It is
obviously an idiom of the language in which the
Book was written, and one to which the writer much
inclined, that is thus employed.

But then an idiomatic usage of this kind is not an
affair of chance.   The word "and" has a meaning.
It does express the idea of connection ; and it would
not occur so often in the Book of Jonah had not the
mind of its author been much occupied with the
sequences and concatenations of Providence, and with
the relationship of things and persons and events to
each other.   The ship, the sea, the wind, the lot, and
the fish were all connected with each other, and with
the sailors, and with the prophet, and with Jehovah ;
so that the repetition of the conjunction was natural
and necessary, and should not be lost sight of by any
reader of this Book.

" And the word of the Lord came unto Jonah," as
as it had come in previous times to Enoch and
Moses, to Samuel and David, to Elijah and Elisha,

and to many others before Jonah, and as it came to
many others in succeeding generations. It came on
this occasion in the shape of a remarkable and unwelcome commission, and my remarks in this lecture
will relate to the commission thus addressed to Jonah,
and to the prophet's disobedience.

I.

You see what the commission was. "Arise, go to
Nineveh, that great city, and cry against it; for their
wickedness is come up before Me." We learn from
the language thus addressed to Jonah that the city
to which he was commissioned was remarkable for
its magnitude and its wickedness, and we know that
it was further remarkable as being the chief city of
the heathen world. It was a great, guilty, Gentile
city, and as such we have now to think of it in connection with the command imposed on the prophet
by the Most High.

1. Nineveh was a great city in many respects; one
of the very greatest cities of ancient times.

It was of great antiquity, having been founded by
Nimrod at least a thousand years before the time of
Jonah. An account of its origin is given in the
book of Genesis,[1] and a very interesting account it is.
As our version describes the matter, he and another
chieftain built four cities apiece; Nimrod building
Babel, or Babylon, and three others, and Asshur
building Nineveh and three others. But really
Nimrod was the founder of all the eight cities
mentioned by the sacred writer; though it is not
improbable that the two groups of cities described

[1] Gen. x. 9-12.

were, strictly speaking, only two great cities. Babylon consisted of "Babel, and Erech, and Accad, and
Calneh, in the land of Shinar," while Nineveh consisted of an acropolis of that name, "and the city
Rehoboth, and Calah, and Resen between Nineveh
and Calah." The beginning of Nimrod's kingdom
was the Babylon he founded in the land of Shinar ;
and afterwards "he went forth from that land to
Assyria, and builded Nineveh . . . the same is a
great city." When this account was written by
Moses, or by the writer whose account he embodied
in his own, Nineveh with its suburbs was already a
great city. The circumstance that it was a Tetrad
may not be without a significance of its own to those
who are versant with the numerical symbolism which
pervades the Scriptures ; and that it really was such
appears from the fact that around the site, and among
the ruins, of ancient Nineveh, are four great mounds,
called respectively Kouyunjik, Nimrud, Karamless, and
Khorsabad, and doubtless corresponding with Nineveh
proper, Rehoboth, Calah, and Resen, which together
made up the great city of which I am speaking.

Nineveh was a great city in respect of its power.
In the time of Jonah it was the chief city of the
mightiest monarchy in the world. This was a circumstance which was likely to impress the prophet's
mind. Jeroboam II. might prevail against the
Syrians, but the Assyrians were a far mightier
people ; he might have nothing to fear from Damascus, but Nineveh was assuredly to be feared by him
and such as he ; and we need not doubt that both he
and Jonah did regard it with patriotic dread.

It was a great city also in respect of the wealth

and splendour for which it was distinguished. This
has been rendered sufficiently clear by the researches
recently made among its ruins by European explorers,
which show that it was enriched and adorned with
all that wealth and art could effect.

Nineveh was great, moreover, in respect of its
extent. It is described in this Book as " an exceeding
great city of three days' journey." A day's journey
was twenty miles, and Nineveh was therefore a city
of sixty miles, *i.e.*, sixty miles in circumference. An
immense space this for a city to occupy! but we
must remember that its walls would include not
only buildings and streets, but gardens and pastures ;
so that, in the event of a siege, its people would have
a supply of food at hand in the " much cattle " thus
accommodated. An immense space indeed! but that
it really was sixty miles in circumference is asserted
by profane writers,[1] and thus our view of the meaning
of the inspired description is confirmed.

Finally, Nineveh was great in respect of its popu-
lousness. It contained upwards of 120,000 young
children, and therefore, in all probability, some
600,000 persons resided within its walls.

2. Nineveh was a guilty city; so guilty that God
said of its inhabitants, " Their wickedness is come
up before Me." The peculiar expression thus employed by the Most High will have to be considered
presently;[2] but let us now direct our attention to

---

[1] Pusey says that Diodorus (probably on the authority of Ctesias)
states that the whole circuit of its walls was 480 furlongs.

[2] לְפָנָי should be compared with the expression in the next verse,
מִלִּפְנֵי יְהֹוָה. God speaks as the enthroned King of Israel and the
nations. See subsequent part of this lecture.

any evidence which may be accessible concerning the nature of the wickedness thus noticed. Jonah was not the only Hebrew prophet who was concerned with the wickedness of the Ninevites. Nahum and Zephaniah, who lived after the time of Jonah, denounced the posterity of those who repented at his preaching for their cruelty, pride, fraud, and lust. The Ninevites had doubtless relapsed into the vices to which they were prone when Jonah was commissioned to cry against their city. They were characteristic vices, and especially their cruelty was a characteristic vice. It was so characteristic that their city was likened to a lion's den, full of the strangled and mangled victims which have been dragged into it for the lionesses and their whelps.[1] The impress of its founder's disposition had been so stamped upon the city that at the end of a millennium the ideal Ninevite was still a Nimrod.

We must suppose that the cruelties perpetrated in Nineveh were chiefly inflicted on captives and criminals and slaves and other subordinate persons; but in truth no man in Nineveh was secure from the violence to which its people were prone. Neither his citizenship, his royalty, his warlike fame, nor the sanctity of the place in which he was engaged in worship at the time, protected the great king Sennacherib from the violence of his foes; and the men who slew him were they of his own household.

3. Nineveh was a Gentile city, and it was this circumstance which chiefly rendered the commission addressed to Jonah so remarkable. Had he been sent to Samaria or to Jerusalem, there had been nothing

---

[1] Nahum ii. 11, 12.

exceptional in the duty imposed upon him; but he was sent to Nineveh, which was not only the capital of the Assyrian empire, but of the Gentile world; and with the ideas in which he had been educated, it was undoubtedly a startling direction which now bade him betake himself to that great city. Yes, it must have startled Jonah; but does it startle us? It is not to be supposed that God was indifferent to the welfare of the Gentiles during the ages which preceded the dawn of the Christian dispensation. Jonah's mission was a peculiar one, certainly; but the careful reader of the Old Testament does not fail to remark that God's chosen people were employed as the medium of possible blessing to their Gentile neighbours from the first. Think of Joseph in Egypt, and Moses in Midian; of Daniel in Babylon, and Mordecai in Shushan the Palace. Sometimes the Hebrews were sent among the heathen, while at other times the heathen were brought among themselves; and, in harmony with all such providential arrangements, the great prophet Jonah was now sent to Nineveh to cry against it by reason of its wickedness, which was, in effect, to cry against the wickedness of the entire heathen world. Thus did God display His interest in the welfare of mankind at large, even in that unripe epoch; and was doubtless prompted by the selfsame feeling as that which found expression in the fulness of time to which the world had attained, when His incarnate Son addressed His disciples in the memorable words, " Go ye into all the world, and preach the Gospel to every creature."

The Israelites were slow to learn that God did thus interest Himself in the welfare of the Gentiles. It

was with the air of one who had made a great dis-
covery, that the Apostle Peter exclaimed in the house
of the Gentile centurion, " Of a truth I perceive that
God is no respecter of persons, but in every nation
he that feareth Him and worketh righteousness is
accepted with Him." But the simplicity and slow-
ness of heart which even devout Israelites displayed
in learning this lesson, should find nothing to corre-
spond with it in ourselves. We should perceive the
truth which Peter expressed with a clearness that
must render it impossible to take that contemptuous
view of certain races which the advocates of a science
falsely so called affect to consider worthy of their
intelligence. It behoves us to " honour all men," as
for other reasons, so also by reason of the interest
which is manifestly taken in their welfare by Him
who " hath made of one blood all nations of men
for to dwell on all the face of the earth, . . . that
they should seek the Lord, if haply they might feel
after Him and find Him, . . . and now commandeth
all men everywhere to repent ; because He hath
appointed a day in the which He will judge the world
in righteousness by that Man whom He hath ordained ; whereof He hath given assurance unto all
men, in that He hath raised Him from the dead."

We should be in sympathy with the feeling thus
displayed by the Almighty Ruler of the Universe the
more thoroughly by reason of the circumstance that
we ourselves are Gentiles, though happily not heathen.
Of our own, as of many another nation, it may be
said, " The people that walked in darkness have seen
a great light : they that dwell in the land of the
shadow of death, upon them hath the light shined."

But our sympathy should not be barren. It should find expression in connection with those grand missionary enterprises which the Church is increasingly busied with in these days. Gratitude for the mercy we have ourselves obtained, demands that we should do all that may be in our power to make known to the other nations of the earth that they also may obtain it.

II.

The disobedience of Jonah to the mandate thus addressed to him must now be considered. " Jonah rose up to flee unto Tarshish from the presence of the Lord."

"Jonah rose up," and thus far there was no disobedience on his part. The first word which the Lord is recorded to have spoken to the prophet was an impressive one. "Arise!" It was by no means the first time that the Most High had aroused one of His servants with this word. He had said to Jacob long before, while yet the patriarch lingered in Padan-aram, "Arise! get thee out from this land, and return unto the land of thy kindred." To Joshua He had said, "Arise! go over this Jordan, thou and all this people, unto the land which I do give to thee." To Gideon, respecting the host of the Midianites, "Arise! get thee down unto the host, for I have delivered it into thine hand." To Samuel, respecting Saul, "Arise! anoint him, for this is he." To Elijah, reposing by the bed of Cherith, "Arise! get thee to Zarephath, which belongeth to Zidon, and dwell there : behold ! I have commanded a widow woman there to sustain thee." So also, long after Jonah's time, did the

incarnate Son of God employ this word to arouse
various persons. To one He said, "Arise ! take up
thy bed, and go unto thy house." To His disciples on
the night of His betrayal, "Arise ! let us go hence."
The word thus spoken by the Lord was never disregarded. Even the dead were roused thereby.
"Damsel, I say unto thee, Arise ! " "Young man, I
say unto thee, Arise ! " No wonder, then, that when
the Lord said to Jonah, "Arise ! go to Nineveh," the
prophet immediately "rose up."

The dove had been reposing with folded wings, but
now rose high in the air at the call which startled
him. Jonah's home mission work was over for the
present. The result of his going hither and thither
among his countrymen, had been that the coast of
Israel was restored ; and he had been taking needful
rest at Gath-hepher, or elsewhere, till he instinctively
spread his wings at this stirring cry, and "rose up,"
as a dove is apt to do. For a moment it was not clear
which way the messenger would take. For a little
while, we may suppose, the prophet was undecided as
to the course he would adopt. Which should it be ?
over the land eastward to Nineveh ? or over the sea
westward to Tarshish ? Alas that such a question
should occur ! Alas that there should be a doubt as
to the course of that startled dove ! Alas that a
wrong decision should presently be reached, and that
the messenger should wing his way for the sea, and
for distant Tarshish ! Better not to have arisen at
the word of the Lord, than to have arisen for this, O
Jonah ! Come back, O fugitive prophet ! Return,
O wandering dove ! Return, disloyal messenger !
Was there no such summons sent after him ? If so,

it was disregarded, and the dove was presently far
on his way from the presence of the Lord, if that
might be.

The prophet's object was to flee from the presence
of the Lord. Was he then bent upon finding some
place, Tarshish or another, which was absolutely
destitute of the Divine Presence? No. A heathen
might have made such an attempt. It was the idea of
those who worshipped gods many and lords many that
each of their imagined deities pervaded some particular region or sphere. But Jonah was a Hebrew and a
prophet, and was therefore well aware that Jehovah is
omnipresent. Whether he was or was not acquainted
with Psalm cxxxixth, he was assuredly acquainted
with the truth expressed by its author in the passage
which so readily occurs to us in connection with this
part of his history, " Whither shall I go from Thy
Spirit? or whither shall I flee from Thy presence?
If I ascend up into heaven, Thou art there: if I
make my bed in hell, behold Thou art there! If I
take the wings of the morning, and dwell in the
uttermost parts of the sea; even there shall Thy hand
lead me, and Thy right hand shall hold me." Not
for a moment did the prophet doubt the Divine
omnipresence

Then, was Jonah bent on getting as far as possible
beyond the range of those *manifestations* of the
Divine presence which were peculiar to Palestine and
its neighbourhood? Probably. It is not unlikely
that he entertained a very similar notion of the
presence of the Lord to that which obtains among
ourselves. We pray that the Divine presence may
be vouchsafed to us in the house of God; but this

does not imply ignorance, or forgetfulness, or mis-apprehension, or disbelief, on our part, of the doctrine that God is everywhere. What we mean, and are understood to mean, is to ask that He will *manifest* His presence to us in a certain peculiar manner of which His people have experience. We pray for a sense or consciousness of the Divine presence, and it is probable that Jonah sought to escape from such a consciousness of that presence as he had been accustomed to experience in his own country, and may have regarded as peculiar to it. But why should he wish to escape from that? Why? The reason is plain enough to those who know that the manifestation of God's presence will produce exactly opposite effects on different persons. It will delight those who are in sympathy with Him and torture those who are estranged from Him. Although Cain went out from the presence of the Lord with the feeling that his punishment was greater than he could bear, that punishment would have been still greater had he been compelled to remain where that presence was revealed. There will be mercy as well as vengeance displayed in the case of those "who shall be punished with everlasting destruction from the presence of the Lord;" and, when His advent takes place, they themselves will be heard to raise the despairing cry to the mountains and rocks, "Fall on us, and hide us from the face of Him that sitteth on the throne, and from the wrath of the Lamb!" It was not wonderful that the presence of the Lord had become intolerable to Jonah from the moment that his want of sympathy with the Divine will in relation to Nineveh had become apparent to himself. God desired him

to go thither, whereas he desired not to go, and
determined to disobey the Divine command.   But
if he would not go to Nineveh, he could not remain
where he was; for there the Divine presence was
revealed, and that had now become unbearable.   So
" Jonah rose up to flee unto Tarshish from the
presence of the Lord."

But there is more to be said respecting this matter.
Jonah was an official of high rank in the theocracy.
The commonwealth of Israel had Jehovah for its
Lord High Protector.   The kingdom of Israel had
God for its King.   As the ministers of an earthly
monarch stand in their master's presence, so it is
with those of the Divine King.   Thus Jonah's great
predecessor, Elijah, "said unto Ahab, The Lord
God of Israel liveth, before whom I stand."   Thus,
too, the angel said to Zacharias, " I am Gabriel, that
stand in the presence of God."   It was Jonah's duty
and privilege thus to stand before God, and he had
been content to do so until the affairs of Nineveh
were found to have engaged the particular attention
of the Most High, and the prophet was commissioned
by Him to betake himself thither.   " Arise ! go to
Nineveh, that great city, and cry against it, for their
wickedness is come up before Me."   " If the wickedness of Nineveh is come up before Thee, I will cease
to stand before Thee.   If my official duty requires
me to proclaim Thy word in Nineveh, I will resign
my office."   That appears to have been the thought
in Jonah's mind, and the thought on which he acted
when he " rose up to flee unto Tarshish from the
presence of the Lord."

The prophet had, of course, no right to resign the

office he held in the service of Jehovah.   It appears
that he ventured to remonstrate with the Most High
in relation to the duty imposed upon him,[1] but it
appears also that his remonstrance did not prevail.
That he should thereupon attempt to desert the path
of duty altogether was certainly a piece of gross presumption on his part.   We read in Holy Writ of
others who displayed reluctance to engage in particular ministries to which they were divinely called,
and of the manner in which they demurred to the
duty assigned them.   Thus Moses endeavoured to
excuse himself from demanding the dismission of the
Israelites at the hands of Pharaoh, and Jeremiah
pleaded his inability to undertake the office entrusted
to him, and Ananias of Damascus deprecated the
errand on which he was sent to Saul of Tarsus.   But
when the Lord insisted on their doing so, as He
did in each of the cases now mentioned, these men
addressed themselves to their appointed tasks.   Not
thus did Jonah.   Commissioned to go to Nineveh,
he remonstrated ; and, finding his remonstrance disregarded, he " rose up to flee unto Tarshish from
the presence of the Lord."

The guilt and presumption of the prophet are
apparent, but have you not been as guilty and presumptuous as he ?   There was a time, I will venture
to say, when " the word of the Lord came to " you
as truly as it " came to Jonah " long ago.   It came
to you in some crisis of your experience when the
precepts of Holy Writ, and the testimony of your own
conscience, and the counsel of your best friends, and
the aspect of Divine Providence, all combined to

---

[1] Chap. iv. 2.

4

point out a particular course of conduct as the path
of duty. But you shrank from that path. You
remonstrated with God in relation to it. You anticipated its dangers with dismay, and its difficulties
with despair, and its other disadvantages with disgust. You were too timorous or slothful or fastidious
to enter upon it, and you had the amazing impudence
to adopt another and an opposite course to the one thus
indicated. In this respect you followed Jonah when
you should rather have followed One greater than he.
Jonah pleased himself instead of that Divine King in
Whose presence he had been privileged to stand;
whereas "Christ pleased not Himself," but "came
down from heaven, not to do His own will, but the
will of Him that sent" Him, "and hath left us an
example that we should follow in His steps." The
question, then, may well be addressed to you, In
what path are you walking now? Are you pursuing
a course which carries you further and further and
further still from the post of duty, or are you retracing
your steps? "Thus saith the Lord, Consider your
ways." It is happily always possible for the transgressor to return: therefore "let him return unto the
Lord, and He will have mercy upon him; and to our
God, for He will abundantly pardon." It is possible
that you have not yet declined to discharge a particular duty which has been divinely imposed on you.
You are only tempted to do so; only disposed to
adopt some other course than the one ordained. In
that case, may the Lord Himself prevent you from
doing as Jonah did when he "rose up to flee unto
Tarshish from the presence of the Lord"!

IV.

THE VOYAGE.

"And [Jonah] went down to Joppa ; and he found a ship going to Tarshish; so he paid the fare thereof, and went down into it, to go with them unto Tarshish from the presence of the Lord. But the Lord sent out a great wind into the sea, and there was a mighty tempest in the sea, so that the ship was like to be broken. Then the mariners were afraid, and cried every man unto his god, and cast forth the wares that were in the ship into the sea, to lighten it of them. But Jonah was gone down into the sides of the ship; and he lay, and was fast asleep. So the shipmaster came to him, and said unto him, What meanest thou, O sleeper ? arise, call upon thy God, if so be that God will think upon us, that we perish not. And they said every one to his fellow, Come, and let us cast lots, that we may know for whose cause this evil is upon us. So they cast lots, and the lot fell upon Jonah."—JONAH i. 3-7.

UNLESS God change His mind, it is useless for any man whom He has called to the performance of any duty to attempt its neglect. It was God's purpose to employ Jonah in the interests of the Gentiles, and therefore He directed him to go to Nineveh, the capital of the Gentile world, and preach to its inhabitants. The prophet in vain adopted another course. He was ultimately compelled to preach in Nineveh ; and, moreover, his attempt to shirk that duty was the means of bringing him into contact with that Gentile captain and his crew of whom we read in the text. As these men are represented as calling upon different gods when they felt the need of Divine deliverance, we may infer that they

belonged to different countries. They certainly
visited different countries in the exercise of their
calling. Mention is made here of two seaports,
Joppa and Tarshish, otherwise Jaffa and Tartessus.
Joppa was in Palestine and Tarshish in Spain, and
therefore the whole length of the Mediterranean lay
between them. Now, the Mediterranean was in
Jonah's time the Great Sea. But little was known of
the Atlantic, or of any other ocean, to the mariners of
his day. They found enough scope for their energy in
coasting the countries washed by the sea just mentioned, for on its shores were clustered all the principal
ports in the world. The sailors who had the intercourse with Jonah which is described in the text would
assuredly make known the truth acquired by its means
in all the ports of the three continents they subse-
quently touched at in the exercise of their calling.
Thus, not only from Nineveh, but from many another
populous place between that great city and the
Pillars of Hercules, was the truth sounded forth
through the medium of that prophet who shrank
from all contact with the Gentile portion of mankind.
Assuredly God was no more indifferent to the welfare
of the heathen in those days than He is in our own.

The embarkation, the slumber, the awakening, and
the detection of the prophet are the incidents to
which attention will be now directed.

I.

The embarkation of the fugitive is the first thing
to be considered. " He went down to Joppa and
found a ship going to Tarshish ; so he paid the fare
thereof, and went down into it."

It was a downward course which Jonah thus adopted. He went down to Joppa, and down into the ship. Down. Down in more than one sense. Down literally and down spiritually. Down, down, down. Does any one object to this manner of dealing with the narrative? It is open to objection, I admit, but not surely to serious objection. In a narrative penned for ethical purposes, the mention of any physical change or movement is apt to suggest some corresponding moral change which it is adapted to illustrate. This is how it comes to pass that more than one accomplished expositor of the Scripture before us has seen in this going down on the prophet's part another and more serious descent. I cannot consent to conceal this view of the subject, either because some may think it over-fanciful, or because it has already been exhibited by others.

Disobedience to God is always debasing to the person guilty of it. From what we significantly call the Fall of Man down to the present time there has been no member of our race who has not been degraded by every several act of disobedience. It is by righteousness that men and nations are exalted, and by transgression that they are debased. There are some of those whom I now address who have been going down for twenty, thirty, forty, or fifty years, or for a still longer period ; constantly approximating to perdition and despair; and the final plunge may be nearer than you think. At this moment, however, your course may be reversed. You may begin to ascend. You may climb high. You may soar to heaven itself. Where is Christ at this moment, and what is it that He says to you as often as His Gospel is preached ? He is at the right hand of God, and He says, " Come unto Me ; come up hither; set your affections on things above; lay up for yourselves treasures in heaven."

There may be some, too, whose case resembles that of Jonah more closely than the one just described. They were ascending patiently the path of their appointed duty, but they have ceased to do so, and are pursuing a downward course at present. This is a melancholy but by no means a hopeless case. A man who has been in those high places where God holds communion with His people may be expected to return thither, for God may be expected to call him back to them as He did His servant Jonah, and as He has called back many another who has wandered from them. It is well that God is so ready to reclaim His erring servants, for the going down of which I am speaking is a fearful thing. It is sufficiently sad when a man goes down as regards his temporal condition, but it is infinitely less deplorable for a rich man to become poor than for a good man to become bad.

The embarkation of Jonah appears to have been easily effected. An ancient and familiar proverb assures us that a downward course is an easy one ;[1] and the prophet does not appear to have experienced any difficulty in connection with the matter when he " went down to Joppa, and found a ship going to Tarshish, and paid the fare thereof, and went down into it." It is plain that God was allowing His disobedient servant to have his own way to a certain

---

[1] *Fācilis descensus Averni.* The descent to hell is easy.

extent, and we may profitably consider the facility with which he pursued it.

He "went down to Joppa." Nothing was allowed to hinder him from reaching that port. Men have often been prevented from reaching the places they wished to visit. They have fallen sick on the road, or an accident has befallen them, or circumstances have compelled them to return. There was a time when Paul and Silas "assayed to go into Bithynia, but the Spirit suffered them not;" and the Apostle was hindered more than once from getting to Thessalonica by the artifices of Satan. But Jonah was neither prevented by the Holy Spirit nor by the Evil One from reaching Joppa when he fled thither from the path of duty.

On his arrival at Joppa he "found a ship going to Tarshish." I suppose there were always vessels to be found there, but it was not always that a vessel suitable for the long voyage he meditated was to be met with in that port. This particular vessel was, as it needed to be, a decked vessel,[1] and doubtless a vessel of considerable magnitude. "The ships of Tarshish" were the largest vessels afloat, and (in the nautical language of modern times) A. 1. It is not surprising to find that this particular vessel was furnished with oars as well as sailing apparatus, for that was then and long afterwards a customary arrangement. Three hundred years ago such vessels were still employed, and some of the largest ever launched were found in the celebrated, but not "invincible," Spanish Armada.

---

[1] סְפִינָה, *Sephinah*, a decked vessel, as distinguished from אֳנִיָּה, *onyyah*, the ordinary Hebrew word for ship.

Having found the ship, " he paid the fare thereof," which the prophet might have been unable to do. The passage from Joppa to Tarshish was, no doubt, an expensive one, and Jonah might have been unable to meet the expense. Prophets were sometimes poor men ; and even if Jonah were well provided with money when he began his journey, he might have lost it before his arrival at Joppa. But it was not so. He found a ship going to Tarshish, and he paid the fare thereof.

Moreover, he "went down into it." It has happened before now that fugitives from justice have secured a passage in some outward-bound vessel by paying the fare thereof at the appointed office, only to be arrested as they set foot upon its deck, without being allowed to descend to the cabin at all. But no divinely commissioned pursuivant laid hands on Jonah as he climbed to the deck of the vessel mentioned in the text, and he was not prevented in any other way from going down into it.

Is there any one here who has resolved on the adoption of a wrong course ? I do not anticipate the intervention of any insurmountable obstacle. Do you intend to defraud a neighbour, or to introduce discord into a church or family, or to gratify some particular evil inclination ? It is probable that you will readily find the means of doing so. It is the business of the devil to furnish men with facilities for the wrong doing on which they are resolved ; and it is a principle of the Divine government that those who turn away from God shall "eat of the fruit of their own way, and be filled with their own devices."

Nothing having occurred to prevent his embarka-

tion, Jonah was presently at sea.   At sea!   Many of
the most interesting incidents in human experience
have been associated with the sea.   Many of the
most interesting chapters of human history relate to
the adventures, exertions, discoveries, and calamities
of those who go down to the sea in ships and do
business upon the great waters.   Some of the greatest
men produced by our own country have displayed
their genius in connection with the mighty deep.
The allusions to it in the Bible render the Sacred
Volume far more attractive to some of its readers
than it would be without them.   I suppose that there
are especially two classes of persons who value these
allusions, viz., sailors and children.   The most
wonderful yarn that ever engaged the attention of
a knot of sailors is not more wonderful than the
account of Jonah's voyage, and Robinson Crusoe
does not more fascinate its youthful readers than
the Book in which that voyage is described.   But
why speak only of particular classes?   Would any
of us like to be deprived of this Old Testament story,
or of the New Testament account of the Sea of
Galilee and the doings of Christ and His Apostles
in connection with it, or of the narrative of Paul's
voyage and shipwreck?   I trow not; and I think
that before we have obtained some insight into the
meaning of the intimation, we are apt to regard as
most unwelcome the assurance given by John that
in the renovated universe he beheld in his prophetic
vision " there was no more sea."

II.

The slumber to which the prophet resigned himself is the next thing to be noticed. Having "gone down into the sides of the ship," Jonah "lay, and was fast asleep." He must have been fast asleep indeed, or his slumbers would have been disturbed by the tumult and disorder occasioned by the storm which came upon the vessel in which he lay. Before he fell asleep the sky had been clear, the wind fair, and the sea smooth. But while he slumbered a tremendous change took place; for "the Lord cast along a great wind into the sea, and there was a mighty tempest in the sea, so that the ship was thought to be broken." But the prophet knew nothing of the great wind or the great tempest, so profound was the slumber in which he was buried. It was very different with his fellow-voyagers, however.

The terror of the sailors was in strong contrast with the insensibility of the prophet. "The mariners were afraid;" but Jonah experienced no corresponding emotion, for "he lay, and was fast asleep." Sailors are not readily terrified by winds and waves; but these men had reason for the fear attributed to them, for the violence of the storm was such that "the ship was thought to be broken." There is no suggestion of cowardice in relation to them. They were afraid, but they did not allow their fear to master them. They were not paralysed by it, or unfitted for the duty which devolved on them by reason of the storm which occasioned it. There was nothing therefore in it which was unworthy of them

as men and seamen, and they were not in any sense
dishonoured thereby. It may appear paradoxical to
say so, but these sailors were none the less brave for
the terror they displayed. The brave man is not one
who is merely calm in time of peril; for such calm-
ness may result from insensibility, or from that
felicitous physical attribute which we term " nerve."
The brave man is he who, while fully sensible of the
peril in which he is placed, and distressed by the
consciousness of that peril, persists in discharging
the duty which devolves upon him at the time. The
sailors mentioned in the text displayed a courage
which we may all emulate with advantage to ourselves and others as often as circumstances call for
its display.

The supplications of these mariners were in strong
contrast with the silence of the prophet. They
" cried every man unto his god; . . . but Jonah
. . . lay, and was fast asleep." The poor heathen
did as they had been taught, and as well as they
could. The worst that can be said of their prayers is
that they were misdirected, and yet we shall see that
they found their way into the ear of that one true
and living God of whom they were ignorant. This is
a circumstance which may greatly encourage those
who are not ignorant concerning Him to entreat His
protection in time of peril. If pagan petitions were
not impotent, what power there must be in those
which Christians present in the Name of their Master,
and under the influence of His Spirit, to their Father
in heaven !

The exertions of the mariners were in strong contrast with the supineness of the prophet. They " cast

forth the wares that were in the ship into the sea, to lighten it of them; but Jonah . . . lay, and was fast asleep." They would gladly have kept the cargo entrusted to their care; but " skin for skin, yea, all that a man hath, will he give for his life ; " and therefore, with such cries as sailors employ when engaged in such work, the precious bales were hoisted from the hold of the vessel, and heaved overboard as fast as might be. There are persons who pray for deliverance in seasons of danger, but obtain no advantage thereby, because they put forth no effort to improve their own position, or because they refuse to part with the property which they perversely regard as the greatest blessing they can possess. Don't be too fond of ease, or too fond of money, if you would pray to good purpose for deliverance from any spiritual peril of which you may be conscious, but learn a lesson from these heathen sailors. They prayed and laboured at the same time, and they did not cling too closely to the property which encumbered them.

While the seamen thus prayed and laboured, under the influence of the terror which the storm occasioned, Jonah remained fast asleep. His slumber was of immense advantage to him while it lasted, for it afforded him relief, as nothing else could have done, from the remorse resulting from his disloyalty to God. As long as he remained awake he was in misery, and could take no such interest in the coast he was leaving, or in the sea as it heaved around him, or in the movements of the mariners, as that which would have been natural under other circumstances. He could do nothing better than resign himself to slumber as soon as he found that possible, and we need not

wonder that it was possible. Many wrongdoers have
found it impossible to slumber as he did. At times
they have not been able to sleep at all, and at other
times they have slept by fits and starts, the slightest
sound being sufficient to awaken them. But it must
be considered that Jonah was probably weary with a
rapidly-performed journey, and with previous insomnia.
Arising at the call of the Most High, he had never
rested, in his eagerness to get as far as possible away
from the place to which he was commissioned, until
he found himself on board the vessel bound for
Tarshish. Then, as there was no occasion for further
exertion on his part, he became sensible of fatigue,
and was so overpowered thereby as to fall fast asleep.

It is impossible to forget the accounts given in later
Scriptures of One greater than Jonah, Who was exposed to a tempest during a voyage across the Sea of
Galilee, and Who " was in the hinder part of the ship
asleep on a pillow " while the waves beat into it,
filling it with water, and filling the hearts of His
disciples with fear. Jonah fast asleep in a tempest
below the deck of a ship of Tarshish, and Christ fast
asleep in a tempest in the after part of a fishing-boat,
suggest various trains of thought; but the only thought
which now asks for expression relates to the contrast
between the slumber of the prophet and that of our
Divine Lord in one particular. It was hallowed and
honourable repose in the case of Jesus Christ, but the
exact contrary in that of Jonah. Rest is a fine thing
for the weary, but it should be earned as well as enjoyed—earned by the faithful discharge of duty; and
the physical repose we obtain should be associated
with that resting in the Lord which is only possible

to those who possess a conscience void of offence
toward God and men.   The transgressor may enjoy
the slumber permitted him for the present, but the
only permanent tranquillity is that which is associated
with the rectitude of those who are blessed thereby.
" The work of righteousness shall be peace, and the
effect of righteousness, quietness and assurance for
ever.   And my people shall dwell in a peaceable
habitation, and in sure dwellings, and in quiet resting-
places."   " But the wicked are like the troubled sea
when it cannot rest, whose waters cast up mire and
dirt.   There is no peace, saith my God, to the wicked."

III.

The awakening of Jonah was probably not long
delayed.   " The ship-master came to him, and said
unto him, What meanest thou, O sleeper ? arise !
call upon thy God, if so be that God will think upon
us, that we perish not."

The captain[1] might have ordered one of the sailors
to awaken the prophet, but preferred to do so himself.
The reasonable inference has been drawn from this
circumstance that he regarded his passenger with
more than ordinary respect.   There had been something in the appearance and demeanour of the prophet
which impressed him from the first with the idea that
he was no common personage.   Had Jonah been
simply a man who had paid his fare, and paid liber-
ally, the captain would have scarcely observed any
ceremony with him in presence of the awful danger
which menaced all on board.   But he had recognised
in the prophet a man who was entitled to respect, and

[1] רַב הַחֹבֵל, *Rab hachobel*, chief of the sailors, captain.

one who might turn out to be a man of resource, or a good adviser at the very least.

Not seeing the passenger on deck, the captain went to look for him below, and was astounded to find him fast asleep. It is possible that the worthy master had some doubt when he commenced his search whether he should be able to find him at all. The prophet was not upon deck, but it did not follow that he was below, for it was not improbable that he had fallen overboard without being noticed in that awful storm. A landsman might easily experience such a mischance, for even seamen are not always able to keep their footing or their hold on such a tempest-tossed vessel. If Jonah were found below, he might be discovered either cowering with a craven fear of which the captain was perhaps ready to suspect such a landlubber as he, or else praying as the mariners were doing above. But the captain was not prepared to find him, as he actually did find him, asleep; and we may suppose that a certain measure of indignation mingled with his astonishment as he proceeded to arouse him. It may be worth our while to observe the two branches of the address with which he did so.

He commenced with a question. "What meanest thou, O sleeper?" literally, "What is to thee, O sleeper?" *i.e.*, "What is come to thee?" or "What aileth thee, O sleeper?" Very likely the question was accompanied by appropriate action on the captain's part; and we may picture him to ourselves as grasping the prophet by the arm, and shaking him as he shouted the question into his ear. Very likely, too, the question was repeated and varied, rapidly and excitedly. "What aileth thee, O sleeper? Art thou deaf? Art thou faint? Art thou mad? Art thou dead? Dost thou not hear the noise of the storm, the raving of the wind, the raging of the waves, the tramp and the cries of the sailors overhead, and the sound of my voice as I now demand, What aileth thee, O sleeper?" It may be that this question of the captain has an application to some one present— to some Jonah, called, chosen, but not faithful, who has exhausted the energy he ought to have consecrated to the Divine service in such and such an evil course, and is now fast asleep in a spiritual sense. If so, I trust that the discourse now proceeding will be as the cry of the captain's voice and the grasp of the captain's hand, and that the sleeper will be awakened thereby.

To the question was added a word of exhortation. "Arise! call upon thy God, if so be that God will think upon us, that we perish not." The captain did not desire to awaken his passenger for the mere sake of doing so. There was a duty which he wanted him to perform, viz., to add his prayers to those of the seamen; and this would seem to indicate that, heathen as he was, the master had certain ideas of prayer which may be considered with advantage by ourselves.

He appears, *e.g.*, to have attached importance to united prayer. It was not enough for him that his crew were engaged in the exercise : he desired every person on board the endangered vessel to be thus engaged. He was not willing that one should refrain from the supplication which had become expedient ; and it were well if a similar feeling prevailed among our Church officers and members. We meet for the worship of God, and to pour out our common suppli-

cations at His feet, and ought not to be indifferent to
the absence of any one member of the community to
which we belong. One of our number absent and asleep
while the others are at prayer! Ah me! it is not only
one who is thus out of communion with his brethren;
and every one who thus holds aloof should be sought
after and aroused to a sense of his duty by those
who have the welfare of the Church at heart.

It seems also that this captain knew that all prayer
is not equally efficacious. The prayers of his sailors
had not resulted in any good, as far as he could see;
and the reason might either be in the character of the
deities to whom they were addressed, or in that of
the suppliants. The god worshipped by the passenger might be of greater power to aid them than
any of those on whom the mariners were calling; or
the passenger himself might have greater power in
prayer than all those mariners together. If this was
really the captain's idea, it was a correct one, and is
one that should be present to our own minds. The
God of Jonah is the only God who can hear the
prayers of men; and He has respect only to the
prayers of those who, consciously or unconsciously,
pray under the influence of His own Spirit.

IV.

It remains to consider the detection of Jonah.
The mariners had toiled in vain. They had cast
their cargo overboard in vain. They had apparently
prayed in vain. Observe then what they did next.
While the captain was below with Jonah, " they said
every one to his fellow, Come, and let us cast lots,
that we may know for whose cause this evil is upon

us. So they cast lots, and the lot fell upon Jonah."
We don't know the method adopted by these men in
casting lots. They cast lots, however; not drew
them: and the lot fell upon Jonah; not was drawn
by him. The prophet was possibly no party to the
performance of this ceremony. He may have been
entirely passive in the matter, but he had scarcely
staggered up after the captain to the deck of the
vessel when he learnt that the lot had fallen upon
himself. This part of his experience is illustrative of
various truths and circumstances in which we are all
interested.

It is illustrative, *e.g.*, of the inspired proverb,
" The lot is cast into the lap, but the whole disposing
thereof is of the Lord." The experience of others
who are mentioned in the Scriptures illustrates this
proverb no less than that of Jonah. You are familiar
with the accounts which are given of Achan and Saul
and Jonathan and Matthias. In all the instances to
which I now refer the Lord did so dispose the lot as
to make it fall upon the proper person. What then?
Those were the days of miracles, you say, and it
would not be right for us to resort to the lot for the
purpose of ascertaining the guilty person who has
imperilled the community of which he is a member.
Certainly not; but suppose that the lot were resorted
to for such a purpose: it would fall upon some one,
and the probability is that it would fall upon an innocent person. The proverb, however, would not be
falsified by that circumstance. It is true in all ages,
and under all dispensations and circumstances, that
" the lot is cast into the lap, but the whole disposing
thereof is of the Lord." The meaning is that there

is, strictly speaking, no such thing as chance, but
that the Divine Providence embraces us and all our
affairs.   Whether the lot fall upon the guilty person
or an innocent one, it still falls on the person whom
God intends it to fall upon.   It may be the means of
detecting the offender, as in the case of Jonah ; or it
may be the means of exposing an innocent person
to the scorn, anger, or violence of others, and thus
subjecting that person to a trial which God designs
to overrule for his (or her) advantage.

This part of Jonah's experience is also illustrative
of the old and wide-spread notion which our Lord cor-
rected when His attention was called to the horrible
fate of those whose blood Pilate had mingled with
their sacrifices.   The notion is that exceptional calamity is the proof and penalty of exceptional guilt.
The patriarch Job was thought by his friends to have
contracted such guilt because they saw that he was
overwhelmed by such calamity.   The sailors saw in
the storm which had come upon them a proof that
some one in the ship had been exceptionally and
excessively guilty.   But the Galileans slaughtered
by Pilate were not sinners above all the Galileans,
and Job was a better man than either of his friends,
and the sailors ought not to have concluded that the
storm had come upon them in consequence of any
particular crime which had been committed by some
one on board.   You say, " I don't see that ; for
Jonah himself told them, ' I know that for my sake
this great tempest is upon you,' and the whole story
confirms the prophet's assertion."   I repeat, however, that the sailors ought not to have entertained
the notion of which I am speaking ; but then God

knew they would entertain it, and therefore arranged that it should be the means of Jonah's detection. It is by no means a notion to be cherished. The miraculous element which operated in connection with the prophet's experience is not in operation now. Not here, but hereafter, will men be rewarded according to what they have done. For the present, some of the best of men have the largest experience of trouble, and some of the worst attain to wealth and power; but "there are first which shall be last, and last which shall be first."

This part of the prophet's experience is illustrative, moreover, of the inaptitude of men to realize their own guilt so readily as that of their fellow men. It does not appear to have occurred to any of these heathen sailors that his own guilt was sufficient to provoke the punishment threatened by the storm. Each of them appears to have thought the storm was occasioned by the guilt of some other person; and I suppose it will be admitted that a man is usually more apt to behold the mote in his brother's eye than to consider the beam in his own eye, even among ourselves.

Once more, the prophet's experience illustrates the manner in which communities are liable to be injured or imperilled by the presence of individuals who are committed to wrong courses. It was because Jonah was in the ship that his fellow-voyagers lost their cargo and nearly lost their lives. It was because Achan was in the camp that the Israelites were defeated by their foes. It is lamentably true that "one sickly sheep infects the flock and poisons all the rest;" and it is for each of us to say, "God helping me, I will not be the one person who may endanger or corrupt the family, or the social circle, or the Church, or any other community to which I belong."

Finally, the prophet's experience is illustrative of the ease with which God can convict the sinner as soon as it pleases Him to do so. It was a dreadful thing for Jonah to stand before those heathen sailors, detected, exposed, convicted, covered with confusion and shame ; but how easily it was brought about ! Then, " be sure your sin will find you out." Sooner or later, at the day of judgment if not before, it will find you out. It is known to the Most High at this moment, and He will remember it then. You may deny i , conceal it, forget it, but it will be brought home to you then. Would you avoid the shame, the remorse, the misery, and all the other consequences of such conviction ? Repent ! That is the pith of what the modern preacher has to say, as it was of the utterances of the ancient prophets. " Repent; for the kingdom of heaven is at hand ! " " Repent, and believe the Gospel ! " Do you say that you can't repent, or you would ? Then betake yourself in thought to the cross whereon Jesus died, and resign yourself to the influence of the feelings it excites as you behold it, and penitence will pervade your spirit.

V.

CATECHIZED BY THE CREW.

"Then said they unto him, Tell us, we pray thee, for whose cause this evil is upon us? What is thine occupation? and whence comest thou? what is thy country, and of what people art thou? And he said unto them, I am an Hebrew; and I fear the Lord, the God of heaven, which hath made the sea and the dry land. Then were the men exceedingly afraid, and said unto him, Why hast thou done this? For the men knew that he fled from the presence of the Lord, because he had told them. Then said they unto him, What shall we do unto thee, that the sea may be calm unto us? for the sea wrought, and was tempestuous. And he said unto them, Take me up, and cast me forth into the sea; so shall the sea be calm unto you: for I know that for my sake this great tempest is upon you."—JONAH i. 8-12.

EXPOSED as Jonah now was by the lot which had fallen upon him, there was no immediate improvement in the condition of the crew. The captain and his men were not perhaps certain, after all, that their passenger was the culprit whose presence had occasioned the tremendous tempest which had come upon them. But in all probability they had no misgiving on this point, and were morally certain that their peril was attributable to his guilt. Yet they were none the better for that conviction. The wind was as fierce, the sea as rough, and the ship as much imperilled as ever; and what could they do to improve their condition? Jonah himself might be competent to counsel them on this point, and they proceeded to consult him concerning it. Clinging as they best could to rope and bolt and bulwark, the sailors and the prophet carried on the conversation recorded in the text, while the foam flew in their faces, and the wind snatched their words from their mouths before they had time to reach the ears for which they were intended. Substantially there were only three questions put to the prophet by his anxious examiners : " For whose cause is this evil upon us ? Why hast thou done this ? What shall we do unto thee that the sea may be calm unto us ? " To the first and last of these questions the prophet returned replies, but not to the second ; yet was his silence as expressive as his speech.

I.

The first of these questions was put in various forms to the prophet : " Tell us, we pray thee, for whose cause this evil is upon us ? " Had his been the only form in which this question was put, there might have been some doubt in Jonah's mind as to its meaning. He might have understood the sailors to mean, " Is it for thy cause that this evil is upon us, or for that of some other man ? The lot has fallen upon thee, but dost thou own or deny that it has fallen upon thee rightly ? " But the different forms of the question showed the prophet that they did not ask whether he was the man, but who and what he was. " Tell us, we pray thee, for whose cause this evil is upon us ? what is thine occupation ? and whence comest thou ? what is thy country ? and of what people art thou ? "

We are not to suppose that these questions were put to the prophet consecutively, but rather that they were shouted at him by the sailors almost simultaneously, and with the excited manner which was inevitable under the circumstances. Still, there was a certain respect for the prophet apparent in the terms of the leading question, " Tell us, we pray thee, for whose cause this evil is upon us ? " Every modification of this question must have been a stab, however, to the conscience of the guilty man to whom it was addressed ; and it must have been with a strangely blended dignity and shame that he replied, " I am an Hebrew; and I fear Jehovah, the God of heaven, which hath made the sea and the dry land ; and I am fleeing from the presence of Jehovah." These are the first recorded words of Jonah, and their testimony to his character is by no means unfavourable. He might have remained silent. He might have bitterly reproached the sailors for their folly in casting lots and questioning him while the ship required all their attention and energy. He might have told them a falsehood, and endeavoured to persuade them that he was entirely innocent of anything which could have brought that awful tempest upon them. He might have defied them in his despair, and cursed them in his anger. Might he ? Nay. Another kind of man might have acted in some such way, but not Jonah. He was not a bad man, however badly he had behaved in this instance. He was not base enough to speak falsely or unkindly to the men he had imperilled ; and therefore, when they interrogated him, he made a clean breast of it, as we say.

It is well that men should confess the faults they have committed to those who have been wronged by them ; and if there is any one present who is conscious that he has wronged another, let me ask whether he has made confession of his fault to the injured person, and if not, why not.

Perhaps the man you have wronged is ignorant of the circumstance, and you think that " where ignorance is bliss, 'tis folly to be wise." But you should remember that there are various ways in which a wrong may be acknowledged, and that, when conscience does not compel a verbal confession on the part of the offender, he may yet virtually acknowledge his fault by doing all in his power to compensate the injured person.

But perhaps the man you have wronged knows all about what has taken place, and you think it superfluous to tell him what he knows. Not to confess, however, is in such a case really to deny that you have done the wrong, and thus falsehood is added to the original offence.

It is possible that you may shrink from confessing the wrong you have done to another because such confession involves humiliation. So it does ; but did you never meditate upon the Scripture paradox, " He that humbleth himself shall be exalted " ? Moreover, it is not so much the confession of wrongdoing which is humiliating as wrong-doing itself.

It is not improbable that you have a stronger reason for not confessing the fault you have committed. You may be aware that, in your case, confession would be idle without restitution, and that restitution is impossible. If you could put things as they were, you would do so ; but as that cannot be done, confession is worse than useless.

How do you know? "There was a certain creditor which had two debtors; the one owed him five hundred pence, and the other fifty; and when they had nothing to pay, he frankly forgave them both." Would it be worse than useless to confess your fault to the person you have wronged, and thus afford him an opportunity of extending his frank forgiveness to one unable to make restitution?

But perhaps you are able to say to your fellow-men in the words of the prophet Samuel, "Behold, here I am: witness against me before the Lord and before His anointed: whose ox have I taken? or whose ass have I taken? or whom have I defrauded? whom have I oppressed? or of whose hand have I received any bribe to blind mine eyes therewith? and I will restore it you." You may be able to issue this challenge as confidently as Samuel himself; and may be able to say also with the Apostle Paul, "We have corrupted no man; we have defrauded no man." But is there no confession due to God of wrong-doing on your part? Let me rehearse two sentences of Scripture at this point, one from the Old and the other from the New Testament: "He that covereth his sins shall not prosper, but whoso confesseth and forsaketh them shall find mercy." "If we confess our sin, God is faithful and just to forgive us our sin, and to cleanse us from all unrighteousness."

II.

The second question put to Jonah by the sailors was, "Why hast thou done this?" *i.e.*, Why hast thou fled from the presence of the Lord? "For the men knew that he fled from the presence of the Lord, because he had told them." Now this was a question most pertinent to Jonah's case, but not more so than it is to that of many a person among ourselves.

1. Consider the question as addressed to Jonah. "Why hast thou done this?" The prophet returned no answer; perhaps because he had no time; perhaps because he had no power, being overwhelmed with confusion and shame at having exposed himself to it. But can we answer the question why Jonah fled from the presence of the Lord rather than go to Nineveh and cry against it, as he was directed to do? I think we can.

It was certainly not from any pity he felt for the people of Nineveh that he refused to go thither and cry against it. If a good man were commissioned in these days to go from this country to some great and guilty heathen city with such a message as Jonah was entrusted with, he might well be distressed at the anticipation of its destruction. But Jonah did not anticipate the destruction of Nineveh so much as its deliverance, as appears from what is said further on: "Therefore I fled before Thee unto Tarshish; for I knew that Thou art a gracious God, and merciful, slow to anger, and of great kindness, and repentest Thee of the evil."

It is not impossible that the prophet was apprehensive that he would be put to death by the Ninevites; and it certainly was not an unlikely thing that a people prone to acts of cruel violence would slay the man who came into their city to cry against it. We read of no promise to Jonah on God's part that his life should be spared, and if his mission to Nineveh resulted in its destruction rather than its deliverance, it was altogether probable that the pro-

phet would perish at the hands of its people. Such
a fate might well have terrors for Jonah. He was
not, indeed, afraid of death, as we shall see. He was
not even afraid of a violent death, if that must be
encountered in the discharge of his duty. But it
was death at the hands of the heathen that he
dreaded. There was a feeling in the heart of every
Israelite like that which Saul displayed at Gilboa:
" Then said Saul unto his armour-bearer, Draw thy
sword, and thrust me through therewith ; lest these
uncircumcised come and thrust me through, and
abuse me. But his armour-bearer would not, for he
was sore afraid. Therefore Saul took a sword, and
fell upon it." Jonah was too good a man to commit
suicide rather than expose himself to death at the
hands of the heathen ; but he was not too good a
man to decline the duty devolved upon him rather
than do so.

To this personal feeling it is probable there was
added one of a professional character. Jonah was a
prophet, and was directed to predict the speedy
overthrow of the Assyrian capital ; but was himself
under the impression that it was more likely to be
delivered than destroyed as the result of his mission
to it, an idea which was justified by the event. It
would be a great mortification to his professional
pride if it were noised abroad among the nations that
he had predicted the destruction of a city which was
not destroyed within the specified time. Jonah
appears to have thought in this instance less of
God's glory than his own; and that is what we are
all apt to do. We are not willing to suffer shame for
His sake, but we ought to be; and it were well for us

to remember that He Himself has said, " Them that honour Me I will honour," and " he that humbleth himself shall be exalted."

A perverted patriotism had, doubtless, something to do with the flight of which the sailors asked the reason. Jonah had predicted the deliverance of Israel from the Syrian power, and his prediction had been fulfilled. But, as the power of Syria declined, that of Assyria increased. The armies of Assyria went forth and subdued the various countries in its neighbourhood; and, to all appearance, Israel was in danger of subjugation also. The prophet, perceiving the peril in which his own people were thus placed, shrank from having anything to do with Nineveh that would be likely to avert the destruction provoked by the wickedness of its people. He would have rather been instrumental in ensuring its destruction than effecting its deliverance, and he believed that its deliverance would result from his obedience to the Divine mandate which sent him thither. The alternative which presented itself to his mind was the destruction of Nineveh or of Israel; and believing, as he did, that the deliverance of Nineveh would involve the destruction of Israel, as indeed it did, we can understand why he fled from the presence of the Lord rather than be the means of averting the doom of the great city. It was, then, a patriotic motive by which Jonah was actuated, but it was a perverted patriotism he displayed; and there is a patriotism among ourselves which closely resembles it. There are persons in this country who are always thinking of " the balance of power," and always apprehensive that the power of some other country will preponderate to the disadvantage of our own. At one time they are afraid of the United States of America, and at another of the Russian Empire. By so much as another nation prospers will the prosperity of our own be diminished, they think; and they would therefore rejoice in any war, or in any calamity whatsoever, that might humble the power of which they are jealous. A patriotism of this kind is at variance with the spirit of the Christian religion. It is for Christians to love and honour all men, and to pray for the time when nation shall no more rise against nation, but the kingdoms of the world shall have become the kingdoms of our God and of His Christ. That time will surely come; but in the meantime, how is it with you? Does Christ reign in your hearts even now, or are you still in rebellion against Him? Think!

2. The question put to Jonah by the sailors, "Why hast thou done this?" has a great deal of pertinence as addressed to one and another among ourselves.

Has any one of you ceased to hold that communion with God which consists in the habitual study of the Scriptures, the prayer, and the devout meditation to which His people are addicted? "Why hast thou done this?"

Have you ceased to attend the House of God with the regularity you once observed? Your parents carried you to the courts of the Lord's House in your childhood, and in your youth you maintained the habit thus formed; but for some years past you have been absent from the Sanctuary more frequently than present when its doors were open for worship. You have habitually turned your back on the assemblies of God's people, and I ask, "Why hast thou done this?"

There is one who was formerly a member of the visible Church, a professed and recognised disciple of Christ; but he has withdrawn from the fellowship of saints, and has many excuses for the course thus adopted. But his own conscience is not satisfied with such excuses, and his fellow-Christians are not satisfied, and God is not satisfied; in Whose great Name I would say to every such backslider, "Why hast thou done this?"

One of those now addressed was formerly all that has been described and more. You maintained private communion with God. You regularly attended His house. You were His professed servant. Moreover, you justified your profession by the specific services you rendered to His cause. You were active and earnest, successful, respected and happy in the work with which you were thus occupied. But you have abandoned that work. Why? Do not tell me that you have less time than formerly, or less physical strength, but produce the real reason for this change of conduct on your part. "Why hast thou done this?"

There may be one whose case is sadder still; who has turned aside not only from the path of religion, but from that of virtue. You were honest once; but are now guilty of sharp practice and petty fraud, if not of downright theft. Or you were sober once; but have become a drunkard, and bartered health and home and hope for the strong drink which you crave with an unquenchable thirst. Or you were chaste once; but have become a cloth for dirty hands, a mat for dirty feet, a soiled and sullied victim of the vice which has destroyed its tens of thousands. "Why hast thou done this?"

Ah me! while others have, without your advantages, been feeling after God, if haply they might find Him, you have been wandering away from His presence. Return, I beseech you! Come back to Christian virtue and service and fellowship and worship! Do not wait till you are called back by storm and tempest, by disaster and calamity, or by some other experience of the terror of the Lord; and do not drift or drive along your present course to destruction and despair!

III.

The final question addressed to the prophet by the sailors was, " What shall we do unto thee, that the sea may be calm unto us?" There was a feeling which found expression in this question which the sailors assuredly did not pause to analyse, but which we may analyse at our leisure.

There was a consciousness of their own inability to devise a right and wise method of dealing with their passenger which made them appeal in this fashion to Jonah himself. They assumed that they would be obliged to do something to him, but what they were to do they could not tell. Anxious to do right, they would do nothing recklessly even in the serious peril in which they were placed; "for the sea wrought and was tempestuous."

They evidently had confidence in the candour of the man to whom they appealed. If Jonah knew the best course for them to adopt, he would certainly describe it to them, however disastrous it might be to himself; for his answer to their first question had been so frank and full that he had won their con-

fidence thereby.   So they seem to have thought, and
the thought did equal honour to the prophet and to
themselves.

Moreover, there was doubtless a hope on the part
of these men that Jonah's reply to their question
would be prompted by the God he worshipped.   In
consulting a prophet of Jehovah, they considered
that they were really asking counsel of Jehovah
Himself; and they were right.   There was nothing
better for them to do than to ask the prophet this
question, " What shall we do unto thee, that the sea
may be calm unto us ? "

The reply they obtained was a remarkable one:
" He said unto them, Take me up, and cast me forth
into the sea; so shall the sea be calm unto you : for
I know that for my sake this great tempest is upon
you."   Observe the prompt, peremptory, prophetic
and plaintive character of this reply.

Its promptitude was all that the circumstances of
the case called for.   Jonah knew what he had to say,
and had no right to keep the men waiting, and therefore answered their question without a moment's delay.

Its peremptory character was occasioned by his
own position in relation to these men.   He was a
criminal and a convict, but he was also a judge ; the
judge in his own case, and called upon to pronounce
sentence as such upon himself.   But he was not the
executioner.   The sailors would have to give effect
to the sentence, and hence the peremptory manner in
which the prophet addressed them.

Its prophetic character shows that Jonah had not
been able to relinquish his office : " So shall the sea
be calm unto you."   The storm was at its height

6

when he pronounced these words. "The sea was going and whirling" when this messenger of the Most High assured the sailors that it would become calm as soon as they had cast him into it.

But it is the plaintive character of this reply which most impresses me. There was the voice of the dove in it. There was pathos in its humility. Jonah had been wont to look down on the heathen; but, alas! he felt that these poor heathen sailors had discharged their duty better than he had discharged his own. They were therefore more fit to live than himself, and it was well that their lives should be saved by the sacrifice of his own. "Take me up, and cast me forth into the sea: so shall the sea be calm unto you." There was pathos also in the remorse which this reply expressed. Jonah had not meant to injure these men by coming on board their vessel, but he had done so. They had lost their cargo, and had nearly lost their lives, by reason of his presence among them; and their peril was not even yet a thing of the past. It was therefore with remorseful emotion that the prophet said, "I know that for my sake this great tempest is upon you." There was an even profounder pathos in Jonah's willingness to die in order that these men might be saved. Was there? Certainly; but what then shall be said of the willingness of One, who described Himself as greater than Jonah, to die in order that you and I might be saved with an everlasting salvation from that death which is unto death? Was that pathetic? Why, the word is wanting in power, as all words must be wanting in power, to express the truth on the subject of our Redeemer's sacrificial death. But it was indeed a touching display

of Divine love, if we must be content with such
language ; so touching that many members of our
race have found their hearts melting within them as
they contemplated it.   Does it not move you to penitence, to gratitude, and to the devotion of your life
to Him who gave His own life for you ?   It assuredly
ought to do so ; for " God commendeth His love to
us, in that while we were yet sinners, Christ died for
us ; " and Christ Himself has proclaimed that " God
so loved the world, that He gave His only-begotten
Son, that whosoever believeth in Him should not
perish, but have everlasting life."

VI.

OVERBOARD.

"Nevertheless the men rowed hard to bring it to the land; but they could not: for the sea wrought, and was tempestuous against them. Wherefore they cried unto the Lord, and said, We beseech Thee, O Lord, we beseech Thee, let us not perish for this man's life, and lay not upon us innocent blood: for Thou, O Lord, hast done as it pleased thee. So they took up Jonah, and cast him forth into the sea: and the sea ceased from her raging."—JONAH i. 13-15.

LET us not fail to admire all that was admirable in the conduct of this heathen crew. If it is ever my lot to undertake a long and dangerous voyage, I shall be glad to find that the vessel in which I embark is manned by as fine a set of seamen as it comprised. A nobler ship's company was never gathered together. These men found themselves exposed to the fury of a tremendous tempest, and expected every moment to go down. It appeared to them that it was not a common storm which thus menaced them with destruction, but one which had been brought upon them by the exceptional guilt of some person on board. Casting lots to discover the culprit, the lot had fallen upon a passenger and a stranger; and he not only acknowledged his guilt, but assured them that, if they would cast him into the sea, the sea should be calm unto them. "Take me up, and cast me forth into the sea," said Jonah;

and the love of life and fear of death in each of his
auditors inclined them to do as he directed. " Take
me up, and cast me forth into the sea," said the
prophet ; and the wild wind, the furious foam, the
drenching spray, and the whirling waves, responded
with a united, emphatic, and magnificent *Amen !*
Yet no human voice cried across the deck of the
labouring vessel that the man who pronounced this
sentence upon himself must be taken at his word.
With a humane self-restraint which did them infinite
honour, the sailors set to work at an attempt to save
themselves without sacrificing their passenger ; and
it was not till that attempt had completely and manifestly failed that they reluctantly and reverently
consigned him to the deep. Let us admire them,
I say; let us catch their spirit ; let us copy their
example as often as circumstances call for the
exercise of those moral qualities which they displayed.

I.

The noble attempt of the sailors to save the prophet
must first engage our attention, and in particular the
toil involved in it, the risk they ran, the motive they
had, and the failure they experienced. " Nevertheless,
the men rowed hard to bring it to the land ; but they
could not : for the sea wrought, and was tempestuous
against them."

1. It was a noble attempt on the part of these
sailors to save the prophet, by reason of the toil it
involved on behalf of a stranger. They were weary
with the work they had done already, and might have
obtained immediate rest by simply dealing with that

stranger as he himself had directed. And why should
they not have done so? What was Jonah to them?
Why should they have continued toiling on his behalf?
Why should they have " digged " their long and heavy
oars into the sea again and again in their attempt to
keep him out of it? Why? Because they were good
fellows, to be sure. Because they were as unselfish
as we ought to be, and of nobler disposition than many
of us are. There are some persons among ourselves
who will do nothing for any one unless they are paid
for doing it. It may be that a neighbour is in urgent
need of some assistance which they might render if
they would; but he is too poor to remunerate them
for their trouble, and has not the claim of a kinsman
to their good offices, and they are weary with their
own proper work, and so they must be excused from
bestirring themselves on behalf of the man whose
deplorable condition appeals to their compassion.
They are not such fools as to labour for nothing.
They may, however, be greater fools than they think.
It is indeed certain that such selfish persons as we
have in view are not so awake to their own interests
as they suppose themselves to be. The work which
good men do for the benefit of those who cannot pay
for it, does yet obtain ample remuneration. That
remuneration may not indeed assume the form of
money or of money's worth, but it is far better worth
having. Do you ask me what is its nature? I reply
that in this particular, as in so many others, " the
secret of the Lord is with them that fear Him."
Learn to labour unselfishly, in imitation of the sailors
who toiled so hard on Jonah's behalf, and in imitation
of many others who need not now be mentioned, and

you will soon learn the nature of the reward which is thus obtained.

2. It was a noble attempt on the part of these sailors to save the prophet, by reason of the risk to which it exposed them for the sake of one who had occasioned them loss. As long as the fugitive prophet remained on board they were themselves in danger of instant death. There had been great generosity on their part in running this risk if Jonah had been a mere stranger, or had been even of any particular service to them. But it was far otherwise. They had lost their cargo as the result of his presence among them. Could they have anticipated what had since taken place when he first tendered his fare at Joppa, and came on board, they would assuredly have rejected both it and him. But no such anticipation was possible, and the loss of the cargo had now been sustained. Nevertheless, these fine fellows (as I cannot help calling them) risked their lives to save the man whose presence had been so disastrous to them from a watery grave.

It is a noble thing to risk life in an attempt to save the life of another. All honour therefore to the men who man the life-boat as soon and as often as there is a call for their services, and urge it through darkness and tempest toward the sinking vessel which has made signals of distress ! All honour also to the firemen who force their way through scorching heat and suffocating smoke and falling ruins in order to effect the rescue of some woman or child or helpless invalid from the fatal flames ! All honour, moreover, to those who venture down the mine wherein an explosion has just taken place, in hope of rendering

service to such as have survived it ! Yes, all honour
to them ; and all honour to the memory of the men
who risked their lives in Jonah's time in order to
rescue the prophet from the doom he had incurred !

It is a noble thing to return good for evil. There
are those who are never satisfied till they have had
their revenge on those who have injured them. "Eye
for eye, tooth for tooth, hand for hand, foot for foot,
burning for burning, wound for wound, stripe for
stripe," is the law they love. There are others who
will refrain from revenge when they might have it,
but that is all they will do. To expose themselves
to serious peril in the interests of those who have
injured them would seem to them very ridiculous.
But these heathen sailors were thus ridiculous, for
they risked their lives for one who had occasioned
them serious loss and peril.

3. It was a noble motive which prompted these
men to make this attempt to save the prophet's life.
They desired to show their sense of Jonah's own
demeanour in relation to themselves, and to make a
suitable response to it. He was a stranger among
them, it is true, and had been the occasion of loss
to them ; but he had not meant to injure them, and
had displayed a generous desire to save their lives at
the expense of his own. It was this conduct on his
part which called forth the equally generous exertion
of the sailors in his favour. If, in reply to their
anxious question, " What shall we do unto thee, that
the sea may be calm unto us ? " Jonah had protested
that it would be useless to do anything to him, and
had begged them to spare his life, I can scarcely
doubt that at least a part of the crew, if not the

whole of it, would have clamoured for his instant
expulsion from the vessel. But offering himself as
he did, and so frankly, to die in order to effect their
deliverance, these men could not execute the sentence
he had pronounced on himself till they had manifestly done all that was possible to save him.

It was thus that the first Napoleon, returning
from Elba, and meeting the soldiers sent to oppose
and arrest him, opened his coat at the breast, and
bade them put an end to all strife concerning himself
by shooting him then and there. But they neither
would nor could do as they were thus invited. They
were disarmed by this tender of his life on the part
of the great emperor; or, rather, they were induced
by it to place their arms and themselves at the disposal of their old leader. Yet there was in this
behaviour of Napoleon no such generosity as in that
of Jonah; for the emperor as clearly meant to save
himself as the prophet meant to be taken at his word.
But the very appearance of a readiness to die for
others in the one case, and the reality of such readiness in the other, were sufficient to win the hearts of
those concerned.

It is something like this with Christ and His Church.
He described Himself as greater than Jonah, but this
very description implies that there is something in
His conduct or experience which corresponds with
that of the prophet. It is certain that He has won
the hearts of His people by the willingness with
which He endured a violent death on their behalf,
and that they display their sense of His grace by
devoting themselves to His service. There are, alas!
too many human beings who refuse to consider what

Christ has done to render their salvation possible; and they are therefore unaffected by His death, or by the love which prompted Him to endure it. But those who take heed to the testimony and exhortations of the Gospel, "who behold the Lamb of God which taketh away the sin of the world," who "consider Him that endured such contradiction of sinners against Himself," "looking unto Jesus" as their only Redeemer and best Friend, are constrained by His love to devote themselves, heart and hand, to His blessed service.

4. The failure of this attempt on the part of the sailors to save the prophet by no means detracts from the nobility of their conduct. Although they rowed hard to bring the ship to land, they could not do so, for the sea was still going and whirling against them. It does not follow, however, that they had nothing but their labour for their pains. They were morally the better for the purpose they had cherished of saving the prophet, and for the effort they had made to accomplish that purpose. In this respect it was with them as it had been with David before them. When David was forbidden to build the Temple of Jehovah, as he had prepared to do, God said to him, "Thou didst well that it was in thine heart." These heathen sailors also did well that it was in their hearts to save Jonah, although they were not permitted to do so.

Do not be discouraged, brethren, because you have failed in certain attempts to benefit men and glorify God; and do not envy those who have been more successful than yourselves. It is possible that their success was attended with temptations to which they have yielded, while you have not been troubled thereby. If they and you knew more about the matter, it might be apparent that they have far more reason to envy you than you have to envy them; for although you have not done as you desired, you have benefited by the discipline experienced in connection with your efforts, and will yet receive a large reward from Him who shall say to each of His people hereafter, "Well done, good and faithful servant; enter thou into the joy of thy Lord!"

II.

We may now proceed to consider the consignment of Jonah to the sea on the part of the sailors. "They took up Jonah, and cast him forth into the sea." We cannot doubt that they handled the prophet as tenderly as the circumstances permitted. Every precious bale they had previously heaved overboard had been abandoned to the sea with a certain degree of reluctance and regret; but it was with far more intense emotion of the same kind that they now lifted the prophet, leaned over the side of the ship, and laid him as gently as possible on a wave which rose to receive him. Such is the scene which presents itself to our fancy, but we must not dwell upon it. Rather let us direct our attention to the prayer which these men offered before they consigned the prophet to the water, and to the answer they received as soon as they had done so.

1. The prayer of the sailors is replete with interest to those who regard it with attention. "They cried unto the Lord, and said, We beseech Thee, O Lord, we beseech Thee, let us not perish for this man's life,

and lay not upon us innocent blood: for Thou, O
Lord, hast done as it pleased Thee."

It was a prayer addressed to the true God by
these heathen for the first time. "They cried unto
Jehovah." Before this they had "cried every man
unto his god," but now they address their prayers to
the God of Whom Jonah had told them. The prophet
had proclaimed Him as "the God of heaven, which
hath made the sea and the dry land;" and the men
felt that the Deity Who could arouse the tempest to
arrest the flight of a fugitive servant, was One on
Whom the merest prudence should prompt them to
call. It was an experiment, doubtless, on their part,
to call upon Him; but it was a reasonable experiment, and it suggests a word of exhortation which
may be more or less applicable to some among ourselves. Let me ask, Is there any one among us who
has never cried unto the Lord? I will suppose there
is. You have sought help and comfort elsewhere, but
never at His footstool. You have access to the Bible,
in which you are urged and encouraged to call upon
Him, but have neglected to do so. The reason of
this must be unbelief on your part. If you believed
in the utility of prayer, you would pray. I think,
however, that you might learn a lesson from these
heathen sailors. They tried the experiment of praying
to Jehovah, and you also might try it. I earnestly
entreat you to copy the example of these truly sensible men in this respect. If you did but realize
your danger, as they could not fail to realize theirs
in that awful tempest, you would require no urging
to call upon the Lord for help. But you are none
the less in danger because you do not realise it; and

therefore it is well to remind you of the promise, " Whosoever shall call on the name of the Lord shall be delivered."

It was evidently a very earnest prayer which these sailors offered. Of course it was. If they prayed at all, under the circumstances in which they were placed, they would be sure to pray earnestly. They were in an earnest mood, as they were likely to be in that storm ; and therefore, when they rowed, they rowed hard,—"digged," as the word is ; and when they prayed, it was with a fervour that found expression in reiterated entreaty : " We beseech Thee, O Lord, we beseech Thee ! " Now, there are some persons who are more earnest in work than in prayer, and others who are more earnest in prayer than in work ; and those who belong to both classes may learn from these sailors neither to exhaust their earnestness in the one kind of exercise nor the other. But at present I insist especially on the importance of earnestness in prayer. God will give nothing to the man whose prayer is a mere formality, but will give much to one who cries to Him from the heart, who pours out his soul like water before Him, who wrestles with Him as Jacob did with the angel, and who thereby attests his conviction that " the kingdom of heaven suffereth violence, and the violent take it by force."

It was a prayer for their own preservation which these men presented. " Let us not perish for this man's life ! " they entreated. I suppose that this is generally understood to mean, " Let us not perish as a penalty for taking this man's life." They believed that Jonah had directed them to cast him into the sea in accordance with the will of that God Whose servant

he was, but what if they were mistaken? They
wanted to do right, but might do wrong in casting the
prophet into the water; and their petition is understood to mean, " Let us not perish for an act which we
think to be right, but which may indeed be wrong."
This may be its meaning, but may it not rather mean
something else? " ' This man's life ' has, on his own
confession, been one of defective devotion to Thee,
and Thou hast sent this storm to arrest his progress
in this direction; but let us escape his fury; ' let us
not perish for this man's life.' " At all events, the
petitioners prayed for their own preservation; and
that in such a manner as implied the assumption
on their part that the Being they addressed was a
righteous God, and not merely a vengeful one. " Let
us not perish for this man's life."

But it was not only a prayer for themselves which
the sailors thus presented; it was also a prayer for the
prophet. " Lay not upon us innocent blood; for
Thou, O Lord, hast done as it pleased Thee." You see
that they neither complained of Jonah, nor regarded
themselves as responsible for his fate. He was " innocent " of any intention to injure them, and they
were not about to consign him to the sea of their own
will, but in obedience to that of the Lord Himself.
Then what was the precise meaning of this petition?
Did they entreat the Most High to accept the responsibility of what they were about to do? or did they
entreat Him to spare the life of Jonah, even though
they threw him into the sea? They certainly meant
to pray with the former significance, and not improbably with the latter also. They must have felt that
the God Who had displayed His power over winds and

waves in the manner described in this narrative, was
able also to rescue His servant from the sea if He
cared to do so.

Evidence is not wanting that the prayer of these
poor heathen sailors, if I must still call them such, was
prompted by the spirit of grace and of supplications.
It was an appropriate prayer. It was sincere, earnest,
and humane. It expressed a humble consciousness
of ignorance and infirmity on the part of those who
presented it. It recognised the power, mercy, and
justice of Almighty God. It was sustained by suitable
conduct. It was a model of devotion, and may be
studied with great advantage by all who are interested
in the subject of communion with the one true and
living God.

2. The prayer having been offered, and the prophet
cast into the sea, the sailors had not long to wait for
the Lord's reply. " The sea ceased from her raging."
This was, of course, a miracle ; and the mere mention
of a miracle is apt to remind us of two different classes
of persons.

On the one hand, there are those who refuse to
believe that miracles have ever been wrought. Now,
a man who says that he is unable to believe that the
miracles described in the Bible were wrought, might
as well say that he cannot believe the Scriptures to be
true, or that Christ spake and did and bore the things
which they attribute to Him. To a person who really
is in this position, it should be of some use to remark
that the Bible, and therefore the Gospel, is either true
or false ; and that if it be false, it is more wonderful
than it would have been if true. But if a man only
affect the disbelief now noticed, it should suffice to

remind him of the retort which was addressed to
another such person by a member of the Society of
Friends.   A flippant fellow-traveller, having asked
him whether he really believed the Bible account of
many things described in it—the story of David and
Goliath, for example, in which a mere youth is represented as killing the champion, of whom the most
experienced and valiant warriors in his country were
afraid, by a pebble from his sling—the Quaker replied,
" Friend, if the giant's head were as soft as thine, it
was not a very difficult thing to kill him in that way."
The moral is, Do not be sceptical if you can help it,
and at all events do not affect scepticism, lest those
who are wiser and worthier than yourself should deem
you a simpleton for your pains.   The killing of Goliath
was not indeed a miracle, but the point of the story is
not blunted by that consideration, and it may be
remembered with advantage.   A providence which
embraces the miracles described in the Bible is worthy
of Him Whose name is Wonderful ; but a providence
absolutely destitute of such miracles from first to last
would be even more marvellous.

But those who do not believe that miracles have
ever been wrought, or even those who say that they
do not believe this, are few in comparison with those
who are eager for miracles and over ready to believe
in their performance.   Romanists[1] and spiritualists

---

[1] When this lecture was delivered the newspapers were reporting,
and commenting upon, the alleged miracles at the Roman Catholic
Chapel in Knock.   A dispassionate and unprejudiced reader could
only marvel at the credulity, or grow indignant at the knavery,
exhibited in connection with the whole matter.   But one is glad to
take this opportunity of saying that there is doubtless as much disgust

and others are desirous to have it believed that miracles are performed among them now, and many persons are disposed, or half disposed, to believe that such is indeed the case. The truth which should be commended to the consideration of such credulous persons is that the miracles recorded in the Scriptures were so many " signs " as well as " wonders " and " mighty works." They were *signs ; i.e.*, illustrations, or attestations, of certain truths which God thought of sufficient importance to call attention to by their means. If the pretended miracles of our own and other times are also *signs*, it must be confessed that they are only signs of fraud on the part of those who perform or exhibit them, and of folly on the part of those who are deceived by them. The miracle mentioned in the text was, however, one of the many signs to which God Himself was pleased to call attention ; and in what remains of this lecture we may consider the significance that belonged to it.

It was a sign that Jonah was indeed a prophet of Jehovah, and that he had not divested himself of his office by the flight in which he endeavoured to do so. He had said to the sailors, " Take me up, and cast me forth into the sea ; so shall the sea be calm unto you . . . ; and they took up Jonah, and cast him forth into the sea, and the sea ceased from her raging." It was important that the sailors should know that a prophet of Jehovah had been among them, not only

excited in the breasts of our more respectable Roman Catholic fellow-countrymen by such drivelling and devilry as there is in one's own. *They*, indeed, must feel intensely humiliated as often as the attention of the public is called to such matters.

for their own sake, but for that of the many persons
to whom they would afterwards relate what Jonah
had told them concerning the God he had offended,
and their own experience in connection with the
storm here described. It was important also that the
people of Nineveh should know that not only had the
coast of Israel been restored in accordance with one
prediction uttered by Jonah, but that a tempest had
been instantly stilled in accordance with another.

This miracle was a sign, too, that Jehovah is the
Ruler of the sea. Jonah had described Him as its
Maker, and now these sailors perceived it to be under
His control. An appropriate lesson for men of their
calling, was it not? For passengers also, who cross
the ocean, and for visitors to the sea-side, and for all
who dwell upon the coast, and for all who are interested in the welfare of those afloat, and for all whose
capital is invested in ships and their cargoes, it is an
appropriate lesson. Let them learn it, then, and let
all men learn the truth on this subject which the
Psalmist teaches: " They that go down to the sea
in ships, that do business in great waters; these see
the works of the Lord and His wonders in the deep.
For He commandeth, and raiseth the stormy wind,
which lifteth up the waves thereof . . . He maketh
the storm a calm, so that the waves thereof are
still."

Finally, this miracle was a sign that God hears
and answers prayer. Do not waste time in curious
inquiries as to whether it is possible in the nature of
things that prayer should prevail with God. It did
prevail with Him when presented by the sailors
mentioned in the narrative before us. It has pre-

vailed with Him in numberless other instances. It does prevail when offered by many persons who are now living. It will prevail if offered by you. Try the experiment, as the sailors did. Test the truth of that saying of the Saviour thereby : " Ask, and ye shall receive ; seek, and ye shall find ; knock, and it shall be opened unto you ; for every one that asketh receiveth ; and he that seeketh findeth ; and to him that knocketh it shall be opened."

VII.

CONVERSION OF THE CREW.

" Then the men feared the Lord exceedingly, and offered a sacrifice unto the Lord, and made vows."—JONAH i. 16.

CONVERSION is not always experienced in consequence of what is heard or seen in a place of
public worship. Persons who are anxious for the
conversion of their friends are apt to wish that the
objects of their anxiety would but attend such a place,
and this is natural enough. It is certain that the
services of the sanctuary are adapted to effect the
conversion of those who attend them ; but it is not
always that conversion is effected thereby. It was
in the open air, and far away from any place where
the worshippers of Jehovah were wont to assemble,
that God met the patriarch Jacob and won his allegiance to Himself. You know how the patriarch
described and denominated the place where God thus
appeared to him. " He was filled with awe, and
said, How solemn is this place ! This is none other
but the house of God, and this is the gate of heaven !
. . . And he called the name of that place Beth-el."
So, too, with the mariners mentioned in the narrative
before us. They were converted to the Lord on
board their ship ; and this may encourage those who
have friends at sea to pray for their conversion.
That reckless young fellow who despised all counsel in

relation to his own spiritual interests, and would never accompany you to the house of God while he remained on shore, is not one to be despaired of merely because he is now on board a ship, and far away upon the ocean. The Lord may meet with him there, as He met with these mariners in Jonah's time; and I hope it may be found encouraging and instructive to consider what is here said respecting the emotion produced in them by their previously recorded experience, and the manner in which that emotion was expressed: "And the men feared the Lord with a great fear, and sacrificed a sacrifice unto the Lord, and vowed vows."

I.

The emotion roused in these sailors was such as to supply us with an interesting subject for reflection by reason of its nature and intensity.

1. The feeling they experienced was that fear of the Lord concerning which the Scriptures have so much to say. It was not the same kind of feeling as that which had possessed them while the tempest raged. When that tempest came upon them, "the mariners were afraid," but the terror thus occasioned was by no means the same as the fear which filled their hearts when the sea had "ceased from her raging." There is a fear which is terror, and there is a fear which is reverence. A wicked man may fear the Lord in the sense of being terrified at the very thought of Him. A good man fears the Lord in the sense of regarding Him with reverence. The devils tremble with the former kind of fear, and the angels rejoice with the latter.

It is impossible to read of the fear experienced by

these mariners, first in the storm and then in the calm, without thinking of the emotion attributed to the disciples on two occasions during the lifetime of their Lord. On one of them He and they were crossing the Sea of Galilee when a storm arose which filled their hearts with fear, but failed to arouse Him from the slumber into which He had fallen. It was their plaintive demand which awakened Him: "Master, carest Thou not that we perish? And He arose, and rebuked the wind, and said unto the sea, Peace, be still! And the wind ceased, and there was a great calm. And He said unto them, Why are ye so fearful? how is it that ye have no faith? And they feared exceedingly, and said one to another, What manner of man is this, that even the wind and the sea obey Him?" The fear they experienced in the storm was manifestly a very different feeling from the fear they experienced afterwards. On the other occasion the disciples were in the ship without the Master, " and the ship was now in the midst of the sea, tossed with waves, for the wind was contrary. And in the fourth watch of the night Jesus went unto them, walking on the sea. And when the disciples saw Him walking on the sea, they were troubled, saying, It is a ghost! and they cried out for fear. But straightway Jesus spake unto them, saying, Be of good cheer: it is I; be not afraid! . . . Then they that were in the ship came and worshipped Him, saying, Of a truth Thou art the Son of God!"[1] On both these occasions a feeling of reverence for Christ took the place of that terror which had previously been experienced by reason of the peril to which the disciples were exposed.

[1] Matt. viii. 23, and xiv. 22.

In all cases this reverence for the Divine Being, this fear of the Lord of which I speak, is occasioned by some revelation of Him which finds its way to the hearts of those who experience the emotion. It is not enough that God is revealed to men in a Book which describes His nature, character, and will. The contents of that Book must be copied from it, and written upon the heart. It is not enough that God is revealed as the Almighty. That by itself would excite the terror which I am trying to show is not the kind of fear to be desiderated. It is necessary that He should be revealed as infinitely wise and righteous also; but even that is not enough. If that were all, God must indeed be regarded with reverence, but must He not also be regarded with despair? When, however, He is revealed as not merely perfect in power, prescience, and purity, but also in benevolence, and as delighting in the exercise of mercy, the reverence with which He is regarded has in it no element of servile terror. The Psalmist knew this when he said, "There is forgiveness with Thee that Thou mayest be feared;" and this blessed truth was doubtless realized by the sailors when "the sea ceased from her raging." It was plain to them that they were in the power of a Deity Whom they had not served, and Who was yet well disposed towards them, seeing that He had answered their prayers and saved their lives; and their hearts were won by this exercise of mercy on His part. As soon as some such revelation of the Most High reaches the heart of any human being, so soon does the fear of the Lord inculcated in His word begin to operate therein. For it is by no means a dead or inoperative feeling. We shall see

presently that it was not such in the case of these
sailors; but, for the time being, let me show the
effect it has upon God Himself, and, through Him,
upon those who experience it.

Do you want to be safe? It is sad to be in danger,
as was the case with the sailors mentioned in the text
when " the sea wrought and was tempestuous against
them." It is possible, however, that some among
ourselves are exposed to graver peril at this moment
than that which menaced them. There is a spiritual
peril from which all who are exposed to it should be
anxious to escape, and from which all who fear the
Lord are well protected, for " the Angel of the Lord
encampeth round about them that fear Him, and
delivereth them."

Do you want to be wise? Many have desired and
laboured for wisdom in vain. They did not begin
aright, and all their subsequent efforts were in vain.
They did not become wise unto salvation, and were
not therefore wise at all; and why was this? Because
it was their misfortune not to know, or not to
believe, that " the fear of the Lord is the beginning
of wisdom."

Do you want to be rich? There are those whose
desire for wealth is so intense that they will toil and
scheme and sin in order to secure it, and yet they
can never attain thus to the true riches. They may
become wealthy in the ordinary sense of the word,
but cannot become rich towards God. On the other
hand, those who fear the Lord may be as poor as the
Son of Man Himself in respect of the good things of
the present life, and yet they are really rich. In
proportion as they cherish reverence for God will they

approximate to that condition of mind which the Apostle claimed to have reached when he said, " I have learned in whatsoever state I am to be content." The man who is content with his lot, and wants nothing, is a rich man, is he not ?   " O fear the Lord," then, " ye His saints ; for there is no want to them that fear Him."

2. The intensity of the emotion experienced by the sailors deserves our notice. They not only feared the Lord, but feared Him with a great fear ; or, if we substitute the English for the Hebrew idiom, they feared the Lord exceedingly.   It was a profound reverence for the God of heaven which had taken possession of their hearts, and this was in a manner characteristic of the men.   They are described as rowing, as praying, and as fearing the Lord.   When they rowed, they rowed hard.   When they prayed, they prayed earnestly.   When they feared the Lord, they feared Him exceedingly.   It would have been deeply interesting had an account been furnished us of the after lives of these men.   Such an account, however, is unnecessary, inasmuch as we are furnished with accounts of other men who had a like intense reverence for the Lord and acted accordingly.

There was Obadiah, *e.g.*, of whom there was occasion to speak in the first of these lectures.   It is said that " Obadiah feared the Lord greatly," and it is also mentioned that his intense reverence for God occasioned him to befriend certain of God's servants at great risk and expense to himself.   " For it was so, when Jezebel cut off the prophets of the Lord, that Obadiah took an hundred prophets, and hid them by fifty in a cave, and fed them with bread and water."

There are others mentioned in the Scriptures as having feared the Lord exceedingly, although this particular phrase is not employed in connection with their names. There was the prophet Daniel. There were his three youthful friends in Babylon. There were the apostles and martyrs of whom we read in the New Testament. There were others to whom no particular reference is needed just now. All these, like the sailors mentioned in the text, feared the Lord with a great fear.

Moreover, there have been many whose names do not occur in the Scriptures, but who have displayed an intense reverence for the Most High. They were men of whom the world was not worthy; some of them died rather than displease their Divine Friend; and being dead, they yet speak to us in a manner that should make us long to emulate their devotion to His service.

But those who endured persecution in the discharge of their religious duty were not inspired by a deeper reverence for God than some of those who have been held in honour by their fellow men. Having favour with all the people, they were not prevented by that happy circumstance from displaying the utmost reverence for God, and that reverence occasioned them to be incessantly and earnestly engaged in His service. Like their Master, they went about doing good, and it was their meat and their drink to do the will of their Father in heaven.

It is an affecting thought that the poor seamen to whom allusion is made in this passage attained at a bound, so to speak, to the moral elevation occupied by the prophets, apostles, martyrs, and other eminent saints whose name and fame are familiar to us. It is an equally affecting thought that many among ourselves, whose privileges have been far greater and more numerous than those of these sailors, have less reverence for the Lord than they exhibited. How is it with you? Do you fear the Lord exceedingly? Do you fear Him at all?

II.

We have now to observe the manner in which this fear of the Lord on the part of these men found appropriate expression. They " sacrificed a sacrifice unto the Lord and vowed vows."

1. They offered a sacrifice unto the Lord, and we may consider what kind of a sacrifice it was that they offered, and what kind of a sacrifice it behoves us to offer in acknowledgment of our own deliverance from destruction.

The kind of sacrifice which the sailors offered may be learnt from the word employed in the original.[1] It was an animal sacrifice, and yet not that particular kind of animal sacrifice which was denominated a burnt-offering.

The sacrifice spoken of in the text involved the shedding of blood. There were some sacrifices among the heathen as well as among the Hebrews which did

---

[1] זֶבַח, *zebach;* as distinguished from אִשֶּׁה, *ishsheh,* a sacrifice of praise made by fire (which might have been perilous on shipboard); מִנְחָה, *minchah,* a sacrifice not involving bloodshed; עֹלָה, *ôlah,* or Holocaust, the whole burnt-offering, which had to be entirely consumed, as it was entirely devoted unto God; and some other kinds of sacrifice mentioned in the Bible to which present reference is unnecessary.

not involve this. They consisted of flour, oil, salt,
and spice, and need not be considered now. It was
not such a sacrifice that was offered by these sailors.
They doubtless had animals on board so large a
vessel as the one in which they served, as a matter
of ordinary convenience, and one of these animals was
slaughtered by them as an offering to the God Whom
they had learnt to fear. They expressed their reverence for Him in this customary manner, although
ignorant of the truth which the institution of sacrifice
was divinely intended to illustrate ; the truth which
is at the very heart of the Gospel ; the truth that in
His beloved Son, the Lamb slain from the foundation
of the world, God is well pleased.

But though it was an animal sacrifice which these
men offered, it was not a burnt-offering. It might
have been dangerous to offer a sacrifice of *that* kind
on board a ship ; for it was the peculiarity of a burnt-
offering that it had to be completely consumed by
fire ; its complete consumption denoting that the life
of those on whose behalf it was offered was entirely
due to God. There were, however, other animal
sacrifices which were not thus completely consumed.
A portion only of the victim was consumed, and the
other portion was eaten by the persons who offered
it. The idea was that they were reconciled to God,
and permitted (so to speak) to eat with Him ; He
regarding them with complacency, and they regarding
Him with gratitude. This was the kind of sacrifice
offered by the sailors. They feasted thankfully on
their share of the victim ; and if the part devoted to
the Most High was as acceptable to Him as the part
they retained was acceptable to themselves, it was

acceptable indeed. They had had no opportunity of
eating since the storm came upon them, and no inclination to eat while it lasted. In lightening the ship
and in rowing against the wind their labour had been
excessive and exhausting. But now the storm was
over, and the sea calm. Their prayer for deliverance
was answered, and they were out of danger. Their
physical nature now craved for food, while their spiritual nature yearned to express their gratitude to
God. It was natural, therefore, that they should
satisfy their hunger and render thankful homage to
their Divine Deliverer in the manner sanctioned by
ancient and universal custom. " They sacrificed a
sacrifice unto Jehovah."

We, too, my brethren, are under obligation to offer
sacrifice. If we are Christians indeed, and not merely
in name, we are priests. Clergymen are not invested
with any priesthood peculiar to themselves. All
Christians are priests unto God, and are under consequent obligation to offer sacrifices to Him. What
kind of sacrifices ? This is a question I am anxious
to answer, in order to give a practical tendency to
the present lecture ; and I say at once that it is not
an atoning sacrifice that we are called upon to offer.
Do you say that God's people were required to make
atonement by sacrifice under the Old Dispensation ?
I will not merely remark that we are not living under
that dispensation, but will remind you that its atoning
sacrifices were but so many types of the only sacrifice
which really constituted an atonement for sin. The
blood of bulls and goats could never take away sin,
and the sacrificial victims of the Old Testament did
but adumbrate in their death that death upon the

cross which our Lord endured when, "through the
Eternal Spirit, He offered Himself without spot to
God." The atoning sacrifices of the Old Economy
were ceremonial, typical, illustrative, shadowy, and
peculiar to itself. But there are other sacrifices which
have always been required from God's people, as they
are required still; personal, not vicarious; eucharistic,
not expiatory; recommended to others by inspired
servants of the Most High, and resorted to by themselves. In immediate advance of what he says about
"them that go down to the sea in ships," the Psalmist
calls upon such persons to "sacrifice the sacrifices of
thanksgiving;" and a little further on in this story
of Jonah we find the prophet saying to Jehovah, "I
will sacrifice unto Thee with the voice of thanksgiving." If you say that both the Psalmist and the
prophet allude to the presentation of those thank-
offerings which were prescribed by the law of Moses
and peculiar to the Old Economy, I will ask your
attention to what is said in the New Testament
respecting the sacrifices of thanksgiving which are
incumbent upon ourselves. There is a passage in the
Epistle to the Romans which reads thus: "I beseech
you therefore, brethren, as you would acknowledge
the mercies of God, to offer your bodies a living
sacrifice, holy and well-pleasing, unto God, which
is your reasonable worship." [1] There is a passage in

---

[1] So Conybeare and Howson. Rom. xii. 1, and Heb. xiii. 15 and
16. The somewhat free translations of Messrs. Conybeare and Howson are very helpful to those who seek to get beyond the mere letter
of the particular Scriptures with which they deal. The present
author has great pleasure in adding his humble testimony to that
which so many have been constrained to bear to the manifold help-
fulness and interest of their great work on "The Life and Epistles of
St. Paul."

the Epistle to the Hebrews which may be compared with the one just cited. Speaking of Christ, the sacred writer says, " By Him, therefore, let us offer unto God continually a sacrifice of praise,—that is, the fruit of our lips,—making confession unto His name. And be not unmindful of benevolence and liberality; for such are the sacrifices which are acceptable unto God." You see then that the sacrifices of thanksgiving which Christians are required to offer are their bodies, their praises, their confessions, their good works, and their alms.

It behoves all Christians, in grateful remembrance of the salvation they have experienced, to present their bodies unto God. They should consecrate their physical life and health, strength and skill, to His service. They should employ their hands and feet, eyes, ears, and tongue, for the promotion of His glory. One must not pursue this particular train of thought at present, but you see how different the life of a Christian should be from that to which many a human being is addicted, even in respect to bodily behaviour.

Christians should offer the sacrifice of praise also to God. It is verbal praise that is intended, for mention is made of the " fruit of the lips." When the praise of God is sung in the sanctuary, His people should be there, and say " Amen " by their mere presence to the song, if they are unable to actually unite in it. Moreover, there should be regularity in this service of praise, for the sacrifice is to be offered " continually." There may be fine sounding talk on the part of those who neglect the ordinances of public worship as often as they attend them about a spiritual worship, or a grateful mood, which they maintain independently of those ordinances; but such talk is to be regarded with suspicion. The Christian fellowship is necessary to the Christian life, and there is little grace in those who neglect the means of grace.

Among the sacrifices of thanksgiving to be offered by God's people, a confession of His Son has an important place. His divinity and authority, His grace and truth, should be acknowledged heartily, constantly, publicly, and suitably, by all His disciples. He Himself has spoken certain words of emphatic warning in relation to the neglect of this duty, which all who profess and call themselves Christians will do well to ponder.

Good works must be included among the sacrifices of which I am speaking. A good work is that which is such intrinsically, and is performed with a good motive. The grand motive to which a Christian yields in the performance of such works is gratitude to the Saviour. He does not perform them in order to obtain salvation thereby, but in order to express his gratitude for the salvation already obtained.

Almsgiving must not be neglected. The Christian must take care to "communicate" to those in need of his assistance such help as it is in his power to bestow. It may take the form of money, or of food, or of clothing, or of advice, or of protection, or of something else. Every such communication is a sacrifice. It is made to the Christian's fellow-men, but it is made to them for the Lord's sake, and is therefore regarded as made to the Lord Himself. The Apostle knew this when he wrote, "I am debtor both to the Greeks and to the barbarians, both to the wise

and to the unwise." The Apostle's creditor was
Christ, and he knew that Christ would accept any
service he might render to the various classes he
mentions as rendered to Himself. We, too, are under
obligation to communicate what good we can to all
about us, not because *they* have laid us under such
obligation, but because Christ has done so.

2. The reverence of the sailors alluded to in the
text for the God of Heaven occasioned them not
only to offer a sacrifice, but to make vows. A vow
is a promise made to God. It relates to the future.
It is a very serious process. In the case of these
sailors various vows were made ; but it is a reasonable
conjecture that they all had the same general tenor,
and involved the solemn promise that henceforth these
men would worship Jehovah and Him alone, and that
they would proclaim the truth respecting Him, as far
as they themselves were acquainted with it, in all the
places which they visited in the exercise of their
calling.

There are two sorts of vow of which the Scriptures
take notice. There are vows which ought, and vows
which ought not, to be made and redeemed. A vow
of the former kind is attributed to Jacob, and one of
the latter kind to Jephthah. It may be convenient to
notice the latter first.

Jephthah's vow was one of the many rash promises
addressed to God which can neither be redeemed nor
violated without sin. You are familiar with the story.
The warrior now named was about to encounter the
Ammonites, and presumptuously sought to bribe the
Most High to ensure him the victory. " Jephthah
vowed a vow unto the Lord, and said, If Thou shalt

8

without fail deliver the children of Ammon into mine
hands, then it shall be, that whatsoever cometh forth
of the doors of my house to meet me, when I return
in peace from the children of Ammon, shall surely be
the Lord's, and I will offer it up for a burnt-offering."
That was the vow; and having made it, Jephthah
went to battle and to victory, and returned to misery.
"Jephthah came to Mizpeh unto his house, and,
behold, his daughter came out to meet him with
timbrels and with dances : and she was his only
child ; beside her he had neither son nor daughter."
Let those who can do so imagine the anguish of the
chieftain as he saw the maiden approaching him.
Aghast, "he rent his clothes, and said, Alas, my
daughter! thou hast brought me very low, and thou
art one of them that trouble me; for I have opened
my mouth unto the Lord, and I cannot go back."
Jephthah could not violate his vow without sin, certainly; but neither could he redeem it without sin ;
and was in that respect precisely in the same position
as many another human being who has rashly vowed
unto the Lord. But if Jephthah sinned in the matter
of this presumptuous vow, he was severely punished ;
and his punishment should further point the warning
conveyed by the incident to which I allude. It cost
him his daughter to redeem his vow; and she was not
simply his only child, but appears to have been a
splendid girl. Courageous and patriotic, "she said
unto him, My father, if thou hast opened thy mouth
unto the Lord, do to me according to that which hath
proceeded out of thy mouth; forasmuch as the Lord
hath taken vengeance for thee of thine enemies."
She only stipulated for a respite during two months;

" and it came to pass, at the end of two months, that she returned unto her father, who did with her according to his vow which he had vowed." The lesson for each one of us is, " Be not rash with thy mouth, and let not thine heart be hasty to utter anything before God."

The vow attributed to the patriarch Jacob was of a different character, though its true meaning is obscured in our version. "If God will be with me, and will keep me in this way that I go, and will give me bread to eat and raiment to put on, so that I come again to my father's house in peace ; then shall the Lord be my God ; and this stone which I have set for a pillar shall be God's house ; and of all that Thou shalt give me, I will surely give the tenth unto thee." Thus read, the vow amounts to this : " If Thou wilt be mine, I will be Thine." But if a more accurate version were before us, the vow would be seen to have this far more appropriate import : " Since Thou wilt be mine, I will be Thine."[1] It was not a proposal on the patriarch's part, but a response. God had already promised to befriend him, and Jacob in return promised to serve his Divine benefactor."

If you have rashly uttered a presumptuous vow like that of Jephthah, I do not counsel you to redeem it. I simply say that you can neither redeem nor violate it without sin ; and if you ask whether it will be more

---

[1] Kitto, adopting Raphall's Jewish translation, reads Jacob's vow in this way : " If God will be with me, and keep me in this way that I am going, and will give me bread to eat and raiment to put on ; so that I return again to my father's house in peace, and the Lord will be my God ; then this stone which I have placed as a monument shall become God's house ; and of all that Thou shalt give me, I will surely tithe it unto Thee."

sinful to redeem or to violate it, I can only reply that
the answer to this question depends upon the circumstances of the case, and cannot be given here and
now.   But if you have vowed a vow like that of Jacob,
I would say to you, in the words of the inspired sage,
" When thou vowest a vow unto God, defer not to pay
it ; for He hath no pleasure in fools : pay that which
thou hast vowed.   Better is it that thou shouldest
not vow, than that thou shouldest vow and not pay."
The Psalmist said in his day (and which of us is without occasion to say *Amen* to his language ?), " I will
pay Thee my vows, which my lips have uttered, and
my mouth hath spoken when I was in trouble."   You
were in trouble, and may soon be in trouble again.
Let not the trouble which may come upon you be
aggravated by the haunting remembrance of violated
vows.

We have done with these sailors now.   I do not
suppose that their vows were violated.   Those vows
were prompted by that intense reverence for Jehovah
which had been awakened within them by their remarkable experience in connection with His prophet ;
and as it is said that " the fear of the Lord is clean,
enduring for ever," we may conclude that their reverence remained with them, and that their vows were
accomplished.   In taking our leave of them, so to
speak, let us humbly hope that the fear of the Lord
may dwell in our own hearts, that the sacrifices of
thanksgiving which it behoves us to offer may not be
withheld, and that every appropriate vow we have
uttered may be duly redeemed.

VIII.

IN THE SEA.

"Now the Lord had prepared a great fish to swallow up Jonah. And Jonah was in the belly of the fish three days and three nights. Then Jonah prayed unto the Lord his God out of the fish's belly, and said, I cried by reason of mine affliction unto the Lord, and He heard me ; out of the belly of hell cried I, and Thou heardest my voice. For Thou hadst cast me into the deep, in the midst of the seas ; and the floods compassed me about : all Thy billows and Thy waves passed over me. Then I said, I am cast out of Thy sight ; yet I will look again toward Thy holy temple. The waters compassed me about, even to the soul : the depth closed me round about, the weeds were wrapped about my head. I went down to the bottoms of the mountains ; the earth with her bars was about me for ever : yet hast Thou brought up my life from corruption, O Lord my God. When my soul fainted within me I remembered the Lord ; and my prayer came in unto Thee, into Thine holy temple. They that observe lying vanities forsake their own mercy. But I will sacrifice unto Thee with the voice of thanksgiving ; I will pay that that I have vowed. Salvation is of the Lord. And the Lord spake unto the fish, and it vomited out Jonah upon the dry land."
—JONAH i. 17—ii. 10.

LET it be observed that the first chapter ends with the sixteenth verse in the Hebrew Bible, and that the second chapter begins with the mention of the great fish. The section of this Book of Jonah which is now before us is all, therefore, properly included in the latter chapter. But I am not about to deal with the whole of it at present. It is not of Jonah's experience in the great fish that I now propose to speak, but of his experience in the sea. You have, in all probability, seen certain pictorial representations, or rather misrepresentations, of the prophet and the great fish. A whale is depicted at the side of the ship, as ready to receive the prophet when he falls from the hands of the sailors; but I must ask you to observe that there is a double error in this view of the case. The great fish was not a whale, nor did that monster of the deep meet with the prophet immediately after his expulsion from the vessel. We shall now examine the account furnished by Jonah of his experience during the interval between that expulsion and his absorption by the fish. That experience had two aspects, objective and subjective, and each of them calls for remark.

I.

Objectively, the prophet's experience was that of one in the belly of hell, in the midst of the seas, entangled in the weeds, and among the caverns worn by the waves beneath the mountains on the coast.

Jonah was in the belly of hell. There are three words in the original Scriptures represented in our version by the word "hell." One of them is *Sheol*, another *Hades*, and the last *Gehenna*. Gehenna is what we commonly mean by "hell," and is that dreadful place of punishment to which the wicked are finally consigned. It was of it that our Saviour spoke when He said, "Fear Him Who, after He hath killed, hath power to cast into hell." But Sheol and Hades have a different meaning, the latter being the New Testament equivalent of the former. Sheol is the word employed in the text. When Jonah says that he was in the belly of Sheol, he means to say

that he was in the region of the dead, in the unseen
world; and it is not improbable that he regarded
himself as actually dead while there.

Again, the prophet was in the midst of the seas;
literally, in the heart of the seas. He did not remain
on the surface of the water after his expulsion from
the ship. It was not in the nature of things impossible that he should keep himself from sinking by
means of floating timber in that now calm sea. But
he did sink, and afterwards gave this description of
the position to which he was thus reduced: "Thou
didst cast me into the deep, in the heart of the seas,
and the floods compassed me about: all Thy billows
and Thy waves passed over me." Thy billows and
Thy waves! the prophet habitually thought of God
as the owner of the sea no less than of the land. He
had previously spoken of Him to the sailors as the
Maker of both, and he thoroughly believed that "the
sea is His, and He made it." Thy billows and Thy
waves! How often has God employed these mighty
instruments in the chastisement of men! Sailors,
merchants, passengers, and others have been made
to suffer by their means in His providence; and it is
well for us all that He who can wield them delights
in the deliverance of His creatures rather than their
destruction. Even the disobedient prophet was not
destroyed thereby, but only chastised, and he recognised the hand of the Lord in the chastisement they
effected. On the point of committing him to the
deep; the sailors had said, "Thou, O Lord, hast done
as it pleased Thee;" and Jonah exonerated them
from all responsibility in the matter when he said,
"Thou didst cast me into the deep."

It is not the least touching feature in this narrative that its hero was entangled with the sea-weeds.
" The weeds were wrapped about my head," said the
prophet afterwards. His danger was much increased
by this circumstance. Many a strong and skilful
swimmer has been prevented from rising to the
surface of the sea by the weeds which grow beneath
it ; and even when the weeds have been uprooted, as
was probably the case in the instance before us, they
have been the occasion of additional peril to the
person hampered with them. But it is not the
danger attending this incident in the prophet's experience so much as its pathos to which I now call
attention. The head which had been anointed with
holy oil wrapped in sea-weed ! It is deeply affecting
to consider it, but how much more affecting is it to
consider the manner in which the head of One
greater than Jonah was crowned with thorns !

Thus entangled with the weeds which gathered
about his head, the prophet drifted towards the coast,
and was presently carried into some of its submarine
caverns. He says, " I went down to the cuttings-
off of the mountains ; the earth with her bars was
about me for ever." There are certain wonderful
caverns in various parts of our own coast. They may
be entered at low-water ; but woe to the adventurer
who, in his admiration of the architecture they exhibit, forgets the flight of time, for they become his
tomb ! We are to think of some part of the Mediterranean coast, where the mountains rise precipitously
from the sea, their bases being hollowed by the action
of the water into various caves and channels. Into
some of these caves or channels the prophet was

carried by the current, and there he must have perished but for the Divine mercy.

II.

The subjective experience of Jonah beneath the waves was that of a living, conscious, suffering, and suppliant person.

It was a miraculous circumstance that the prophet remained alive in such a position. Things are so arranged by the will of God that life is ordinarily dependent upon certain things being present and certain other things being absent. As a rule, men cannot live without food, or with a virulent poison in their blood, or in fire, or under water. Yet Moses and Elijah[1] lived forty days without food, Paul was unhurt by the viper which had fastened on his hand, the three Hebrew princes remained alive in the fiery furnace, and Jonah remained alive also when submerged in the manner described in the text. It was because God had work for the prophet that He preserved his life, and God is able to preserve our lives until our appointed work is accomplished. "In Him we live and move and have our being," and by His will we remain alive when circumstances threaten to destroy us. "In Him we live;" not in air, in light, in liberty, in the possession of food and shelter; but "in Him we live and move and have our being."

Jonah was not only alive, but conscious, while

---

[1] While this volume was preparing for the Press, a Dr. Tanner was proceeding with a fast of forty days in the United States. It is too soon for a well-digested scientific opinion of this fast to be obtained; but, as far as one can judge, the affair has not made much impression upon those whose opinions with regard to it would be of most interest to Bible readers.

under the sea. This appears from several expressions
in the text, which will have to be more closely considered presently. " I cried out of the belly of
hell; I said, I am cast out of Thy sight; I remembered the Lord." He had been unconscious when
the tempest first smote the vessel in which he set
sail from Joppa, but the captain had aroused him,
and he had remained conscious ever since. Conscious
when examined by the sailors, when they prayed for
deliverance, when they committed him to the deep,
he remained so in the belly of hell. It is a merciful
providential arrangement that drowning men soon
become unconscious. This appears from the circumstance that such men have been rescued in numerous
instances in an unconscious state. If a man drowned
to death were fully sensible of his condition to the
very last, his would be a more terrible fate than it
really is. The agonies of constant suffocation are
terrible to think of, and yet there is no hint that
such agonies were endured by the consciously submerged prophet. The miraculous protection extended
to him preserved him in all probability from those
agonies, as well as from the death in which they are
wont to issue.

The distress he experienced beneath the water
appears to have been spiritual rather than physical.
In reference to it he says, " My soul fainted within
me ; " literally, " was covered within me," *i.e.*, " overwhelmed." As his body was overwhelmed by the
water, his soul was overwhelmed by the consciousness
that he was cast out of God's sight. His experience
supplied an illustration of those words of the Proverbist,
" They shall eat of the fruit of their own way, and be

filled with their own devices." He had fled from the
presence of the Lord, and now he was cast out of His
sight, and consequently overwhelmed with distress.
It is a terrible thing for the soul of a human being to
be thus overwhelmed with the consciousness of being
a castaway from God. The Psalmist had some such
experience, as appears from the passage, "Deep calleth
unto deep at the noise of Thy waterspouts; all Thy
billows and Thy waves are gone over me." He was
not actually under water when this language was applicable to his case, but submerged in sorrow, baptized
in anguish, overwhelmed with spiritual distress. What
can be worse than such an experience? Talk of desola-
tion and bereavement! Who so desolate and bereaved
as the man who is conscious of being cast away from
God? If this consciousness were prolonged, it would
issue in despair, as there is no doubt it has often done.
But it can never do so in the case of any child of God.
The sense of His presence and favour may be lost to
such a person for a time, but it must soon return to
him. The promise can in no case fail of its fulfilment:
"I will not leave you orphans; I will come to you."
The citation of this promise reminds us of our Master,
from whose gracious lips it fell a very few hours before
He Himself was overwhelmed by the consciousness
of estrangement from God. On the cross He was
heard to cry, "My God! My God! why hast Thou
forsaken Me?" We cannot be reminded too frequently that the anguish thus expressed was endured
on our behalf. As we have departed from God, so
would He have departed from us, had His Son not
consented to endure the anguish of an outcast from
the Divine presence on our behalf.

Jonah, conscious and distressed beneath the waters, was saved from despair by the suppliant mood which possessed him. We need despair of no man while he prays, however great his guilt and forlorn his condition ; and no man has occasion to despair of himself while he is able to call upon God. A very instructive account of the prayer which Jonah offered in his extremity may be gathered from the text.

He himself deemed it important to acknowledge that this prayer was occasioned by the trouble which overwhelmed him at the time : " I cried by reason of mine affliction unto the Lord." It is not said that Jonah prayed while yet on board the ship. The sailors prayed in the first instance to the several deities they had been trained to worship, and afterwards to Jehovah. The captain called upon the prophet to pray, but we are not told that Jonah complied with the call. But when he found himself in the deep, he could no longer refrain from prayer. Perhaps the words of the Psalmist came into his mind, but at all events they were peculiarly applicable to his case : " From the end of the earth will I cry unto Thee when my heart is overwhelmed: lead me to the Rock that is higher than I." It is well that such words should occur to any of us in our seasons of distress. We may not be literally at the end of the earth, as Jonah was in the cavern to which he had drifted ; the rock higher than himself, and higher than the sea which covered him, being inaccessible to him at the time. But if our spirits are overwhelmed within us, there is nothing better for us to do than to cry unto the Lord as he did, and there can be no more appropriate petition for us to present than that of the Psalmist : " Lead me to the Rock that is higher than I ! "

Jonah's prayer was accompanied by a look toward the temple of Jehovah. " I will look again toward Thy holy temple," said the prophet in his trouble. Consider well the language he employed. " Thou didst cast me into the deep. . . . And I said, I am cast out of Thy sight, yet I will look again toward Thy holy temple." " I am no longer permitted to behold Thee, but I will look toward the place in which Thou art most graciously revealed." There is no difficulty in understanding why the prophet looked in the direction thus described. The Old Covenant was in force, and its peculiar observances and institutions centred in the temple. It was in the temple that the high priest exercised his more important functions, sprinkling the sacrificial blood and burning incense within the veil, and thus obtaining the right to bless the people in Jehovah's name. You will readily remember that, in his prayer at the dedication of the temple, Solomon repeatedly anticipated a time when God's people from distant places should turn themselves, and stretch forth their hands towards it as they besought His blessing. Accordingly, long afterwards, Daniel prayed in Babylon with his windows open toward Jerusalem, where, indeed, the temple then stood no longer, but where it had been, and where it was destined to be re-erected. So, too, was it with Jonah, who looked toward the temple as he prayed. A look of this kind was a virtual acknowledgment that the supplicant who directed it recognised the mediation of the high priest as the ground for hoping that his own prayer would be accepted. We know

that *that* mediation was only efficacious as represent-
ing the mediation employed by the true High Priest,
even our Lord Jesus Christ, who is represented in the
Gospel as exhibiting His own blood before the throne
of God, and founding upon its sacrificial character the
plea which He urges on behalf of all who entrust their
case to Him. Jonah did not know all that Christians
now know concerning the mediation of our Lord, but
he knew that his prayer could only be accepted because
of something outside himself,—a something expressed
in the services of that holy temple towards which he
looked. But how could the prophet look toward that
temple? He was beneath the waves, and in consequent darkness. He was certainly in ignorance as to
the direction of the temple while in that condition.
Nevertheless he was able to look toward that sacred
edifice with the eyes of his spirit ; and, in the same
way, you and I can look toward the holy temple in
the heavens. With the eye of faith thus directed, no
prayer that any of us offer in time of trouble will be
offered in vain.

Jonah's prayer beneath the water was prompted by
his remembrance of the Lord. "When my soul was
overwhelmed within me, I remembered Jehovah."
In saying this, the prophet did not mean merely that
he remembered the existence of Jehovah. He doubtless meant that he remembered the manner in which
the Divine Being had revealed Himself in the Scriptures and in his own personal experience. The
remembrance of this revelation encouraged Jonah to
cry unto the Lord in his distress. Now, men are apt
to forget God in prosperity, and to remember Him
in adversity; and it is a happy circumstance for them

that He does not so resent their forgetfulness as to refuse them His aid when they remember Him. You have learnt something, my brethren, concerning the Lord from the Scriptures, and you should not forget that your Bible is a larger one than Jonah's. The Sacred Volume assures you that God is willing to receive all who apply to Him into His family, that He sent His Son into the world in order to effect their redemption, that He regenerates and sanctifies them by the agency of His Spirit, that the chief of sinners is not excluded from His grace, and that He delights in the exercise of lovingkindness and judgment and righteousness in the earth. The testimony of the Scriptures respecting Him has been enforced by that of your personal experience. You have found His service pleasant, His promise faithful, and His grace sufficient. You have been conscious of His presence, which is sweet; of His favour, which is life; and of His lovingkindness, which is better than life. Then do not abandon yourselves to despair in the deepest distress to which you may descend, but call to remembrance all that you have learnt concerning the Lord, and call upon Him to deliver you in full assurance that He will comply with your entreaty.

The prayer of the prophet was accompanied by a vow on his part, to which he afterwards made reference in the words, " With the voice of thanksgiving would I sacrifice unto Thee ; what I have vowed I would pay."[1] He had, therefore, vowed that he would

---

[1] A more correct reading than the one in our version ; but at this date it is possible that every such note as the present is rendered superfluous by the labours of those engaged in the revision of the Old Testament.

sacrifice unto the Lord with the voice of thanksgiving, if his prayer for deliverance were answered. As the sailors vowed above the water after their deliverance from the storm, so the prophet vowed beneath the water before his deliverance from the belly of hell. What has been said already in the foregoing lecture on the subject of vows renders it needless to say much upon it in the present discourse. But I may remind you that when a man calls upon God in his distress, and enforces his prayer with a vow, he is utterly unable to deceive the Most High in relation to the matter. He may deceive his fellow men in relation to it, and may even deceive himself, but he cannot deceive God. The Lord knows beforehand whether the vow will be redeemed or violated, and this circumstance should render any one who makes a vow very careful to promise nothing more than he is able and resolved to perform.

Jonah's prayer from the belly of hell was answered in a remarkable manner, of which I shall have to speak in the next lecture. He was swallowed by the great fish mentioned in the text, and conveyed by the monster to the country he had left. His deliverance was not perfected till he was cast upon the shore, but it is evident from the language he employed while in the fish that he regarded his very strange position with satisfaction. He appears to have regarded the monster as a messenger of mercy. If he had been swallowed by it as soon as he fell from the hands of the sailors, his feeling might have been a different one. But he had been in the deep for some time, as we have seen; and as compared with his position in the belly of hell, that which he afterwards

occupied in the belly of the great fish was not one
for him to deplore. The trouble which a person is
called upon to experience at any given time is apt
to seem more or less heavy according to the weight
of his previous afflictions. The man who has had
seven burdens to carry rejoices when he has only to
carry one of them ; whereas if he had only had that
one from the first, he would have been aggrieved
thereby at this moment. Thus it was with Jonah,
whose heavier affliction in the deep occasioned him
to regard his lighter affliction as a prisoner in the
great fish as no affliction at all. There is nothing
in his language, at all events, to indicate that he
regarded his embowelment in that monster as an
occasion of distress. There are, on the contrary,
certain grateful reflections recorded in the text as
having been entertained by the prophet while in that
strange position ; and with some reference to them
the present lecture may conclude.

The first of these grateful reflections is, "Thou
hast brought up my life from destruction, O Lord,
my God!" Had Jonah been allowed to drown in
the deep after the ordinary manner of men submerged as he was, his body would soon have become
corrupt. But he was rescued from corruption, as
he says ; and was so sensible of the Divine goodness in this respect that he addressed Jehovah as
his God. It is a blessed thing for a man to be able
to say, "Thou hast done great things for me, O
Lord God;" but it is a more blessed thing for him
to be able to say, "Thou hast done great things for
me, O Lord, my God!" Jonah was now aware that
God had not cast him off altogether, but had de-

9

termined on his deliverance; and it was with
intense thankfulness, be sure, that he said, "Thou
hast brought up my life from corruption, O Lord,
my God!"

The second of these grateful reflections is thus
expressed: "My prayer came in unto Thee, into
Thine holy temple." He had looked toward that
temple as he prayed, and his prayer had not fallen
short of the sacred edifice, or failed to find an entrance,
but had passed right in to the Deity whose earthly
throne was there. Through waves and walls and
other barriers the prayer had penetrated into the
very presence of the Most High: that presence from
which the prophet had formerly desired to flee. The
prayer of faith is a wonderful thing, whether it proceed from a prophet or an ordinary servant of the
Lord. It can find its way into God's holy temple in
the heavens, and can influence God Himself in the
welfare of the person who utters it, so as to procure
for that person deliverance, consolation, enlighten-
ment, or whatsoever other blessing he may most
desire and need for the time being.

The third of these grateful reflections is: "They
that observe lying vanities forsake their own mercy."
The prophet was conscious when he gave utterance
to it, that the estrangement which had recently taken
place between himself and God was not because God
had forsaken him, so much as because he had forsaken
God. The word rendered "observe"[1] is a very
forcible one. It means "give themselves up to," or
"devote themselves to," in this connection. They
that devote themselves to lying vanities, as a parasite

---

[1] מְשַׁמְּרִים, from שָׁמַר.

devotes himself to the patron on whom he depends, forsake their own mercy, *i.e.*, the mercy of God, which, but for their misplaced regard for other things, they would have enjoyed. God had allowed trouble and disaster to come upon Jonah; not that He was less merciful than before, but because His servant had forsaken Him and His service in deference to those considerations which had obtained the mastery of his mind. The sentiment to which the prophet had surrendered himself, that everything was to be done for Israel and nothing for Nineveh, that the former was to be delivered and the latter destroyed, irrespective of all moral considerations, was a lying vanity; and there are many such lying vanities observed among ourselves. Men adopt certain ideas, opinions, prejudices, and sentiments, regulating their own conduct accordingly, requiring others to do the same on pain of their displeasure, and forsaking the plain path of duty as often as walking in it is found to be incompatible with their own favourite notions. Worldly fashions, sacerdotal assumptions, and various forms of selfishness, which are not known to be such by those committed to them, are so many lying vanities which cannot be observed without loss. The grateful reflection in Jonah's mind was that, while all his recent afflictions were attributable to his own perversity, God was no less disposed to be merciful than before.

The last of these grateful reflections was, " Salvation is of the Lord;" literally, " Salvation unto Jehovah!" Salvation is attributable to the Lord. Salvation is well-pleasing to Him. This is the idea which pervades the Book of Jonah, as it pervades the

Bible at large. It is interesting to remember that what the prophet thus said in darkness and solitude was afterwards sung by that vast and brilliant throng which John beheld in vision. As he looked on those who constituted it, " they cried with a loud voice, saying, Salvation to our God, which sitteth upon the throne, and unto the Lamb!" It is well that this saying, "Salvation is of the Lord," should be rehearsed before saints and sinners pretty frequently; before saints to keep them humble, and before sinners to make them hopeful. "Salvation is of the Lord," and must not be ascribed unto men. "Salvation is of the Lord," and the most abandoned sinner upon earth may obtain it from Him. Was the poet thinking of Jonah's experience and John's vision when he wrote the following familiar hymn?—

> " Salvation! oh, the joyful sound!
>   'Tis pleasure to our ears;
> A sovereign balm for every wound,
>   A cordial for our fears.
>
> " Buried in sorrow and in sin,
>   At hell's dark door we lay;
> But we arise by grace divine
>   To see a heavenly day.
>
> " Salvation! let the echo fly
>   The spacious earth around;
> While all the armies of the sky
>   Conspire to raise the sound."

IX.

THE GREAT FISH.

" Now the Lord had prepared a great fish to swallow up Jonah. And Jonah was in the belly of the fish three days and three nights. Then Jonah prayed unto the Lord his God out of the fish's belly. . . . And the Lord spake unto the fish, and it vomited out Jonah upon the dry land."—JONAH i. 17, and ii, 1 and 10.

IN these four sentences we have a remarkable account of a remarkable experience. It is said that truth is stranger than fiction, and it was assuredly a very strange thing for such an experience as this to befall a human being. But is not this narrative, then, to be regarded as a fable, an allegory, or something of the sort ? No. There are such things in the Bible, to be sure, but this is not one of them. Truth may be taught by means of fiction (however paradoxical this may seem), as well as in other ways. Christ taught certain truths of the utmost importance through the medium of those fictitious narratives, His parables ; and the Old Testament contains various lessons which are set forth in the same general form. There is, *e.g.*, Jotham's fable of the trees which went forth to choose a king. But the Book of Jonah is not a fictitious narrative, nor is this particular part of it such a narrative. It is veritable history, and it is wonderful that so remarkable an experience should have been recorded by its subject in such brief and simple fashion. The man who denies the historic character of the narrative before us should be prepared to show that the account given of Christ in the New Testament is fictitious, for Christ is represented as saying that Jonah was in the position here described. The historical character of the Gospels involves that of the Book of Jonah; but we need not dwell on this point. Let us take the four sentences which constitute the text, and see what may be learnt from them when carefully considered.

I.

" The Lord had prepared a great fish to swallow up Jonah." *Prepared.*[1] The word is repeatedly employed in this Book. God prepared the gourd, the worm, and the east wind, as well as the great fish. The original word has various meanings. *Prepared* is one of them; *appointed* is another; *divided*, or *separated*, is another. We may therefore read the sentence before us in either of three ways. The Lord had prepared, or appointed, or set apart, a great fish to swallow up Jonah. The huge creature was not conscious of its commission, and the majority of God's creatures are unconscious of the several commissions indubitably imposed upon them. But it is well for us to consider that there is a vocation which belongs to every creature after its kind, and that every human being is especially called to the discharge of some duty which no inferior creature could perform. The man who is conscious of his consecration to some particular office

---

[1] מָנָה, *manah.*

and work in the service of the Most High should
never cease to remember the consequent and corresponding responsibility which rests upon him.   It was
in this respect that Jonah failed in the deplorable
manner described in the Book before us.

But we must now keep our attention fixed on the
great fish which the Lord had prepared to swallow up
the prophet.   It was by no means the only instance
in which He was pleased to commission fish to play
a miraculous part in His providential arrangements.
Twice in the course of our Saviour's earthly ministry
did He enable His disciples to haul in a miraculous
draught of fishes.   Twice also did He miraculously
multiply a few fishes, and a corresponding quantity of
bread, into a superabundant meal for several thousands
of persons.   On one occasion a fish was commissioned
to bring a coin in its mouth, in order that the Apostle
Peter might be enabled to meet the demand of those
who collected the temple tribute.

Nor were fish the only creatures thus miraculously
employed in God's service.   He somewhat frequently
commissioned other creatures to chastise or assist
members of the human race.   Thus the Egyptians
were plagued with frogs and flies, lice and locusts,
and the children of Israel with fiery flying serpents.
A lion was sent to slay that disobedient prophet, who
was first tempted and then denounced by a fellow-
prophet.   Two she-bears were commissioned to destroy
two-and-forty of those youthful sons of Belial who
insulted the prophet Elisha ; while another prophet
thus describes the mischief done by various vermin
employed in the chastisement of his countrymen :
" That which the palmer-worm hath left hath the

locust eaten, and that which the locust hath left hath
the cankerworm eaten, and that which the cankerworm hath left hath the caterpillar eaten." [1] So, too,
it is said of that vainglorious Herod, who drank from
the cup of flattery tendered to him till he was intoxi-
cated, that " he was eaten of worms, and gave up the
ghost."   On the other hand, the ravens were commanded to feed the prophet Elijah while he tarried by
the brook Cherith, and did actually supply him with
bread and flesh, morning and evening, for a considerable length of time ; while, in the case of Jonah also,
this great fish was appointed to rescue the prophet
from the dreadful position described in his own
prayer.

All these incidents may serve to impress upon our
minds the truth that all His creatures are under the
complete control of the Creator.   Usually He leaves
them to the dictates of their own instinct, but that very
instinct is simply the expression of His will concerning them.   In the cases to which reference has been
made, however, the creaturely instinct was checked
or quickened so as to produce the exceptional procedure described.   It was by no mere accident that
the great fish and the prophet met beneath the water.
Accident !   No ; for " the Lord had prepared a great
fish to swallow up Jonah."

II.

Now take the second textual statement.   "Jonah
was in the belly of the fish three days and three
nights."   The nature, significance, and immediate
utility of this miracle will require some remark.

[1] Joel i. 4.

1. Respecting its *nature*, you will be aware that a
miracle is not necessarily involved in the swallowing
of a man by a great fish. The infidel's argument
that a whale is so formed as to be unable to swallow
a man has been abundantly answered. One gets
somewhat weary of pointing out that there is no
mention of a whale in the Book of Jonah, and that our
Lord did not say that the prophet was in the whale's
belly, although our version of His language on the
subject employs that phrase. The word He actually
used[1] is the exact equivalent of the one that occurs in
the text, and may mean a whale, or seal, or shark, or
dolphin, or any other marine creature of considerable
size. Now, it is quite possible for a shark to swallow
a man whole, and the thing has often been done.
The body of a man, complete in itself and completely
clad, has been found in a captured and opened shark.
Even the complete carcase of a horse has been found
in the body of a shark. There was therefore no
miracle in the mere circumstance that Jonah was
swallowed whole by the great fish. Neither was
there any miracle in the circumstance that the
prophet was disgorged by the monster and survived.
In the year 1758, A.D., a sailor fell overboard in the
Mediterranean. He was able to swim, and would
have been presently rescued by his messmates, if a
shark had not gulped him down before their eyes.
Then a very strange thing took place. The captain
shot the shark in a sensitive part of its body, so that
it vomited the sailor forth, and he was rescued after
all. The fish was secured, dried, and presented to
the man who had had this narrow escape from death;

[1] Κῆτος, *Kētos.*

and he went about Europe with it, obtaining a great
deal of money by its exhibition. It was twenty feet
long, and weighed nearly four thousand pounds; and
yet this huge creature was small in comparison with
some specimens of its own species, which have been
found to weigh as much as ten thousand pounds.[1] If,
then, some monster of the deep—say a white shark—
swallowed Jonah without killing him, that was not a
miracle in itself. The miracle was in the circumstance that the prophet remained alive for so long a
time in such a position: for "Jonah was in the
belly of the fish three days and three nights."

2. This duration of the prophet's embowelment
had much to do with the *significance* of the miracle
involved. The miracle was also a sign, and our Divine
Master once delivered this prediction of His own
burial: "As Jonah was three days and three nights
in the belly of the great fish: so shall the Son of
Man be three days and three nights in the heart of
the earth." The buried Jonah, then, was a type of
the buried Christ. The circumstance that the prophet was in the great fish for the space of time
mentioned was an antecedent illustration of the
burial of our Lord. I suppose, too, that we should
not lose sight of another circumstance connected
with this subject. It is true of the type, as of the
Antitype, that " he saw no corruption " while thus
entombed. Much emphasis is laid in the Scriptures
upon the incorruption of the body our Lord had
assumed, notwithstanding its interment. ' Thou
wilt not leave my soul in hell, neither wilt Thou

---

[1] See the interesting illustrative facts collected and authenticated
in Pusey on Jonah in *" The Minor Prophets."*

suffer Thine Holy One to see corruption," said the
patriarch David ; and Peter declared on the great day
of Pentecost that the Psalmist spake these words as
the mouthpiece of Christ.   David himself did see
corruption, but David's Son and Lord saw none, and
the embowelled Jonah saw none.   The same miraculous operation of Divine power as that which prevented the prophet's body from rotting in the belly
of the great fish also prevented the body of our Blessed
Lord from decomposing in the heart of the earth.

It must be acknowledged, however, that the
miracle wrought in connection with Christ's entomb-
ment was greater than the one wrought in connection
with that of the prophet.   Jonah was kept from
corruption by being kept alive, whereas Jesus Christ
was actually dead, and yet His body was not only
preserved from corruption, but was also endowed
with certain properties which it had not previously
possessed.   When Jonah came forth from the fish he
was as liable to death as ever, and did doubtless die
in due time like any other man.   But when Christ.
came forth from the sepulchre, He was found to be
immortalised, and in a position to say, as He afterwards did, " I am He that liveth and was dead, and
behold, I am alive for evermore ! "

But that which it most concerns us to remark in
the superiority of the Antitype is that whereas we are
not ourselves affected by the experience of Jonah, we
are immensely affected by that of Christ.   His resurrection is the earnest of that which His people also
shall experience in due time.   There is the same
kind of connection between Him and them as there
is between the first-fruits and the harvest.   " Now is

Christ risen from the dead, and become the first-fruits of them that slept . . . . Every man in his own order : Christ the first-fruits; afterward they that are Christ's at His coming . . . . For this corruptible must put on incorruption, and this mortal must put on immortality . . . . Thanks be to God, which giveth us the victory through our Lord Jesus Christ." But though the burial of Christ was connected with greater wonders than that of Jonah, it was adumbrated thereby; and when it is said in the New Testament that Christ rose again the third day according to the Scriptures, one of the Scriptures to which reference is thus made is the very sentence now before us : " Jonah was in the belly of the fish three days and three nights."

3. If any one inquire as to the *immediate utility* of this miracle, an answer can be readily given. Jonah was in need of an asylum and a conveyance, and his absorption by the great fish secured him both these things. It is difficult to imagine any way in which he could have been rescued, rested, and restored to land and light, if this great fish had not been commissioned to carry him back. Cleaving its way with ease through the mighty deep, the monster rendered a service to the prophet which might well occasion him to exclaim, as we have seen he did, " Salvation is of the Lord!" This particular miracle resembled the other Divine miracles described in the sacred volume in this respect, that it was immediately beneficial as well as perpetually significant. I do not forget that some of the miracles to which I refer were injurious to certain persons, as when Elijah called down fire from heaven to consume his enemies,

and as when Christ allowed the demons to enter into
the herd of swine. But even these miracles were
more beneficial to some than they were injurious to
others ; or, at least, they were adapted to be so ; and
the circumstance to which I thus call attention may
be regarded as bearing witness to the blessed truth,
that God's power is exerted in such a way as to promote the welfare of all human beings who do not
oppose themselves to Him, or flee from the path of
duty as Jonah did.

III.

The next of these sentences is, "Then Jonah prayed
unto the Lord his God out of the fish's belly."

Human beings have addressed their prayers to the
Most High from all kinds of places ; and prayer is
prayer, come whence it may. From sick beds, from
tempest-driven vessels, from deep and darksome
mines, from the recesses of dense forests, from moun-
tain solitudes and dreary wildernesses, from dismal
dungeons and more dismal haunts of vice and crime,
has prayer gone up to God. Such prayer has, in
many instances, been found to be as acceptable to
Him, and as effectual in obtaining His blessing, as
any which has ascended from homes of the most
respectable character, or from churches resonant with
harmony and beautiful with the adornments of architecture. We may be certain that Jonah prayed as
acceptably and effectually from the belly of the fish
as he could have done from the courts of the temple
itself. I am aware that the doctrine thus illustrated
may be abused. Men may employ it in order to
excuse their own neglect of the house of God. They

may say, "It is not necessary for us to go thither, for we can pray at home, or in the open air, or in any place where we chance to be." Quite true; but the answer to all such talk is obvious. Men who really do pray in such places as have just been mentioned are precisely the persons who are glad to come to the house of God as often as possible. When a man says, "I never attend a place of public worship because I can pray at home," he should not be surprised to find his neighbours sceptical as to his praying anywhere. Private and public prayer have their several peculiar advantages, and those who love to pray at all will be glad to do so in public as in private, in the house of God as well as in their own.

Although it is said that "Jonah prayed to the Lord his God out of the fish's belly," there is no petition in the language he is recorded to have used. There is reference in that language to the prayer he had previously presented when in the belly of hell, but it would seem itself to be rather the language of praise than of prayer in our sense of the latter word. It is probable, therefore, that the word[1] rendered "prayed" in this passage is one that denotes more than the mere presentation of petition to God. It is not the word always employed in the Old Testament when any one is said to have prayed. It is, however, the word employed when we are told that Hannah prayed. If you read her prayer at your leisure, you will find that it is so far like the prayer of Jonah that it contains no petition. It would seem, therefore, that the word of which I speak denotes any kind of address to God, whether a petition, confession, or thanks-

1 פָּלַל, *palal.*

giving. But may I not say more than this? Is it not true that any confession or thanksgiving which may be appropriately addressed to God involves a prayer? Surely the man who acknowledges his sin to the Most High thereby virtually entreats that that sin may be forgiven, and that he may sin no more. Surely, too, the man who thanks God for His past mercy thereby virtually prays that such mercy may be continued.

It is said that "Jonah prayed unto the Lord his God out of the fish's belly." The Lord his God. I do not want to repeat what was said on this point in the foregoing lecture, but may just observe that the Lord does not cease to be our God when we cease to be His servants. Jonah was by no means the only one of God's ancient servants who ceased to serve Him. Moses and Aaron did so, as did David and Solomon, Asa and Josiah, Mark and Peter, and a great many others. But the Lord remained their God, although they ceased to be His servants, and by His grace they were restored to the path of duty from which they had wandered. It has been with some of us as it was with those just mentioned. You and I, my brethren, have left the right path again and again, but have we not to acknowledge that we have been as often restored to that path by the Lord our God? Or is there any one among us who is saying sadly to himself that he has wandered so far and so long from the way of rectitude that he cannot hope to regain a place among the people of God? I say to him that he has no need to despair. He who restored Jonah will restore him. Of Jonah's God it is still as true as it was in the time of the Psalmist, that " He restoreth the outcasts of Israel." Be of good cheer, for as surely as you desire to be restored, you shall be so.

IV.

It remains to consider the last of these textual sentences. " The Lord spake unto the fish, and it vomited out Jonah upon the dry land." We are not told how He spake to the monster, but it is surely not difficult to believe that He did speak to it. If a man can speak to his dog in such a way as to be intelligible to the brute, why should it be hard to believe that God was able to speak thus to the great fish? It is not hard, you say: but I may remind you that there are persons who appear to think it impossible for God to speak to any of His creatures, even to such creatures as ourselves. Tell them that the Bible is the Word of God, in which He addresses us in the language of command, counsel, invitation, and encouragement; and they will deny that the Bible has a more Divine origin than many another book or collection of books. They will tell you, moreover, that it is ridiculous to suppose that God really addressed Himself to particular persons in the manner described in the Bible. But to say that a thing is ridiculous is not to prove it to be so, and we may fairly retort that it is ridiculous to suppose that the Creator is unable to hold intercourse with any of His creatures as often as it pleases Him to do so. The Lord speaks to us in the Bible and otherwise; and the Lord spake unto the fish in some way that was suitable to the creature's nature and to the other circumstances of the case.

Nor did He speak in vain. His command was obeyed. The monster would rather have retained the man it had swallowed, we may suppose. But "the Lord spake unto the fish, and it vomited out Jonah upon the dry land." I do not suppose the obedience of the fish to have been voluntary. It had to do what God willed in this matter. When Jonah was directed to betake himself to Nineveh in the first instance, he had the power of choice as to whether he would obey or not. There was a difference between him and the great fish in that respect, and there is a like difference between ourselves and those below us in the scale of creation. Ravens, lions, locusts, and fish must do as they are commanded. Men may obey or disobey as they please. The consequences of disobedience will be serious, but choice is allowed them. God's object is not to compel our obedience, but to win our sympathy; so that a mere formal and heartless obedience on our part to the letter of His law is so far from being well pleasing to Him that it is abhorrent in the extreme.

The subordination of this fish to the will of Jehovah was adapted to make a profound impression on the minds of those who dwelt in those regions in that age of the world. We know that those who dwelt on the eastern shore of the Mediterranean were worshippers of fish. The Philistines, *e.g.*, called their national divinity " Dagon," which some say means *great fish* and others *little fish*, but which was certainly a fish-god. It appears from the sacred Scriptures, as well as from certain pictorial representations of the fish-gods formerly worshipped thereabouts, that Dagon was a kind of merman, having in part the form of a

10

man and in part that of a fish.   A great fish like the
one mentioned in the text was likely to be regarded
with religious reverence as the actual deity which
Dagon represented.   Think then.   It was the popular
notion that each region had its own god, and we have
seen how the storm-tossed mariners called upon the
several deities they had been trained to worship in
their respective countries.   Jehovah was regarded as
the God of the Hebrews, and Dagon as the God of
the Philistines and others.   When the Hebrews
triumphed over the Philistines it was thought that
Jehovah had overcome Dagon ; and when the Philistines triumphed over the Hebrews it was thought that
Dagon had overcome Jehovah.   This notion was
deeply dishonouring to the one true and living God ;
and on various occasions He displayed His superiority
to Dagon in a very striking manner.   It was in the
temple of Dagon that Samson performed the last of
his mighty acts ; pulling down the edifice and crush-
ing all who were assembled in it, himself among
them ; and this would be understood as an advantage
gained by the God of Samson over that of Samson's
foes.   It was in the temple of Dagon that the Philistines put the Ark of Jehovah after they had captured
it in battle ; but the result was that Dagon fell to
pieces before the Ark, and the Philistines sent it
from place to place, and finally sent it back to the
land of Israel.   In harmony with the records which
relate these things is the one before us.   Jonah was
Jehovah's messenger to the heathen ; and it was
shown by this part of his experience that Dagon,
and what Dagon represented, could be dealt with as
Jehovah pleased.   It was partly on this account, we

may assume, that this great fish was employed to carry the prophet back to the country he had left. The supremacy of the true God was rendered apparent by the incident mentioned in the sentence before us ; " The Lord spake unto the fish, and it vomited out Jonah upon the dry land."

But was this incident known at the time to any considerable number of persons ? Yes. At least there is reason to think so. There are certain traditions which have come down to us, and which appear to be traceable to the event described in the text. It is probable that there were other and kindred traditions which have perished, but which were for a long time much before the people of those parts.

There is a somewhat doubtful tradition, among others, to the effect that Hercules,[1] of whom so many wonders are related, was overtaken by a tempest, swept into the sea, swallowed by a great fish, and afterwards cast uninjured upon shore.

Then there is the story of Arion.[2] He was a great musician, and such a person was regarded by his heathen contemporaries as divinely inspired. Arion had enriched himself by the exercise of his art in Italy and Sicily, and had committed himself and his treasure to the care of a crew bound for Corinth. The sailors resolved to murder him and take possession of his wealth. Being directed by them to leap into the sea, he asked permission to array himself in

---

[1] A patristic allusion to Hercules, mentioned disparagingly by Pusey as not made till the end of the fifth century, is as follows :—" Hercules is sung, when his ship was broken, to have been swallowed up by a ketos, and, having come within, was preserved."

[2] Herodotus, Book I., 23, 24.

his best robes and sing them a parting song. He
was allowed to do this; and when his song was
finished, he flung himself overboard, harp in hand.
A dolphin, which had been fascinated by the music,
received Arion upon his back, and carried him into
Corinth before the arrival of the vessel from which he
had been expelled. When its crew was landed the
murderous miscreants were confronted by Arion in
presence of the chief magistrate of the city, covered
with confusion by his accusation, convicted of their
crime, and condemned to death by crucifixion.

There is also a Babylonian tradition, which should
not be overlooked in connection with this subject. It
is said that an extraordinary being named Oannes [1]
(which may easily be only another way of spelling
Jonah), having the body of a fish, but the head,
hands, feet, and voice of a man, emerged from the
sea, arrived in Babylon, and taught the people of that
city various things of the utmost consequence to
them. This association of a reformer with a fish, an
emergence from the sea, and a ministry in one of the
capitals of that great monarchy, which first had its
seat in Nineveh and afterwards in Babylon, is assuredly due to the actual history of the prophet Jonah.

Now these traditions suggest two considerations,
with which this discourse may fittingly conclude.
One is, that the heathen world was not so utterly destitute of religious truth under the Old Dispensation as
people are prone to suppose. It repeatedly rang with
tidings of what had been said and done and experienced by the servants of the living God.

The other consideration is of more practical con-

[1] Kitto. " *Daily Bible Illustrations.*" Article *Dagon.*

sequence to ourselves. It is that the Holy Scriptures infinitely transcend in value any mere tradition, and that we ought, therefore, to be devoutly thankful to have them in our possession. It is plain that the traditions respecting Hercules, Arion, and Oannes, underwent many alterations as they were handed down from one generation to another. They differ from each other at least as much as they differ from the true account of Jonah which is furnished in the Book before us. This circumstance enables us to understand how the truth concerning One greater than Jonah would have been obscured but for the Scriptures in which it is preserved. Suppose the four Gospels had not been written, or that they had not been preserved : in that case there might have been various traditions relative to the incarnation, miracles, crucifixion, burial, resurrection, and ascension of our Divine Lord. But they would have differed as much from the truth concerning Him as do the traditions relative to Jonah from the Scripture account of that prophet. Indeed, there are some such traditions concerning Christ which have come down to us,[1] and we have only to compare their testimony respecting Him with that of the New Testament to perceive their worthlessness and its exceeding value. The Christ described in the Gospels is One worthy of our supreme affection, confidence, and reverence ; and the more we consider their testimony concerning Him, the more are we likely to devote ourselves to His service, and to rejoice in His salvation.

---

[1] See the *Protevangelion* and other Apocrypha of the New Testament.

X.

THE PREACHING OF JONAH IN NINEVEH.

" And the word of the Lord came unto Jonah the second time, saying, Arise, go unto Nineveh, that great city, and preach unto it the preaching that I bid thee. So Jonah arose, and went unto Nineveh, according to the word of the Lord. Now Nineveh was an exceeding great city of three days' journey. And Jonah began to enter into the city a day's journey, and he cried, and said, Yet forty days, and Nineveh shall be overthrown. So the people of Nineveh believed God, and proclaimed a fast, and put on sackcloth, from the greatest of them even to the least of them. For word came unto the king of Nineveh, and he arose from his throne, and he laid his robe from him, and covered him with sackcloth, and sat in ashes. And he caused it to be proclaimed and published through Nineveh by the decree of the king and his nobles, saying, Let neither man nor beast, herd nor flock, taste any thing : let them not feed, nor drink water : but let man and beast be covered with sackcloth, and cry mightily unto God : yea, let them turn every one from his evil way, and from the violence that is in their hands. Who can tell if God will turn and repent, and turn away from His fierce anger, that we perish not ? "—JONAH iii. 1-9.

FEW of us have failed to feel the force of the familiar saying very keenly at certain times, " Better late than never." It is, of course, desirable that every one who receives a Divine call should at once respond to it. Promptitude is better than procrastination in relation to it. But many of God's servants have been faulty in this respect, and the prophet Jonah was one of them. Divinely directed to go to Nineveh, he at first declined to do so, and we have seen some of the consequences of his disobedience. But when the Lord repeated the com-

mand, the prophet obeyed. It was better late than
never in his case, but it had been better still if he
had obeyed in the first instance. The word of the
Lord has come to some of you more than once. It
has come to you the second time. Has it not come
to you the hundredth time? It has called you to a
life of consecration to His service, and to the discharge of some particular duty in that service. But
have you even yet obeyed? Alas for those who refuse
to do so! The time is coming when the Lord shall
say to them, "Because I have called, and ye refused
. . . . I also will laugh at your calamity; I will
mock when your fear cometh." It will be too late
then, but it is not too late now, to respond to the
Divine call which has been addressed to you. It is
late enough, however, even now; but still I say,
Better late than never; and I beseech you to postpone no longer your approach to God, and your
entrance upon the work to which He has called you.
Well, Jonah went to Nineveh when the word of
the Lord came to him the second time, and preached
in that great city in accordance with his commission.
It is of his preaching that I am now to speak; and
my remarks will relate to its substance, its suitableness, and the manner in which it was supplemented.

I.

The substance of Jonah's preaching in Nineveh
was simply this: "Yet forty days, and Nineveh shall
be overthrown!" The prophet was not, therefore, a
preacher of the Gospel. He could not introduce his
announcement to the Ninevites with any such remark
as that which the angel long afterwards addressed to

the Jewish shepherds: " Behold, I bring you good
tidings of great joy ! " On the contrary, it was a sad,
solemn, and startling cry which rang out in the streets
of the great city when the prophet proclaimed, " Yet
forty days, and Nineveh shall be overthrown ! " and
there was not a word on his part to soften its character
as such.

Try to realize the prophet's progress through
heathen Nineveh. I have already had occasion to
comment on the magnitude of the city; but let us
return (as the sacred narrative itself does) to that
subject for a moment. " Now Nineveh was an exceeding great city of three days' journey. And Jonah
began to enter into the city a day's journey; and he
cried, and said, Yet forty days, and Nineveh shall
be overthrown ! " Remember that a day's journey
was twenty miles, and that Nineveh was sixty miles
in circumference. Had it been a circular city, its
diameter would have been twenty miles, and a day's
journey would have just taken the prophet through
it. It was, however, rather square than circular,
though by no means exactly square. But then it is
probable there was no thoroughfare from one of its
gates to another which observed an exactly direct
course, and therefore the prophet would find that his
passage right through it did just amount to a day's
journey. It was indeed a remarkable and memorable
day's journey which he thus performed. We don't
know whether his entrance into the city attracted
much attention; but those who observed him saw a
stranger clad in the peculiar garb of a Hebrew prophet,—a mantle of camel's hair with a leathern girdle,
—and we may be sure that before he had gone

very far into the city, he did attract a great deal of
attention. The very first time he raised that por-
tentous cry, " Yet forty days, and Nineveh shall be
overthrown!" the crowd would gather round him;
and as he paced along his way, past places of residence, of business, of worship, and of amusement,
that crowd would largely increase. As the day wears
on, the ordinary business of the city is suspended.
Its inhabitants are sensible that something unusual
is taking place before they know precisely what it is.
The rumours which run in all directions along its
streets are at length united in the one piece of intelligence that the prophet is passing through it. The
hum of the advancing crowd announces his approach
to those who await his coming. The street is kept
carefully clear before him. He will come round yon
corner presently. Hark! he is coming; see! he is
here. Less noise there in the by-streets! Ye children, cease from play! What ho there! check that
chariot; stop that music; keep that hammer still;
silence in yonder balcony! Silence! silence! silence!
The prophet is now at hand, and the cry which has
been heard in the distance comes clearly from his
lips: " ŌD ARBAIM YOM VENINEVEH NEHPĀCHETH!" "Yet
forty days, and Nineveh shall be overthrown!" That
is all. There is no comment, no enlargement, no
condition, no qualification. The mere announcement
made, the preacher passes on, and repeats it at inter-
vals, until his day's journey is accomplished, and he
goes forth from the city, leaving its inhabitants to
talk and think over what he has said.

I am not about to speak in this discourse of the
effect produced by Jonah's preaching. That will

occupy us in another lecture; but we may so far
anticipate the subject as to glance at the text of the
next discourse : " And God saw their works, that
they turned from their evil way ; and God repented
of the evil that He had said that He would do unto
them; and He did it not." So then, although Jonah
said, " Yet forty days, and Nineveh shall be overthrown !" the forty days went by, and the city
continued to flourish. This consideration prepares
the way for two remarks of some importance, and
germane to the subject of the present lecture.

The first remark is that *Divine threats are conditional.* It is with them in this respect as it is with
the promises recorded in the Scriptures. Both
promises and threats are conditional. Take the
promise recorded at the close of the fifth Psalm:
" Thou, Lord, wilt bless the righteous ; with favour
wilt Thou compass him as with a shield." Now I
say that this promise is conditional, though no condition is stated; and I vindicate this assertion by an
appeal to the language of the Lord Himself to His
servant Ezekiel : " When I shall say to the righteous
that he shall surely live ; if he trust to his own
righteousness and commit iniquity, all his righteousness shall not be remembered; but for his iniquity
that he hath committed, he shall die for it." So, on
the other hand, is it with God's threats, for He goes
on to say, " Again, when I say unto the wicked, Thou
shalt surely die; if he turn from his sin, and do
judgment and justice; if the wicked restore the
pledge, give again that he had robbed, walk in the
statutes of life without committing iniquity, he shall
surely live, he shall not die. None of his sins that

he hath committed shall be mentioned unto him : he hath done that which is lawful and right ; he shall surely live." The appropriate condition is implied, whether it is mentioned or not, in all the promises and in all the threats which are recorded in the Scriptures as coming from God. Thus, when Jonah passed through the great heathen city proclaiming the simple threat, "Yet forty days, and Nineveh shall be overthrown," there was an implied, though not a formulated, condition that it should be spared if its people repented.

Is not this a doctrine which has deep interest for ourselves ? A man is now living in sin and in estrangement from God. He has reason to tremble, for God threatens such as he with the fierceness of His anger; but he has no reason to despair, for the Divine threats are conditional, and the penitent transgressor will be delivered from the consequences of his transgression. I proclaim this truth for the admonition and encouragement of all who hear me, and especially for the benefit of those who are now consciously living in estrangement from God.

The other remark to which I would bespeak your particular attention is that *Divine threats are merciful.* It was in mercy that God sent His servant Jonah to cry in the streets of the great and guilty Gentile city, "Yet forty days, and Nineveh shall be overthrown!" The threat thus fulminated was the means of bringing the Ninevites to repentance, and saving their city from destruction, as it was intended to be. What if the menace had not been addressed to them? What if no prophet had been sent to cry among them as Jonah did? Such silence on God's part would have been severity, for the unwarned city would have been destroyed. But the warning which Jonah rehearsed in its streets was as merciful a proclamation as any promise could have been.

It is the preacher's consolation that the Divine threats are always merciful. It is distasteful to him to repeat them. Distasteful! it is most distressing; most distressing to transform his pulpit into an Ebal, from which the curses of the law are sounded forth. But he has his consolation, I repeat, in the conviction that God threatens in mercy, and that it would be more unkind on his own part to remain silent on the subject than to warn his fellow-sinners of the doom they have provoked.

It is not only distasteful to himself, but to his hearers, when the preacher makes mention of the wrath to come. They would rather hear of the glory to be revealed to God's people hereafter than of the shame and everlasting contempt with which sinners will be overwhelmed. They would rather hear of the Divine lovingkindness than of the Divine vengeance; rather hear of heaven than of hell. Naturally. Nevertheless the preacher must preach the preaching that God bids him, and may rejoice (though Jonah mourned) in the conviction that the very warnings he repeats are adapted to save those who receive them from the doom to which they point.

This adaptation is, however, lost sight of by some persons. They regard it as unwise on the part of one who wishes to induce men to serve the Lord to discourse concerning the sinner's doom. They think him likely to defeat his own purpose by doing so. They are never weary of reminding him that

" he that winneth souls is wise." Well, well. I suppose that Jesus Christ understood the business of soul-winning better than any one else, and yet some terrible threats and denunciations fell from His lips in the course of His personal ministry in the world. It is of course true that men can only be won by love; but will they be likely to love the Lord before they realize in some degree the awful character of the doom from which He desires to save them? Of what use is it to cry " Peace, peace!" when there is no peace? What wisdom is there in refraining from a warning cry when you observe a blind or heedless person approaching the brink of a precipice? It is a wise thing, then, on the preacher's part to warn the sinner of his danger, as it is a merciful thing on God's part that he is commissioned to do so. Not morosely do I say to those who are living in sin, but in quite an opposite mood, " You are drifting to destruction; you are in danger of the fiery Gehenna."

II.

The suitableness of Jonah's preaching in Nineveh is the next thing to be noticed. We know that God designed to save Nineveh, and that He designed therefore to bring its people to repentance. It might have been thought, however, that this design would be rather frustrated than fulfilled by the preaching of Jonah; for was not his preaching quite as likely to amuse or annoy the Ninevites as to effect a reformation on their part?

Under certain circumstances, the people addressed by the prophet would assuredly have been amused by

his preaching. A stranger comes into the great city
and cries, "Yet forty days, and Nineveh shall be overthrown." "Overthrown! By what? By whom?
Ha, ha! Say that again, stranger. You are a very
amusing fellow indeed. Ha, ha, ha!"

The Ninevites were more likely, however, to be
annoyed than amused by the preaching of Jonah.
For one who was not of their nation to enter their
city, and threaten it with destruction in less than six
weeks, might easily have been regarded by them as
the height of presumption on his part, and have been
fiercely resented as such. If not mobbed and molested
in the streets, the magistrates might be expected to
deal with him as a disturber of the peace.

But nothing of the kind occurred. Jonah went
through the city and delivered his message, being
neither insulted nor injured by those he addressed;
and the question arises, How is this to be explained?
I have said that the prophet's preaching was suitable
to the circumstances of the case; and was it not so?
Our Lord says that "the men of Nineveh repented at
the preaching of Jonah," and it is certain that the
preaching of no other person would or could have produced the same effect. The message of the prophet
derived the major part of its impressiveness from the
known facts of his own history. The prophet's text
was the startling cry, "Yet forty days, and Nineveh
shall be overthrown;" the prophet's sermon was
himself. That is what underlies the assertion of the
Lord Jesus Christ that "Jonah was a sign unto the
Ninevites." A sign, a living miracle, an incarnate
illustration of certain truths which immensely enforced
the verbal warning he addressed to them. Consider

what these truths were. They related principally to the Divine attributes, or to some of them.

Jonah was a sign unto the Ninevites of Jehovah's power. The Ninevites had been accustomed to think of Him as the God of the Hebrews, while they thought of Nisroch as the god of their own nation, of Rimmon as the god of the Syrians, of Dagon as the god of the Philistines, and of other deities as severally related to particular countries. But Jonah's recent experience afforded ample evidence that the God he worshipped had power in all directions, and was indeed the God of heaven, of all the earth, and of the sea. He who could raise a tempest when He pleased, and allay it when He pleased, was surely equal to the work of executing the sentence with which His servant now startled the men of Nineveh : " Yet forty days, and Nineveh shall be overthrown ! "

Jonah was also a sign unto the Ninevites of Jehovah's justice. The prophet had disobeyed the Deity whose servant he was, but surely such a person as himself might do that with impunity ? Was he not a favoured servant of Jehovah ? Might he not, then, hope to escape the chastisement deserved by his transgression ? No. It was known that he had been overtaken by a tempest, compelled to pronounce sentence upon himself, and cast into the sea by the sailors in accordance with the terms of that sentence. What miseries he had experienced in the deep, in darkness, in the belly of hell, could only be conjectured ; but it was certain that they had constituted an appalling punishment of the transgression he had committed. If, then, even Jonah, so honoured as a prophet of Jehovah, might not sin with impunity by reason of the justice of that

Deity, what hope could the Ninevites have that their crimes would escape punishment, if they themselves ever fell into the hands of that dread Being?

The only hope they had was in the mercy of Jehovah, and Jonah was a sign unto them of that mercy. God had not, indeed, allowed the prophet to sin with impunity, but neither had He allowed him to be destroyed. There he was in Nineveh, alive and well, notwithstanding all that he had gone through. He had obtained mercy as soon as he had sought it, and might the people of Nineveh not hope to obtain it also? Ah! that was the question. Might they? Jonah was a sign unto them of Jehovah's readiness to extend mercy to His anointed ministers, and even to His chosen people; but was he a sign unto them of anything more than this? Was he a sign of God's readiness to extend His mercy to such Gentiles as should seek it at His hands? Certainly. The heathen sailors with whom he had been brought into contact had sought mercy from the God he worshipped, and their prayer had not been despised. Their lives had been spared, their worship accepted, and the people of Nineveh might fairly infer that their own entreaty for Jehovah's mercy would not be disregarded.

The Divine power, justice, and mercy, are matters in which we are no less deeply interested than the ancient Ninevites; and it is very spirit-stirring to listen to the proclamation of the Psalmist with regard to them: "God hath spoken once; twice have I heard this; that power belongeth unto God. Also unto Thee, O Lord, belongeth mercy: for Thou renderest to every man according to his work."

III.

We may now consider the manner in which the preaching of Jonah was supplemented in Nineveh. The prophet himself passed through the city, proclaiming, as he paced its principal thoroughfare, " Yet forty days, and Nineveh shall be overthrown ! " Then he went out of the city, and his voice was heard no more within its walls. But other voices were heard. A royal proclamation was issued, and the voices of the heralds resounded in all directions, supplying an effective supplement to the preaching of the prophet himself.

The manner in which this royal proclamation was produced deserves consideration. It was not produced by the king alone, but by the king and his nobles. The monarch heard of what had taken place in the city, and may have heard it in sufficient time to betake himself to some vantage-ground for listening directly to the prophet's cry. What was to be done ? Calling his counsellors around him, those magnates of the monarchy deliberated as to what course they might adopt. It was well for themselves, for their master, and for his subjects that they counselled him to issue the proclamation described in the text. They had often deliberated on matters of state before, but had never previously resolved on a measure so fraught with blessing to the community as the one of which I now speak. It is well for a commonwealth when its rulers and statesmen do what lies in their power to reform the manners of its people. It is not, however, probable that those who occupy the high places of the state will care about the promotion of

11

virtue unless they are themselves virtuous men.   We
should therefore pray, my brethren, that those who
are called to the counsels of our own Sovereign may
be men who fear God and love their country, rather
than men who are mainly bent on serving their own
selfish interests.   "God save the Queen!" say I;
and save her from advisers who delight in war, who
oppress the weaker nations of the earth, who tarnish
the lustre of the British crown by their deceit and
cruelty, and who employ the prerogative of their royal
mistress to make themselves as nearly despotic as
they can.   God save the Queen!   and when her
advisers gather in council, may it be to emulate the
example of the nobles of Nineveh, who displayed such
wisdom and suitable feeling in relation to that city
after the prophet had passed through it with his
warning cry![1]

The *drift of this royal proclamation* may be regarded as either imperative or hortatory.   It contains
a number of what some may call commands, and
others counsels.   The counsels given by a king are
apt to have the force of commands; but it seems
more suitable, on the whole, to speak of counsels
rather than commands in the case under consideration.

This proclamation contains a counsel to fast.   As
a feast is regarded as an appropriate celebration in a
season of triumph and rejoicing, so a fast is appropriate to a season of humiliation and sorrow.   The
deeper the humiliation, and the keener the sorrow,
the more rigid is the fast likely to be; and it was a

---

[1] This discourse was delivered during the progress of the General
Election in the earlier part of the present year, 1880.

very rigid fast to which the people of Nineveh were called by their king and his nobles. They were not to affect fasting. They were neither to eat nor drink. They were not so much as to taste anything. Their condition was all but desperate, and this was the manner in which they could most fittingly acknowledge it to be such. Christians are neither commanded nor counselled to fast in the New Testament. They are at liberty to fast, or to abstain from fasting; but there are suitable ways in which humility and contrition may be expressed before God, and each of us must judge for himself which of them it becomes him to adopt.

The Ninevites are further counselled in this proclamation to cover themselves with sackcloth; or, as we say, to go into mourning. The king himself set an example in this matter, for "he arose from his throne, and he laid his robe from him, and covered him with sackcloth, and sat in ashes." It must have been very affecting. It must have produced a profound impression. It was most appropriate. But it is not the kind of thing which is required of those who now humble themselves on account of their sins before Almighty God. If the spirit is clad in mourning, we may dispense with sable drapery for the body. "The Lord looketh upon the heart," and "the outward appearance" is but of little consequence in comparison with the condition of the inward man. Is the hidden man of the heart clad in mourning in the case of any one among ourselves? Remember the beatitude, "Blessed are they that mourn, for they shall be comforted." The God of all consolation shall give to those who mourn in Zion "beauty for ashes, the oil of joy for mourning, the garment of praise for the spirit of heaviness."

The people of Nineveh are counselled also to pray in the proclamation before us. It urges them to cry mightily unto God, and no better counsel could be given. The meaning of the fasting and the sackcloth would find further expression in the words of prayer employed by the people. It was public prayer to which they were thus called, no doubt; and it was a "cry" which they sent up to God for His mercy. Thus the cry of the prophet was followed by the cry of the people he had threatened with the destruction of their city. His cry had called them to repentance, as their cry now called God to repentance; and both cries were effectual, as we shall see.

The proclamation counsels the people addressed to reform their manner of life. The reformation advised was practical. They were not only to fast and wear sackcloth and cry mightily unto God, but to "turn every one from his evil way and from the violence that is in their hands." The reformation was also to be personal. Every one was to turn from his evil way. Every one. If every citizen of Nineveh reformed, the city would soon experience a reformation; and it is as well for us to remember the truth illustrated by the familiar and homely proverb, "Let each one sweep before his own door, and the street will be clean."

Finally, the proclamation counsels the Ninevites to associate the very brutes with themselves in their appeal to God: "Let neither man nor beast, herd nor flock, taste anything: let them not feed nor drink water; but let man and beast be covered with sack-

cloth, and cry mightily unto God." The poor
brutes would cry in their hunger, as their masters
would cry in their fear; and we shall find that the
cry of the flocks and herds was not sent forth in
vain.

*The reason which the proclamation gives for acting
as it counsels* is couched in very plaintive terms:
"Who can tell if God will turn and repent, and turn
away from His fierce anger, that we perish not?"
It is impossible to forget, as we read this, the language of David in reference to his own conduct during
the illness of his beloved and dying child. "I said,
Who can tell whether God will be gracious to me that
the child may live?" As long as David hoped he
prayed; and the Apostle Paul says that "we are
saved by hope." It is certain that if the Ninevites
had only feared in consequence of the prophet's proclamation, they would have perished in despair. But
they hoped as well as feared, and the hope they
cherished is touchingly expressed in the concluding
portion of the royal proclamation: "Who can tell if
God will turn and repent, and turn away from His
fierce anger, that we perish not?" It was language
equally removed from despair and presumption; and
it may be profitably compared with an address employed by God Himself, and recorded by the prophet
Joel: "Therefore also now, saith the Lord, turn ye
to Me with all your heart, and with fasting, and with
weeping, and with mourning: and rend your heart,
and not your garments, and turn unto the Lord your
God: for He is gracious and merciful, slow to anger,
and of great kindness, and repenteth Him of the evil.
Who knoweth if He will return and repent, and leave

a blessing behind Him?" Who knoweth? Who
can tell? There should, after all, be no uncertainty
with respect to this subject on the part of those who
are acquainted with the Gospel. Who knoweth?
Who can tell? We know; we can tell; that is to say,
we know that God will return unto us if we return
unto Him, and we can tell that He will in all cases
receive to His mercy those who seek it in the
appointed way. I will not now describe that way to
you at any length. It will suffice to remind you of
those majestic words of the Lord Jesus Christ, "I
am the way, the truth, and the life: no man cometh
unto the Father but by Me." From God as the
Ruler of the Universe you may have much to fear,
but from God as the Father you have nothing to fear;
and if you come to Him through Jesus Christ, you
will find in Him a Father and a Friend.

XI.

REPENTANCE, HUMAN AND DIVINE.

" And God saw their works, that they turned from their evil way ; and God repented of the evil, that He had said that He would do unto them ; and He did it not."—JONAH iii. 10.

THOUGH Jonah declared that Nineveh should be overthrown within forty days, his prediction was not fulfilled. Was it not? Think. The city was certainly not overthrown in one sense, but was it not overthrown in another? Was there not a revolution within its walls? Unquestionably. It was, indeed, a moral revolution which took place, but it was a revolution. Nineveh was overthrown, and the occasion of its overthrow was the prediction which some may say was not fulfilled. Nineveh was overthrown by the preaching of Jonah, as long afterwards the world was said to be turned upside down by that of the Apostles. It must be acknowledged, however, that this was not the kind of overthrow to which the prediction of the prophet pointed. He evidently meant, and was understood to mean, that within forty days the great city would be destroyed. It was not, however, destroyed, inasmuch as its inhabitants repented, and by so doing occasioned

God Himself to repent of His purpose in relation to them. There is, then, such a thing as repentance, not only on the part of human beings, but also on that of the Divine Being; and we are led by the language of the text to consider both the repentance of the Ninevites and that of Jehovah.

I.

The repentance of the Ninevites may engage our attention with great advantage, and the subject will now be set forth in a series of observations which I trust will prove to be of some practical value.

It was a sincere repentance on the part of the Ninevites: "God saw their works, that they turned from their evil way." This settles the matter. They might have deceived each other and deluded themselves, but it was impossible for them to deceive God. It has happened before now that both individuals and communities have been terrified by some peril which menaced them; and while their terror lasted, there was some evidence of penitence on their part; but as their sense of danger subsided, there were no "fruits meet for repentance" found among them. Men must frequently wait before they can fairly judge of the sincerity of repentance in their neighbours or even in themselves; but God is not obliged to wait. He is able to perceive at a glance whether a person's penitence is sincere or not; and He saw that the people of Nineveh did really repent at the preaching of Jonah, as long afterwards His Son acknowledged that such was the case. There is in our fallen nature a tendency to the hateful sin of hypocrisy, and there are two kinds of hypocrisy which call for some remark at this point. There is the hypocrisy which affects holiness, and there is that which affects penitence. The latter is the more artful, as it is the more heinous. A man who merely wishes to deceive the World will pretend to be holier than his neighbours, but the man who wishes to deceive the Church will pretend to be deeply penitent on account of his transgressions. The latter scoundrel has studied his part carefully, or else he has a certain insight into its requirements which is the very genius of hypocrisy. He knows that the best men have been the most conscious of their own depravity, and the most ready to acknowledge it. He knows that the Apostle Paul, *e.g.*, said that he was unworthy to be called an apostle ; that he was less than the least of all saints ; and that he was the chief of sinners. He resolves, therefore, that he will speak of himself in the same way ; and by this artifice he is enabled to deceive many who are far better than himself. But he cannot deceive God, to whom all things are naked and open ; and who has searched him, and known him, and is acquainted with all his ways. " They that worship Him must worship Him in spirit and in truth," or their worship will not only not be acceptable to Him, but abhorrent. You know what the poet says of hypocrites :—

> " Their lifted eyes salute the skies,
>   Their bended knees the ground ;
> But God abhors the sacrifice
>   Where not the heart is found."

You know, too, what the Apostle says to those who claim to be disciples of Christ : " Let your loins be girt about with truth," *i.e.*, with sincerity. Let there be no pretended penitence on your part, for that kind of play will end in disaster to the players.

The repentance of the Ninevites was occasioned by their faith in God. The prophet said, " Yet forty days, and Nineveh shall be overthrown ! And the people of Nineveh believed in God." That is what is said. Faith in God is certain to produce repentance from sin, and hence the close and constant connection we find between repentance and faith in the New Testament account of these things. When Peter's conscience-stricken hearers on the day of Pentecost demanded of him and his colleagues, " Men and brethren, what must we do ?" his reply was, " Repent !" When the Philippian jailer said to Paul and Silas, " Sirs, what must I do to be saved ?" their reply was, " Believe !" How came Peter and Paul to reply to the same question thus differently ? Why should Peter say, " Repent," and Paul, " Believe" ? The explanation is that repentance and faith involve each other. A man cannot repent without repenting of his unbelief in God and in God's Son. Belief in Them, as they are revealed in the Scriptures, is not an instinct with fallen humanity, but results from a change of mind ; and what is repentance but a change of mind ? Paul assured the Ephesian elders that he had kept back nothing that was profitable in his preaching and teaching among them and their people, and then explains this assurance by reminding them that he had been found " testifying, both to the Jews and also to the Greeks, repentance toward God and faith toward our Lord Jesus Christ." The author of the Epistle to the Hebrews represents " repentance from dead works and faith toward God" as funda-

mental to the religion he inculcated. You will never
attain to genuine repentance till you have attained to
faith in God; and therefore I will say to you, my
hearers, in the words of the Divine Master, "Have
faith in God!" Does the secret of such faith appeal
to you worth finding out? Do you ask me how the
people of Nineveh came to believe in God? I reply
that they were affected by the preaching, the presence, and the personal experience of the prophet
Jonah, which all combined to furnish them with a
true idea of the Most High; their faith being the
surrender of their hearts to the influence of that idea.
But how much more ample is our opportunity of
acquiring true ideas of God, and what superior motives
have we to surrender ourselves to the influence of
those ideas! They had the testimony of one prophet; we have that of all the prophets, and we have
also that of patriarchs, apostles, evangelists; above
all, we have that of the Lord Jesus Christ. If this
testimony be duly considered, faith in God will be
found inevitable, and faith will involve repentance.

The repentance of the Ninevites was universal.
They seem to have done as the royal proclamation
counselled, and to have turned every one from his
evil way. It is probable that the case of Nineveh is
unique in this respect. To what other community of
like magnitude can we point as having repented in
the mass after this fashion? But the circumstance
that one such community did thus repent is enough
to show that it is not impossible in the nature of
things that entire populations may be converted to
God. It is not impossible that the entire population
of Swansea, for example, or Cardiff, or Bristol, or even

London, may be brought to repentance; and therefore
it is by no means impossible that that of our own little
town should be thus blessed.   Do I see an incredu-
lous expression on some of your faces?   There is
probably much incredulity on this subject in some of
your hearts.   But I must not be daunted by any such
circumstance.   I do really think that this universal
repentance of the Ninevites is intended to be regarded
as an earnest of the universal repentance of mankind.
It is intimated in the Scriptures that a time is coming
when "the earth shall be full of the knowledge of the
Lord, as the waters cover the sea."   Let the people
of God, therefore, refuse to be discouraged.   Their
labours are not in vain.   Their example shall not be
thrown away.   Their hopes shall not be disappointed.
The cause to which they have consecrated their best
energies is assured of certain triumph.   The kingdoms
of this world are to become the kingdom of our God
and of His Christ; and when the victory is celebrated,
it shall not be forgotten that you, my brethren, contributed to bring it about by your prayers and works
and alms, and by your persistent pursuit of those things
which make for righteousness and peace and joy in
the Holy Ghost.   "Therefore, my beloved brethren,
be ye steadfast, unmovable, always abounding in the
work of the Lord, forasmuch as ye know that your
labour is not in vain in the Lord."

The repentance of the Ninevites was exceedingly
prompt.   There was, indeed, a necessity for promptitude on their part.   Within forty days their city was
to be overthrown, unless its overthrow might be
averted by their repentance.   Delay in such a case
was certain destruction.   It was not as though the

prophet had cried, " Yet forty years, and Nineveh shall be overthrown! " Had that been proclaimed by him, it is probable that the penitence of the people would have been postponed. It would have been with them as it is with so many among ourselves. Our own observation abundantly confirms the saying of the inspired sage, " Because sentence against an evil work is not executed speedily, therefore the heart of the sons of men is fully set in them to do evil." But men should be reminded that the sentence which impends over them may be executed within forty days, or forty hours, or forty minutes, of the moment now passing. It is their wisdom, therefore, not only to repent, but to repent with the utmost promptitude. Let no one be satisfied with resolving to repent at some future time, is the advice which every preacher of righteousness is bound to give to his hearers with all possible emphasis; and the grounds of such advice are sufficiently obvious. Repentance should not be postponed till a more convenient season, because it is not certain that there will be such a season. " Behold, now is the accepted time; behold, now is the day of salvation." Therefore, " boast not thyself of to-morrow, for thou knowest not what a day may bring forth." Repentance should not be postponed, if only because the futility of such postponement is clearly taught by ample experience. It is very likely, indeed, taught by your own experience. Did you not resolve some years ago that you would repent before the time which is now present? and have you yet repented? If, then, the time you formerly anticipated as the proper period for penitential humiliation on your part has come and gone without such humiliation, and

you are nevertheless disposed as much as ever to procrastination, how great the folly of such delay ! Moreover, it ought to be well considered that a resolution
to postpone the repentance to which God graciously
calls you now is itself a serious addition to your former
offences, and proportionately augments your peril.

The repentance of the Ninevites appears to have
originated at the summit of society, and then spread
downwards to its base : " The people of Nineveh
believed God, and proclaimed a fast, and put on sackcloth, from the greatest of them even to the least of
them." Now, the greatest of them was, of course,
the king ; and accordingly we read that " he arose
from his throne, and he laid his robe from him, and
covered him with sackcloth, and sat in ashes." This
great prince had in all probability led his people to
the battle-field, and placed himself at the head of
their triumphal processions, and assumed his proper
primacy in all the matters covered by his prerogative.
Now he leads them in the great moral movement
described in the narrative before us, and does more
to promote their welfare thereby than he had ever
done before. We all know how readily and mightily
people are influenced by their superiors. There are
many things which they do for no better and for no
other reason than that they are done by those who
are above themselves in rank and station. It is
therefore of immense importance that our own
national aristocracy should be largely composed of
God-fearing persons ; and the same remark applies to
those who have influence in the spheres of literature
and commerce, to all employers of labour, and to all
persons in authority. Moreover, it is of immense

importance that the Christians in a country should addict themselves to prayer for its governing classes; and, in the words of an apostle, " I exhort, therefore, that, first of all, supplications, prayers, intercessions, and giving of thanks be made for all men ; for kings and all that are in authority." It is better to do thus than to indulge in wild revolutionary talk, such as has been sometimes found to precede political convulsions of the most deplorable character. The art of reformation is the art of prayer.

The repentance of the Ninevites, sincere and effectual as it was, did not prevent their descendants from doing all manner of evil, and incurring the destruction of their city. Isaiah, Nahum, and Zephaniah all predicted, after Jonah's time, the overthrow of the Assyrian empire, and Ezekiel employs language which shows that their predictions were fulfilled. The king who repented and called his people to repentance in the time of Jonah had among his successors one who was thus addressed by a later prophet : " O king of Assyria! . . . there is no healing of thy bruise."[1] And there was none. The great city was at length destroyed ; and the lesson for us is that the penitence of our fathers is of no use to us in the absence of our own personal repentance. Piety is not hereditary. The sons of Eli were sons of Belial, and the sons of Samuel were no better. Pious parents cannot bequeath their piety to their posterity, and should therefore labour to train their children in the nurture and admonition of the Lord. There is ample encouragement for them to do so afforded in the Scriptures. It is a familiar, but in-

[1] Nahum iii. 18, 19.

spired, sentence that I am about to cite : " Train up a
child in the way he should go, and when he is old he
will not depart from it." But I am not only addressing pious parents; I am addressing also the children of
such; and I would say to them, Do not presume on the
piety of your fathers and mothers, or that of your remoter
ancestors, who may have been renowned for devotion
to God in their day. Their repentance does not involve
yours, and their salvation does not ensure yours. The
God of your fathers will be your God, but you must
seek Him for yourselves. Your mother's Saviour will
be yours, but you must personally entreat His grace.

II.

We may now pass from the repentance of the
Ninevites to that which is here ascribed to God.
" God saw their works, that they turned from their
evil way ; and God repented of the evil that He had
said that He would do unto them ; and He did it not."
There is manifestly a doctrinal difficulty in connection
with this passage, and it needs to be carefully con-
sidered. The nature of this difficulty is easily stated.
The text belongs to a certain class of passages of
Scripture which attribute repentance to the Most
High, while there is another class of passages in
which it is denied that He does repent.

One passage of the former class occurs very early
in the sacred volume : " It repented the Lord that
He had made man upon the earth." Another occurs
in the account of David's conduct in connection with
a certain census and its consequences : " When the
angel stretched out his hand upon Jerusalem to
destroy it, the Lord repented Him of the evil, and

said to the angel that destroyed the people, it is enough : stay now thine hand." It is said in the Book of Joel that God " is gracious and merciful, slow to anger, and of great kindness, and repenteth Him of the evil." But Joel must have called to mind as he penned this passage the language of Jonah, as recorded in the context: " Thou art a gracious God, and merciful, slow to anger, and of great kindness, and repentest Thee of the evil." These are not the only passages of the class to which they belong, but they will suffice for our present purpose.[1]

On the other hand, we find it repeatedly declared in the Scriptures that God does not, and even cannot, repent. The testimony of Balaam on this subject was as truly inspired by the Holy Ghost as that of far better men. " God is not a man that He should lie; neither the son of man that He should repent." What Balaam thus said to Balak corresponds with what another prophet said to another king. It was Samuel who said to Saul, " The Strength of Israel will not lie nor repent; for He is not a man that He should repent." Then there is the language of God Himself at the close of the Old Testament : " I am Jehovah; I change not; therefore ye sons of Jacob are not consumed." In the New Testament we find one Apostle saying that " the gifts and calling of God are without repentance;" while another says that " every good gift and every perfect gift is from above, and cometh down from the Father of lights, with whom is no variableness, neither shadow of turning." [2]

---

[1] Gen. vi. 6 ; 2 Sam. xxiv. 16 ; Joel. ii. 13 ; and Jonah iv. 2.
[2] Numb. xxiii. 19 ; 1 Sam. xv. 29 ; Mal. iii. 6 ; and Rom. xi. 29.

The difficulty is now fairly before us ; God does and does not repent ; and to any one who demands an explanation of this discrepancy, it might be enough to reply that the truth concerning God is unspeakable ; that the poverty of human language is such as to necessitate many verbal difficulties of this kind; but that they are verbal only, and should not be magnified too much. It would be true enough and fair enough to deal with the matter in this way, if it were impossible to deal with it in a more satisfactory manner. But such is not the case. Truth may be sometimes formulated most conveniently by means of a paradox; and I shall not hesitate to assert that the teaching of the Scriptures with regard to the subject now under consideration is that *God is unchangeably changeable.*

Observe the thermometer. Would you describe it as changeable or unchangeable ? It is certainly changeable, for the mercury it contains is sometimes above fever heat and sometimes below freezing point. But it is just as certainly unchangeable, for it always indicates the temperature to which it is exposed ; the mercury rising as surely as the weather gets warmer, and falling as surely as it gets colder. The action of the instrument is invariable in its character, and yet action itself involves change.

Take another illustration. The tide is a changeable thing, now ebbing and then flowing ; but the tide is also an unchangeable thing, for its ebb and flow are so regular that they can be anticipated with the utmost confidence ; and months, or even years, beforehand, it can be calculated precisely when it will be high-water and when low-water on any part of the coast.

Take yet another illustration. During the reign of the second James and the third William in this country there was a conspicuous politician who was neither Whig nor Tory. He had changed sides so often that he obtained the *sobriquet* of "Trimmer." A changeable statesman, you say. Yes, but he was also as unchangeable in respect of public affairs as any of his contemporaries. He never lost sight of what is known as the balance of power; and the principle on which he invariably acted was that of doing all that lay in his power to preserve or restore that balance. Accordingly, when the Whigs were uppermost, he acted with the Tories; and when the Tories were uppermost, he acted with the Whigs. He was constant in his political inconstancy; and the sentence addressed by the patriarch to his eldest son did by no means apply to "the accomplished Trimmer," as Macaulay calls Lord Halifax : "Unstable as water, thou shalt not excel."

These illustrations may help us to understand the truth about the Most High. He is always displeased with those who transgress His commandment, and always pleased with those who endeavour to obey it. As often, therefore, as a change takes place in a human being from loyalty to disloyalty, or *vice versâ*, a corresponding change occurs in God in relation to that person. This change takes place in the Most High, not because He is changeable, but because He is unchangeable. A mere metaphysician may not be satisfied with such an account of this matter, but a practical person may very well be content with it. Or if such a person be troubled with any misgiving in relation to it, one thinks it is only necessary to direct his attention to the passage I am about to quote in order that it may be removed: "At what instant I shall speak concerning a nation, and concerning a kingdom, to pluck up, and to pull down, and to destroy it; if that nation against whom I have pronounced turn from their evil, I will repent of the evil that I thought to do unto them. And at what instant I shall speak concerning a nation, and concerning a kingdom, to build and to plant it; if it do evil in My sight, that it obey not my voice, then I will repent of the good wherewith I said I would benefit them." [1] That is the changeless principle of God's government, and it explains all the changes in His attitude toward nations and persons. God has often changed in the manner thus described, and that for the simple and sufficient reason that He is unchangeable.

If, then, you have any reason to believe that the Most High regards you with complacency, take heed that you continue in the course which will ensure the continuance of His approbation. I need not tell you that that course is indicated by the sacred Scriptures; and that as long as you cultivate the faith and practice the virtues which they enjoin, their Divine Author will continue to regard you as He now does. If you change, He will change; inasmuch as He invariably does change towards those who change towards Him. On the other hand, if there is one who knows only too well that he is regarded by the Supreme Being with deserved displeasure, let such an one know that a change on his part towards God will result in a corresponding change on God's part towards himself. Try it, O my brother! "and in that day thou shalt

[1] Jer. xviii. 7-10.

say, O Lord, I will praise Thee : though thou wast angry with me, Thine anger is turned away, and Thou comfortedst me." In the name of Him of Whom it is said that " Jesus Christ is the same yesterday, and to-day, and for ever," I say to all whom it may concern, " Turn ye, turn ye from your evil ways ; for why will ye die ? "

XII.

THE PROPHET'S DISPLEASURE.

"But it displeased Jonah exceedingly, and he was very angry. And he prayed unto the Lord, and said, I pray Thee, O Lord, was not this my saying, when I was yet in my country? Therefore I fled before unto Tarshish; for I knew that Thou art a gracious God, and merciful, slow to anger, and of great kindness, and repentest Thee of the evil. Therefore now, O Lord, take, I beseech Thee, my life from me; for it is better for me to die than to live."—JONAH iv. 1-3.

BEING aware of the murmuring of the Pharisees and Scribes at His conduct in eating with publicans and sinners, our blessed Lord spake the parables of the Lost Sheep and the Lost Coin, appending to the latter the very striking assertion, "Likewise, I say unto you, there is joy in the presence of the angels of God over one sinner that repenteth." This is doubtless because the angels are in sympathy with God Himself. They are pleased or displeased with the things which please or displease Him. It is certain also that there are some human beings (I need not say in heaven, but will say on earth) who so far resemble the angels that they are well pleased to learn that sinners have been brought to repentance. Such persons are especially well pleased when they have any reason to suppose that sinners have been brought to repentance by their own instrumentality. Which of

all the men who are now engaged in preaching the
Gospel would not gladly learn that even one of his
hearers had been brought to repentance by his means ?
Which of them would not be overwhelmed with delight
on receiving evidence that a whole community had
been saved by his preaching ? There never was but
one man, however, whose preaching is known to have
resulted in the immediate repentance and deliverance
of a whole city ; and he was, of course, filled and
thrilled with ecstasy and rapture unspeakable. Alas !
no. The man of whom I speak was not pleased, but
displeased, with this blessed and most marvellous
result of his own preaching. "It displeased Jonah
exceedingly." The nature, intensity, and manifestation of the prophet's displeasure are the things which
must engage our attention in this lecture.

I.

The nature of Jonah's displeasure may easily be
misunderstood. There are two kinds of displeasure
which may be felt by any of us. One is wrath, and
the other grief. Which then of these two emotions
did the prophet experience at the result of his mission
to the Ninevites ? We read that "it displeased Jonah
exceedingly, and he was very angry." Does not this
word "angry" settle the matter ? No. The word
employed in the original[1] may either be rendered
angry or distressed. It does sometimes mean "angry,"
and it may be thought to mean this here. But having
regard to the context, and to all the circumstances of
the case as far as they are present to my own mind, it
appears to me that Jonah is described as having been

very grieved rather than very angry. I know of no
circumstance which renders the harsher expression
imperative. It is said in the second verse that God
is "slow to anger," but the word there rendered
"anger"[1] is quite a different word from the one
rendered "angry" in the former verse. That so good
a man as Jonah could be angry with God for sparing
the Ninevites is not to be believed, unless such anger
is unequivocally ascribed to him in the sacred narrative, and such is not the case. It was bad enough for
him to be distressed by the course of events, but not
so bad as it would have been had he been made angry
thereby. Remember what was said in a former lecture
respecting the prophet's name. Jonah means Dove,
and this was an appropriate name for a messenger of
mourning such as he. He was distressed from the
first with his commission to preach in Nineveh; and
now that he had accomplished that mission, he was
distressed with its result: "It displeased Jonah exceedingly, and he was very grieved."

One cannot read of the distress thus experienced
by the prophet without a disposition to adopt the
language of David. A certain choice was allowed
that royal personage, as you will remember, in relation to the punishment he was to receive for his
misconduct in the matter of that census to which I
have already had occasion to refer. The language in
which he announced his decision was that of a wise
and good, if erring, man. "David said unto God, I
am in a great strait: let us fall now into the hand of
the Lord, for His mercies are great: and let me not
fall into the hand of man." It was clearly much

---

[1] אַף, *aph.*

better for the Ninevites to fall into the hand of the Lord than into that of the prophet Jonah.

But another idea is derived from this part of the story before us, viz., the impotence of mere external experience in relation to a person's inward disposition. If we were reading the Book of Jonah for the first time, I suppose that the passage now under consideration would excite our astonishment. We might have read without much surprise of the prophet's displeasure when first directed to go to Nineveh. To err is human, and prophets were but men. It is adapted to surprise us very much, however, when we find that, notwithstanding his so wondrous and so recent experience of the displeasure with which God regarded his shrinking from the duty assigned him, his own displeasure in relation to that duty was not diminished. After the marvellous and gracious deliverance he had experienced from the heart of the seas and the belly of hell, it might have been supposed that he would regard all that was related to his duty with the utmost good humour. But it was not so. The prophet was the same man, and felt in the same way about the people of Nineveh after his tremendous experience as before it. There is a description in the famous Christmas Carol composed by the late Charles Dickens of a man who had devoted himself to the pursuit of gain so much to the exclusion of other things that he had become a monster of selfishness. This man went to sleep one Christmas Eve, and dreamt in a manner so illustrative of the terrible effects of such a life as his, that he awoke with totally different feelings about getting and spending money from those with which he had fallen

asleep. On Christmas Eve he had been a morose
and selfish man; on Christmas Day he had become
a genial and generous one. But no such change is
found to occur in the actual experience of men. I
do not indeed deny the possibility, or even the occurrence, of sudden conversion. Of course not. But a
new convert is never a moral giant. He is a babe,
and must grow; there being no experience of terror
or disaster which can transform him in a single day
from a little child into a full-grown man. Sanctification is a gradual process. It was gradual in
Jonah's case, and will be gradual in our own.

II.

The intensity of Jonah's displeasure is remarked in
the text, and must also be remarked by ourselves:
"It displeased Jonah *exceedingly*, and he was *very*
grieved." Now it has been supposed that the man
of whom this is recorded must have been a flinty-
hearted person, but I shall attempt to show that such
was not the case.

This intense displeasure at the deliverance of
Nineveh was really deep distress on the prophet's
part in the prospect of calamity to his own country.
Jonah would, in all probability, have had no objection
to the deliverance of Nineveh if that had not been
likely to involve the destruction of Israel. His stern-
ness in relation to Nineveh must in truth be measured
by his tenderness in relation to his own people. If
Nineveh had been destroyed, Israel would have had
nothing to apprehend from the Assyrians, and the
prophet would thus have been relieved from a reasonable and patriotic anxiety. It is true, indeed, that

another idea should have had weight with him. If the repentance of the Ninevites ensured their deliverance, so would that of the Israelites ensure their own. But Jonah knew his countrymen too well to have much hope that they would repent. He knew also that, unless they did repent, God would have no alternative than to destroy them. All the signs of the times, moreover, were such as to indicate that the Assyrians would be chosen to crush the commonwealth of Israel by way of punishment for its rebellion against its God. We may find in these circumstances, and especially in the prophet's conviction that the continued impenitence of his own people would provoke their destruction at the hands of the Assyrians, the real and ultimate reason of his deep distress at the deliverance of the Assyrian capital.

Another thing to be remembered is that the destruction of an impenitent heathen community would not have appeared to Jonah so terrible as such a thing must appear to ourselves. It would, of course, appear very terrible even to him; but the worst that he would think of as befalling those involved in such destruction would be their death. Why should not such persons be put to death? The world would be well rid of them, and they richly deserved such a fate. But we cannot take this simple view of such a matter. We know that death is not the end, or the whole, of it; but that there is something worse beyond in the case of all such offenders. But little was known in Jonah's time concerning the future state of the wicked in comparison with what has been revealed to ourselves; and for any of us to be displeased at the deliverance of penitent sinners from destruction under any circumstances would be something far more horrible than Jonah's displeasure at the deliverance of the Ninevites.

It must be considered, further, that if Jonah was grieved at the escape of the Ninevites from death, he was himself anxious to die. The prayer for death, which is recorded in the text as having been presented by him, will receive our attention presently. For the moment, I remark that he did not desire a worse fate for them than for himself. Or rather, he desired to die if they lived, and to live if they died. Death was not in itself the greatest evil of which the prophet had any knowledge, and his view of things appears to have been something like this : The cause of Israel was the cause of God. It was for God's glory that Israel should repent, and return to the path of obedience. If Israel did not repent, however, what would become of God's cause and covenant? If Israel were destroyed, how could that cause be carried on, and that covenant confirmed? Is it then so wonderful that the man who would have rather died himself than witnessed the extinction of God's cause should have been displeased at the deliverance of those who appeared likely to effect its extinction? I see in this great grief of the prophet, unbecoming as it was, such regard for the Divine glory as could only have been cherished by a subject of Divine grace.

Finally, it may be well to consider in connection with the intense displeasure ascribed to the prophet that there are some men of whom it is said that " their bark is worse than their bite," and that Jonah was possibly such a man. The familiar manner in

which God communed with him makes it apparent
that he was by no means the merciless monster that
some readers of his history have deemed him.   In
one of our Saviour's parables we are told of a king
who refused mercy to a servant by whom it had been
refused to a fellow servant; and on the principle thus
illustrated we may be certain that, if Jonah had been
as callous and cruel as some have thought, God would
not have held such intercourse with him as He did.
You know how it is at times with some among ourselves.   They read that a murder has been committed,
and that the murderer has escaped.   As long as the
papers are unable to report that the criminal has been
arrested, these men speak sternly of the man and of
their own desire that he should die upon the scaffold.
But when they do at length read of his capture, his
conviction, and his capital sentence, a change takes
place in their sentiment with regard to the guilty
wretch.   Pity has taken the place of that vindictive
feeling with which they formerly thought of him, and
it is as likely as not that they will sign a petition
to the Home Secretary on his behalf.   It does not
follow, therefore, because Jonah was displeased with
the deliverance of the Ninevites, that he would
have rejoiced over their destruction.   There are some
men who deem themselves to be better than they
are, and there are others who deem themselves to be
worse than they are.   Repeatedly has it happened
that men who have undertaken to assassinate princes
have found their way into the presence of their intended victims only to discover that they were not
sufficiently resolute in wickedness to carry out their
fell purpose.   It is on record, that when Marius was

in prison, a soldier was employed by the enemies of that illustrious Roman general to murder him. When, however, the man came into his presence in such a way as plainly to betoken his intention, he lost all power of carrying it into execution. The aged and unarmed hero did but look in his face and demand, "Man! wilt thou slay Caius Marius?" and, lo! the soldier flung down his weapon, rushed forth from the prison, and exclaimed, "I cannot kill Caius Marius!" So it seems to me that Jonah was not so callous in relation to human suffering as he seemed; and that he would, in all probability, have been even more distressed by the destruction of Nineveh than he actually was by its deliverance from the doom he had predicted.

III.

The extreme distress thus experienced by Jonah found expression in the prayer recorded in this passage: "It displeased Jonah exceedingly, and he was very grieved; and he prayed unto the Lord." The terms of the prayer are preserved for our advantage, and we had better examine them.

1. The prayer contains a reference to a former saying of the prophet himself: "I pray Thee, O Lord, was not this my saying when I was yet in my country?" What was this "saying"? It was doubtless to the effect that his mission to Nineveh would surely result as it had done, that its people would repent and be spared, and that his own country would be endangered by its deliverance. The saying, therefore, showed that Jonah was a true prophet. It was likely enough that some people would sneer at his

mission to Nineveh, and at his announcement in its
streets. He had gone a long way to make that
announcement, and it was falsified by the event.
Although he had said, "Yet forty days, and Nineveh
shall be overthrown!" no such speedy overthrow
took place. He himself had been aware, however,
that his prediction was conditional, and that it would
not be fulfilled. He was no deceiver; for if the
Ninevites had remained impenitent, their city would
have been destroyed within the appointed time. He
was not deceived, for he could appeal to God in relation to this matter in the words before us : "I pray
Thee, O Lord, was not this my saying when I was
yet in my country?"

2. The prayer, too, contains an account of his
flight : "Therefore I fled before unto Tarshish."
The prophet did not suppose that he was imparting
any information to the Most High in saying this ;
but he said it in the way of appeal to Him. In effect
he says something like this : "Consider, O Lord,
what my distress is at this moment. It is just as
deep as when I took the desperate course involved in
my flight rather than do what I have now done. I
have not repeated my disobedience ; I have accomplished my mission ; I have preached in Nineveh ;
but my anguish is no less acute than before." Now
the heart that is burdened with sorrow can do nothing
better than cast that burden on the Lord, however
the sorrow has been occasioned. Let no one try to
lighten the load of grief by some kind of wrong-doing,
as Jonah did in the first instance ; but rather let the
matter be laid before the Lord in prayer, in imitation
of the prophet's after conduct. Not for the informa-

tion of the Deity, but for your own relief, pour out
your heart like water before Him. God knows all
about your affliction already, but none the less for
that circumstance will you find it beneficial to rehearse
the whole matter to Him.

3. This prayer contains an account of Jonah's conviction concerning the Divine character : "I knew
that Thou art a gracious God, and merciful, slow to
anger, and of great kindness, and repentest Thee of
the evil." It was a remarkable instance of human
perversity that a man who had this conviction should
have attempted the flight to which reference has been
made, but we will not revert to that just now.
Rather let us feast for a time upon the truth which
Jonah so poorly digested, in hope that we may be
greatly strengthened in spirit thereby.

It is a great thing to know that the Lord is gracious.
He is spoken of in the Scriptures as the God of all
grace ; and His manifold grace has found manifold
expression. It will be sufficient to refer broadly at
present to the ministry of His Son and Spirit, and
to the account of their ministry which we have in
the Gospel. There was no such manifestation in
Jonah's time of the Divine grace as that which has
been vouchsafed to ourselves ; nor was any one then
in a position to say, as we are permitted to do, that
" the grace of God which bringeth salvation hath
appeared unto all men." Well might the poet
sing,—

> " Grace, 'tis a charming sound,
>   Harmonious to the ear;
> Heaven with the echo shall resound,
>   And all the earth shall hear."

And well may I beseech you, friends and neighbours, that ye receive not the grace of God in vain.

It is a great thing also to know that the Lord is merciful. Even a holy angel needs Divine grace, but sinful men need Divine mercy. It is said of God in the Scriptures that His tender mercies are over all His works, and that His mercy endureth for ever. There is no occasion to prove that you and I have a deep personal interest in this doctrine, for the manifest truth is that "it is of the Lord's mercy we are not consumed, because His compassions fail not." We have broken His law and deserved His wrath, but in wrath He has remembered mercy. I will say no more to you on this subject at present than was said by the Apostle long ago to the Christians in Rome: "I beseech you, therefore, brethren, by the mercies of God, that ye present your bodies a living sacrifice, holy, acceptable unto God, your reasonable service."

It is a great thing, moreover, to know that the Lord is slow to anger. The long-suffering of the Most High is much expatiated on in the Scriptures, but alas for those who take advantage of that long-suffering! The Lord is slow to anger, but there is such a thing as the wrath of God. There is such a thing as the wrath of the Lamb. There is such a thing as the wrath to come. There is such a thing as "the winepress of the fierceness and wrath of Almighty God." If we are conscious that we have deserved to be cast into that winepress, we must also be constrained to rejoice that the Lord is slow to anger.

It is a most blessed thing to know that the Lord is

13

of great kindness. Kindness! The term may seem inadequate, but must not any term appear such to those who well consider what God's kindness really is? Think of the kindness which God has displayed as your Creator, Preserver, and Redeemer, your Father and King, and then say Amen to the assertion of the Psalmist, "Thy lovingkindness is better than life."

We have already had occasion to dwell on the truth that God repents Him of the evil. I will only repeat, before turning from this part of the subject, that as surely as the Lord repented of the evil that He had said that He would do unto the Ninevites, when they on their part turned from their evil way, so surely will He repent of the evil He now intends to bring upon any transgressor among ourselves, if that transgressor will cease from his wickedness and implore the Divine mercy.

4. The prayer on record in the text contains a petition on the prophet's part for death: "Therefore now, O Lord, take, I beseech Thee, my life from me; for it is better for me to die than to live." This was the very pith, you perceive, of the prophet's prayer, " Take, I beseech Thee, my life from me."

It was a very unusual prayer which Jonah thus addressed to God. Very likely many of you, brethren, have prayed for life, but how many of us have prayed for death? A human being is far more likely to say to his Maker, " Let me live," than " Let me die." The example of Hezekiah has been followed far more frequently than that of Jonah; nor is this wonderful, for whereas the prophet prayed for death, the monarch prayed for life.

It was an unbecoming, as well as an unusual, prayer which Jonah thus presented. He told God that it was better for him to die than to live ; meaning that it was better for him to die then than to live any longer. But this was presumption on his part, inasmuch as he was neither called upon to judge of this matter, nor capable of doing so.

But however unbecoming this prayer was, it was the petition of a noble-minded man, and as such we may linger by its record for a little while. It was evidently presented by one who had no dread of anything on the other side of death. Jonah had no such revelation as we possess respecting what is there, but he had confidence in the grace of God ; and his faith was grand in proportion to the paucity of the revelation he possessed.

This prayer was offered by one who was too well aware of the sanctity of his own life to commit suicide. He was not such a man as Saul the rejected king, or as Judas the recreant Apostle. I have little doubt that Jonah longed for death from the moment that he was first directed to go to Nineveh and predict its overthrow. As he commenced his flight, he doubtless expected to be slain for his disobedience to the Divine mandate. Knowing, as he did, how another disobedient prophet had been slain by a lion by direct Divine appointment during the reign of the first Jeroboam, he might naturally expect to be also punished with death, and never would have fled in the way attributed to him but that he desired death rather than life. When Jonah was aroused by the captain from his slumber in the sides of the ship, and became aware of the tempest which had overtaken him, he doubtless supposed that his hour had come; and it was with a certain sombre satisfaction that he said soon afterwards to the sailors, "Take me up, and cast me forth into the sea; so shall the sea be calm unto you: for I know that for my sake this great tempest is upon you." Had the choice been allowed him, he would rather have been drowned to death than effected the deliverance of the Ninevites by preaching in their city. Accordingly, when he had effected their deliverance, he prayed for death on the ground that life was no longer worth having: "O Lord, take, I beseech Thee, my life from me; for it is better for me to die than to live." If, however, the sailors could not, and the Lord would not, take his life, he was too good a man to commit suicide; and it were well if all the people we know were equally impressed with the sanctity of the life with which God has been pleased to endow them. There are, alas! many among us who are as really committing suicide by the several forms of intemperance to which they are addicted as the person who pistols himself or cuts his own throat. Your life belongs to God, and it is for you to be its careful custodian on pain of His displeasure.

This prayer was offered by one whose distress, as we have seen, was occasioned by his despondency in relation to the cause of God. Jonah felt, as Elijah had felt before him, that the cause of God was on the verge of destruction; and prayed, as Elijah had done, for death as preferable to the misery of surviving that cause. The despondency of these two magnanimous persons was transient, but their interest in the Divine cause was permanent; and there is more for us to imitate in their example than to avoid.   Be sure that God perceived all that was good in Jonah, as well as all that was defective, and that it would be well for us if the Most High could perceive in us anything like that interest in His cause which distinguished that prophet.

XIII.

THE BOOTH.

"Then said the Lord, Doest thou well to be angry? So Jonah went out of the city, and sat on the east side of the city, and there made him a booth, and sat under it in the shadow, till he might see what would become of the city."— JONAH iv. 4-5.

UNLESS what was said in the foregoing lecture respecting the word rendered "angry" in this narrative be remembered, the purport of the passage to which your attention is now invited will be partially missed. The question God addressed to the prophet was, "Doest thou well to be grieved?" and it is a question which is always applicable to any one who is in anguish of spirit. God does indeed often ask this question through the medium of the sufferer's conscience; and it is one that suggests the presence of a moral element in the emotions we experience from time to time. It suggests that grief, *e.g.*, is blameworthy or praiseworthy, as the case may be. The distress experienced by the Psalmist was commendable when he said, " Rivers of water run down mine eyes because they keep not Thy law." The distress displayed by the Jewish rulers on account of the preaching of the Apostles was culpable. But was Jonah's grief commendable or culpable ? I think that we know enough about it by this time to be aware that it was a mixed emotion as regards its moral character. It was culpable, no doubt; but not wholly so. For a moment, however, let us turn from the case of Jonah to that of any distressed person now addressed. "Doest thou well to be grieved?" Yes, if thou art numbered with those who sigh and cry for the abominations that be done in the land. Yes, if thou canst say, "I beheld the transgressors and was grieved." Yes, if, in accordance with Scripture requirement, thou dost weep with them that weep. But no, if thy sorrow is selfish, or rebellious, or intemperate, or ungrateful. Bethink thyself, therefore, O child of sorrow, and return a conscientious reply to the question thus put to thee by thy Father in heaven, "Doest thou well to be grieved?"

Jonah returned no reply to this question, and yet we must not regard him as refusing to reply to it. He meant only to postpone his reply until the course of events should enable him to vindicate his distress or compel him to confess its impropriety. He would wait awhile, and then reply to the question addressed to him; and that he might have some shelter while he waited, he proceeded to erect the booth of which we read in the passage before us. The present discourse will relate to the construction, position, and utility of this booth.

I.

The construction of this booth was not a circumstance which need occasion us any surprise. An Israelite who desired to spend a short time in any place without consorting with its people would, quite

as a matter of course, do as Jonah did. The first time
we read of booths in the Bible is in connection with
the patriarch Jacob. We are told that " Jacob jour-
neyed to Succoth, and built him an house, and made
booths for his cattle : therefore the name of the place
is called Succoth," *i.e.*, booths. It was in booths like
those thus provided by the patriarch for his cattle
that his descendants appear to have lodged in the
wilderness of their wandering. Booths were much
more easily provided than tents, which were far more
elaborate and durable structures. It was of booths
rather than tents that the Apostle Peter was thinking
when he said to his Master on the Mount of Trans-
figuration, " Lord, it is good for us to be here ; and
let us make three tabernacles,[1] one for Thee, and one
for Moses, and one for Elias." Peter, like Jonah
before him, had doubtless been used to the process of
booth-building in connection with the Feast of Tabernacles. This was one of the three great annual festivals
ordained by the law of Moses, and its institution is
thus recorded : " In the fifteenth day of the seventh
month, when ye have gathered in the fruit of the land,
ye shall keep a feast unto the Lord seven days : on
the first day shall be a sabbath, and on the eighth
day shall be a sabbath. And ye shall take you on the
first day the boughs of goodly trees, branches of palm
trees, and the boughs of thick trees, and willows of the
brook ; and ye shall rejoice before the Lord your God
seven days. And ye shall keep it a feast unto the
Lord seven days in the year. It shall be a statute for

---

[1] סֻכָּה, *sukkah*, booth ; אֹהֶל, *ohel*, tent; σκηνή, *skēnē*, tabernacle.
The Greek word may be regarded as the equivalent of either of the
two Hebrew words here given.

ever in your generations : ye shall celebrate it in the
seventh month.   Ye shall dwell in booths seven days ;
all that are Israelites born shall dwell in booths : that
your generations may know that I made the children
of Israel to dwell in booths when I brought them out
of the land of Egypt."   An account of the revival of
this observance in the time of Nehemiah is thus given :
" They found written in the law which the Lord had
commanded by Moses, that the children of Israel
should dwell in booths in the feast of the seventh
month ; and that they should publish and proclaim
in all their cities, and in Jerusalem, saying, Go forth
unto the mount, and fetch olive branches, and pine
branches, and myrtle branches, and palm branches,
and branches of thick trees, to make booths as it is
written.   So the people went forth, and brought them,
and made themselves booths, every one upon the roof
of his house, and in their courts, and in the courts of
the house of God, and in the street of the water gate,
and in the street of the gate of Ephraim.   And all the
congregation of them that were come again out of the
captivity made booths, and sat under the booths : for
since the days of Joshua the son of Nun unto that day
had not the children of Israel done so."   This last
remark of the sacred writer would seem to show that
the prophet Jonah, who lived between the time to
which he refers and that of Joshua, had had no experience of booth-building in connection with the
Feast of Tabernacles.   But when the remark is compared with certain other passages of Scripture,[1] it
becomes evident that its meaning can only be that
the particular festival to which it relates was the

---

[1] See, in particular, Ezra iii. 4.

most impressive that had taken place since the time
of Joshua.　It is almost certain that it was regularly
observed in Jerusalem during the lifetime of Jonah;
and quite certain that, if such was the case, that good
man would make a point of attending it.

During the observance of this festival, Jerusalem
presented an exceptional and interesting appearance.
In certain of its thoroughfares, in the court of its
temple, in the courts of many of its houses, on the
flat roofs of its other houses, as well as on its walls,
and in the country just outside them, the booths were
erected, and both citizens and visitors lodged in them.
Those booths were in sharp and instructive contrast
with the buildings proper to the city in two respects.

The booths were temporary, and the city buildings
permanent; which reminded the people of God's goodness to their ancestors, in causing them to exchange
the weary wanderings and poor accommodation of the
wilderness for a permanent abode in the land flowing
with milk and honey, which He gave them for a possession.　But this is a matter in which we too are
interested; for the experience of God's ancient people
was an adumbration of our own.　We are assured in
the Scriptures that God intends us to pass from the
wilderness of this world into the celestial Canaan, and
that we shall exchange the earthly house of this tabernacle for an house not made with hands, eternal in the
heavens.

The booths occupied by the Israelites during the
Feast of Tabernacles were all pretty much alike in
size, shape, and material; whereas the buildings be-
longing to the city presented a great variety in these
respects.　This was adapted to remind the people that

their ancestors had in some respects been on a level which had not been preserved to their own time. There were, indeed, gradations of rank in the wilderness, but there was little difference between the dwellings of the princes and the poor ; while all classes and conditions of persons had the same meat and drink. It was not so afterwards. In Jerusalem were some who dwelt in palaces, and others who dwelt in hovels. But at the Feast of Tabernacles they recognized the essential equality of all Israelites by dwelling, like their ancestors, in booths. The lesson for ourselves is not hard to learn. Those who are Israelites indeed differ from each other in various respects. Some are richer than others, stronger than others, wiser than others, and so forth. But as regards things of the highest importance, all God's people are on a level. They are all children of God, brethren of Christ, and possessors of that Holy Spirit Who is the earnest of their inheritance.

But we must return to Jonah, who found it as easy to erect a booth in the neighbourhood of Nineveh as in that of Jerusalem ; and who postponed till after he had accomplished this task an answer to that Divine demand, " Doest thou well to be distressed ? "

II.

The position of Jonah's booth is not a little suggestive. It was extra-mural, elevated, and solitary ; and each of these circumstances will be found to deserve attention.

1. It was erected outside the city : " Jonah went out of the city, and sat on the east side of the city, and there made him a booth." There were three

courses open to the prophet after he had completed his errand in Nineveh. He might have remained in the city for a time ; he might have at once returned to his own country; or he might have done as he did. We know why he did not at once return to the land of Israel; he wanted " to see what would become of the city." But why did he not remain in the city? Why did he go forth and build a booth beyond its walls ? There may have been several reasons for the course he thus adopted.

Perhaps he shrank from more than a bare discharge of the duty which had been imposed on him. He had preached in the city, but did not care to explain, enforce, illustrate, or qualify the announcement he had made to its inhabitants, lest it should be rendered more effective than he desired it to be.

Or the prophet may have shrunk from accepting the hospitality of the people he had warned. In their penitence before God we may be certain that they would be ready to treat the man He had sent to warn them with kindness and respect. But Jonah was conscious that he had not really been anxious for their welfare, and that there would be a want of magnanimity on his part in accepting their hospitality.

Or, once more, the prophet may have shrunk from the ceremonial defilement so easily contracted in such a place as Nineveh. That was a fear always apt to haunt a devout Israelite who found himself among strangers. Thus the Apostle Peter declined to eat with Gentile converts, lest he should be defiled by his intercourse with them; and Jonah might well be animated by the same kind of feeling when he went forth from Nineveh to build his booth.

But the prophet's principal reason for the course he adopted was probably a regard for consistency. He had proclaimed as he passed through the city, "Yet forty days, and Nineveh shall be overthrown!" It did, indeed, become clear to him, when he saw the repentance of the people, that the city would not be overthrown. But the people themselves could not be sure of this, for God had not afforded them any intimation that it was to be spared. Even the prophet could not be absolutely sure of it, although he was morally certain in relation to it. It assuredly behoved him to leave the city after predicting its destruction within forty days, lest the people should suspect that he disbelieved his own proclamation. There would have been no consistency or propriety in remaining within a place which he had said was about to be destroyed. Now then, brethren, reflect. Did consistency require the prophet to leave the city which he had said would be destroyed? Then what shall be said respecting the consistency of certain preachers and professors of religion among ourselves?

There is a city which Bunyan called *the City of Destruction*, but which is more frequently called *the World*. There are men who preach, and there are others who profess to believe, that this world is to be destroyed; that the city of destruction is rightly named. Consistently enough, such persons in some instances take care to come out of the world; but, alas! in others they remain in it. How is it with you? If you profess to believe that the world will be destroyed as the Scriptures say, come out of it. You are not, of course, required to commit suicide. You are not even required to isolate yourselves after the fashion of the monks and nuns and hermits who have sought for sanctity in solitude. You are simply required to cease from the foolish customs which characterise the world, and to devote yourselves to the service of God in the manner directed in the Scriptures. In this way you may separate yourselves from the world; but if the separation is not effected, you need not expect that sinners will take warning by your professed belief that the world is to be destroyed. It will be thought that if you really deemed it a city of destruction, you would come out of it.

There is also another city which consistency requires those who profess to believe the Word of God to abandon. It is called *Babylon* in the Bible, after the ancient city of that name, to which God's people were carried as captives. The ancient Babylon has long since been destroyed, and its antitype is doomed to destruction. A voice from heaven has been heard to cry, " Come out of her, my people, that ye be not partakers of her sins, and that ye receive not of her plagues ! " But what are we to understand by this mystical Babylon ? The Church of Rome ? Certainly; but the appellation must not be too rigidly applied. There are many who are in external communion with the Church of Rome, and yet have no sympathy with its grosser superstitions, and no feeling but shame and horror for the crimes which have been perpetrated by many of its agents. On the other hand, there are persons who have never formally united themselves to the Romish Church, and are yet manifestly blinded by its errors and dominated by its spirit. Oh the folly, as well as the

inconsistency, of those who profess and call themselves Christians, and yet remain in that Babylon
which is to be destroyed !

2. Jonah's booth was erected on an elevated spot.
He wanted to see what would become of the city,
and it was therefore natural that he should station
himself on its eastern side, inasmuch as the ground
sloped upwards in that direction. The booth thus
made by the prophet was at a greater elevation than
any palace in Nineveh, and the prophet himself was
at a greater moral elevation than any of its inhabitants. Do you doubt this? Do you say that Jonah
was a very faulty person, and in a very culpable
mood, while the Ninevites were in the first ardour of
their repentance ? But there are other circumstances
to be taken into account, if we desire to get at the
truth on this subject.

Jonah's moral elevation was greater than that of
the Ninevites, because his piety was more intelligent
than theirs. The prophet knew far more than they
did of the one true and living God. They had but
just become aware of His power, His justice, and His
mercy ; whereas the nationality, office, ministry, and
experience of Jonah had enabled him to learn a great
deal of the Most High. There are among ourselves
some whose piety is more intelligent than that of
others ; and I would urge you to acquaint yourselves
as fully as possible with God. Do all you can to
obtain enlarged ideas of His power and wisdom, love
and holiness. Seek the truth respecting Him, and
then more of it, and then more. Seek, and ye shall
find. Seek, and the very search shall elevate your
character in proportion to its diligence and persistence.

Again, Jonah's moral elevation was greater than that of the Ninevites because his piety was more confirmed than theirs. Theirs had just been planted, whereas his had taken root. Men do not attain suddenly to the condition of those who have long been exercised in the ways of God. The only progress possible to His people is of such a nature as to require patience on their part. It is well for young Christians to understand and remember this. They are apt first to presume and then to despond. They presumptuously propose to play a part which is only possible to persons at a far superior elevation to their own; and then, in the hour of inevitable disappointment, they abandon themselves to a despondent emotion which is equally unbecoming. Patience and humility are what they need in order to make a progress which is slow but sure, and to reach the elevation to which they aspire.

Once more, Jonah's moral elevation was superior to that of the Ninevites by reason of the more positive character of his piety. They were but just turning from their evil way; whereas he had been walking in the way of righteousness (though not without some deviation) for a long while. They had ceased to do evil; he had learnt to do well. It is not enough for men to render a certain obedience to the negative precepts of Divine law (Thou shalt not do this, Thou shalt not do that), but regard must be had to its positive aspect. Separation from sin is not enough; there must be consecration also to God's service.

3. Jonah's booth was erected in a solitary place. He would, indeed, have been solitary in a certain

sense if he had remained in the crowded city. There is such a thing as solitude in society; and the Hebrew prophet in the heathen city would have been separated from its people in other respects, if not in space. But outside the city he was absolutely alone. Ah, no, that is wrong, for God was with him there ; but with that important exception, Jonah was alone.

There are some persons who long for society, and others for solitude; the longing in each case resulting from an experience of the opposite condition of things. There are others, again, whose circumstances are such as to enable them to pass from society into solitude, or from solitude into society, as they please. How is it with you, my brethren ? Do you find yourselves compelled to remain in comparative solitude ? This is the case with many who mourn over the circumstances which occasion this state of things with exceeding bitterness. Talk to them of the blessings incident to solitude, and one of them is almost sure to reply, in the words of the poet, and in no mere facetiousness, —

> "O solitude ! where are the charms
> 　That sages have seen in thy face ?
> Better dwell in the midst of alarms
> 　Than reign in this horrible place."

If a time should come in your experience when you are confined to your own chamber, and regard that chamber as a " horrible place " by reason of its sameness and solitude, it will be well to remember that you are no more in absolute solitude than Jonah was when he built his booth beyond the walls of Nineveh. You may acquire, even then and there,

14

the power to adopt the Master's words, "Alone; and yet I am not alone, because the Father is with me."

Or do you find yourselves compelled to remain in the society of other human beings almost incessantly? In that case, you are doubtless apt to desire some means or opportunity of escaping from those about you. It was thus with the Psalmist at one time, and he has left on record the language he then employed: "I said, Oh that I had wings like a dove! for then would I fly away, and be at rest. Lo, then would I wander far off, and remain in the wilderness." Is this how you feel? Ah! be content; you would soon desire to come back to the crowds of which you complain; and the desire would be a healthy one, for God has fitted you for such fellowship with your neighbours as is fraught with blessing to them and to yourselves.

If you are so circumstanced as to be able to secure the advantages of society or of solitude at your own pleasure, be thankful; and consider that in solitude you may prepare to acquit yourselves in society as becomes the professed servants of God, and in a manner that bears witness to your remembrance of those words of the Lord Jesus: "Let your light so shine before men, that they may see your good works, and glorify your Father which is in heaven."

III.

The utility of Jonah's booth will be apparent as soon as we have considered the working and waiting involved in his experience in connection with it.

1. The prophet's labour in constructing the booth was assuredly of great service to him. He had to

find certain trees, and then deprive them of the branches he required, and then convey the materials thus obtained to the spot where he intended the booth to be. Now it is certain that there were no trees very near that spot; none immediately below it, or he could not thence have surveyed the city by reason of their intervention; none immediately above it, or on either hand of it, for its erection would then have been unnecessary. It is clear, therefore, that there was considerable exertion required merely to get the materials for the booth to the place where it was to be set up. Being brought there in the burning heat, some of them had to be pointed and driven into the ground, and all of them had to be trimmed and trained and twisted into the shape that suited the prophet's purpose. All this did indeed involve labour; but wherein did its utility consist? Why, in the diversion of thought it secured for the time being from the subject which troubled him, and in the relief it afforded to his overwrought spirit.

It often happens that a man is fascinated, so to speak, by some painful circumstance connected with his experience, and is like to be driven wild with vexation in consequence. What, then, is to be done? It is easy to say that his thoughts must be diverted from the thing which troubles him; but how shall this be effected? The tempter says, *Drink!* but God says, as in other ways, so also by this story of Jonah, *Work!* The prophet was in deep distress by reason of the shape things were taking in the Divine Providence; and the more he thought upon the subject, the more distressed he was. When God asked him, " Doest

thou well to be grieved ? " he could not bear to reply,
" Yes " or " No ; " he refrained from words, and set
to work.   Take the hint, I beseech you, brethren, as
often as circumstances may render it desirable for
you to do so.   If there be any course or combination of such circumstances as compel your sustained
attention, and at the same time fill your heart with
anguish, do as Jonah did, and set to work.   What
work ?   Why, your own work to be sure.   Let the
cobbler stick to his last, the carpenter to his bench, and
the fisherman to his nets !   Let the shopman betake
himself to his counter, the clerk to his desk, and the
farmer to his fields !   Let the merchant, the minister,
the magistrate, and the medical man devote themselves to the discharge of their respective duties !   It
matters little what the nature of the work may be.
It may be exceptional or commonplace.   It may be
exalted or homely.   It may be conspicuous or obscure.
But if the work be good in itself, and work to which
you are called, work away !

It is always well that excessive emotion should
find a vent.   What kind of vent ?   Well, consider.
Hannah poured out her soul before the Lord in
prayer.   David danced before the Lord with all his
might.   The children of Jerusalem rent the air with
their Hosannas.   The man who had been lame till
Peter bade him arise and walk in the Name of the
Lord Jesus entered the temple walking and leaping
and praising God.   Jonah built a booth.   A man
should always turn any excessive emotion of which
he is the subject to account, and may always do so
by letting it find vent in some useful work.   It is
morally deleterious to allow any vehement feeling

which has been aroused within one to subside without such effort being put forth as it plainly suggests. Even a wicked emotion should not be experienced without a resolute endeavour on the part of its subject to overcome the innate evil in which it originates.

But the experience of the prophet in connection with his booth involved waiting as well as working. He built it in order that he might wait under its shadow until he should see what would become of the city which he had said should be destroyed. But did he not know that Nineveh was to be spared? Was it not precisely that knowledge which occasioned his grief? I reply that he was morally, but not absolutely, sure that the city would be spared. God had not said so, and there was a possibility that it would be destroyed after all. An earthquake might engulf it, or a fire consume it, or a hostile army dismantle it, or a revolution among its inhabitants result in its ruin. Jonah would wait and see. The forty days would soon pass; and even if Nineveh were not destroyed in the interval, it might be made clear to the prophet that its deliverance was preferable to its destruction. Jonah was thus really waiting upon God while he sat in his booth, and this consideration may suggest a concluding meditation.

It is possible for any human being who is acquainted with the Gospel to construct a booth in which he may wait upon the Lord with greater comfort to himself than would be otherwise possible. Christ is the Tree of Life, and you may approach that Tree and obtain from it the materials for the booth of which I speak. Then will the sweet old promise be fulfilled in your experience: "There shall be a booth for a shadow in the daytime from the heat, and for a place of refuge, and for a covert from storm and from rain." Let me urge you, then, to approach the Tree of Life, and to build yourself a booth with the hand of faith; for faith in Christ shall enable you to sit under His shadow with great delight, and it shall be to you as the shadow of a great rock in a weary land.

XIV.

THE GOURD.

"And the Lord God prepared a gourd, and made it come up over Jonah, that it might be a shadow over his head, to deliver him from his grief. So Jonah was exceeding glad of the gourd."—JONAH iv. 6.

RESOLVED to see what would become of the city, Jonah sat under the booth he had erected on the eastern side of Nineveh. But how long would that booth remain serviceable to him? It could not, in the nature of things, last very long. It certainly could not be expected to continue comfortable for forty days. The leaves and branches of which it was constructed would soon lose the moisture they at first possessed, and a mere skeleton of the tiny tenement he had erected would remain to the prophet. The booths erected for the Feast of Tabernacles were only wanted for eight days, but Jonah might have to remain in the neighbourhood of Nineveh for five times that length of time. What course, then, would he have to adopt with regard to his booth? Would he have to procure fresh materials for its repair or reconstruction? Nay; for "the Lord God prepared a gourd, and made it to come up over Jonah, that it might be a shadow over his head, to deliver him from his grief." (To deliver him from his grief, you observe; not to deliver him from his anger.) " So Jonah was exceeding glad of the gourd." It is to this gourd that I now direct your attention; and I shall ask you to consider what it was, how it was produced, and the purpose it served.

I.

Some have supposed that this gourd was an ivy bush, others a cucumber plant, and others a vine. But some very learned men, whose opinion on such a matter is entitled to peculiar respect, assert with considerable confidence that it was the castor oil plant. They have compared this passage in the Book of Jonah with certain passages in various Greek, Latin, and other ancient authors, and have reached the conclusion that the *Kikajon* mentioned here is the *Croton* of the Greeks, the *Ricinus* of the Latins, and the *Castor Oil Plant* of the English. It seems that this plant is still found growing in the neighbourhood of ancient Nineveh. It is of very rapid growth, attaining in a very few days to its full height of from eight to twelve feet. Its leaves are broad and green and juicy, and therefore it was admirably adapted to afford the prophet the shadow of which he was in need.

The ancient Latin name of this plant was the *Ricinus*, but Christian writers who employed the Latin language gave it another name, which has been extensively adopted. They called it the *Palma Christi*, *i.e.*, the Hand of Christ. The anglicised form of the word is Palmchrist; and the plant appears to have been thus denominated by reason of the shape of its leaf, which bears considerable resemblance to a man's hand, and perhaps also in part by reason of the oil which it yields. Its leaf was taken, in short, to resemble the Hand of the Anointed One, which is stretched forth to bless the people of God. That Hand, which was once nailed to the Cross, conveys the Holy Spirit, the Oil of Gladness, to all on whom it rests in friendly fashion from time to time.

Do you say that this is an arbitrary association of ideas? I shall not resent the imputation. Do you say that to represent the leaf of Jonah's gourd as illustrative of Christ's grace-dispensing Hand is a far-fetched conceit? Well, perhaps it is; but, in making you a present of that admission, I must be allowed to narrate two anecdotes in self-defence. The one relates to a personal friend of mine, who, though an excellent preacher, or perhaps because of that circumstance, once had an uneasy consciousness that a certain illustration he had occasion to employ was a little strained. So he said to his hearers, "Some of you, my friends, may be disposed to complain that this illustration is somewhat far-fetched; but you will have the kindness to remember that I had the trouble of fetching it." The other anecdote relates to the great and good Andrew Fuller. He had heard a sermon preached on some occasion by a younger minister in whom he was deeply interested, and with whom he gently remonstrated because he had said nothing about Christ in his sermon. His friend, however, replied that Christ was not mentioned in the text. Then said Fuller, pointing to a lonely house on the side of a distant hill, "Do you see that house?" "Yes," was the reply." "Well," said the great

theologian, "you may be sure that there is a road
from that house to London, and that there is a connection between your text and Christ." You may
think what you please about the matter, but it seems
to me that it was by a sure and sound spiritual
instinct that those who called this gourd the Palmchrist attained to such an association of ideas respecting it and the Saviour of mankind as that to
which reference has been made. At all events, I am
glad to take, or to make, an opportunity of saying
something about our Blessed Lord before passing on
to new points in the story of Jonah.

God's people all resemble the prophet in one respect,
if not in others. They are alive to God, but their
spiritual health is liable to be impaired. When they
are well, they rejoice in the Lord; but when they are
sick, they abandon themselves to a grief like that
which overwhelmed Jonah. Then is the time for
them to adopt the prayer of the Psalmist: "Restore
unto me the joy of Thy salvation." In response to
this petition the blessed Hand of Christ has been
stretched forth in numberless instances; and by its
means have been communicated "beauty for ashes,
the oil of joy for mourning, and the garment of praise
for the spirit of heaviness." Are you, my brethren,
in any kind of distress at this moment? Let but
Christ's Hand be extended to you, and that distress
shall be removed. Is your trouble occasioned by
some disappointment you have experienced with
regard to the pursuits in which you are customarily
engaged? The Hand of Christ can bestow upon you
a greater blessing than the one you vainly hoped to
secure. Or is your grief the result of some positive

loss you have sustained? The Hand of Christ can more than compensate you for the most serious loss that can be experienced by any of His people. Or is your distress attributable to some peril in which you are placed? It is certain that God's people are frequently menaced by physical, social, commercial, or spiritual danger; but it is also certain that the Hand of Christ is that of One who "is able to save unto the uttermost all who come unto God by Him." Perhaps your anguish arises from a perception on your part of the scorn with which you are regarded by those whose respect you would gladly enjoy. In that case, let me remind you that the Hand of Christ is that of One Who was Himself "despised and rejected of men," Who can therefore sympathise with you in respect of this particular sorrow, and Who will one day confer upon you a crown of glory which shall never fade away. Or your neighbours may not so much contemn as hate you, and you are profoundly afflicted by reason of your inability to win their goodwill. The Hand of Christ can bring you comfort, however. It belongs to one who said to His disciples while He was personally with them, "If the world hate you, ye know that it hated Me before you," and Who is well able to cheer you with such tokens of His own love as to make the hatred of others a matter of comparatively small consequence. Your case, indeed, may be more distressing than I have yet supposed. You may be the prey of a remorse, for which there is only too much reason in some secret wrong-doing of which you have been guilty. But still I say that the Hand of Christ has only to be exhibited to the eyes of your faith in order to

afford you strong consolation; for does it not retain
the print of the nail which fastened it to that Cross
on which He died in order to procure your redemption
from all iniquity? Oh blessed Hand of Christ! touch
every troubled child of God, and sorrow and sighing
shall flee away. Oh blessed Hand of Christ! do but
rest lightly on the head of each afflicted servant of
the Most High, and nothing more shall be needed to
enable the sufferer to rejoice even in tribulation with
a joy that is unspeakable and full of glory. Oh true
Palmchrist! wave above our drooping heads, that
we may enjoy a better shelter from the scorching heat
of adversity than we can secure for ourselves.

II.

In considering how this gourd was produced, we of
course take notice of the record that " the Lord God
prepared a gourd;" but that record does not of itself
enable us to answer a question which has been often
asked respecting its production. Did the preparation
of this gourd involve a miracle? Some say " Yes;"
and others "No." In the context we find it said
that the plant " came up in a night and perished in a
night;" or, more exactly, that it "was the son of
the night." But this is clearly a poetic expression;
and the question as to whether it should be understood that the Palmchrist came up in the course of a
single night is not decided thereby. If it did come
up with such exceeding rapidity, assuredly a miracle
was wrought; but if it took a few days—say a week—
to attain to its full size, no miracle was wrought. I
will not undertake to express an opinion on this
subject, but the uncertainty there is in relation to it

may suggest one or two lines of thought replete with profit to those who devoutly pursue them.

God does not work miracles when they are not necessary to the end He has in view. In the New Testament narrative of the raising of Lazarus from the dead, our Lord Himself is represented as doing what He alone could do, but as leaving others to do what they were able to accomplish without miraculous assistance. He worked no miracle to open the sepulchre, but said, " Take ye away the stone." He worked no miracle to liberate Lazarus from the grave-clothes in which he was wrapped, but said to them, " Loose him, and let him go." But in the interval between these two directions to the bystanders, He did work a stupendous miracle, speaking the words which others would have spoken in vain, but which He did not speak in vain, " Lazarus, come forth ! " If then there was no necessity for the miraculous production of this Palmchrist, we may assume, on the principle just illustrated, that it was not miraculously produced.

On such an assumption, however, the account before us is assuredly none the less instructive and interesting. If the preparation of the gourd was a natural, rather than a supernatural, operation of Divine providence, it the more impressively exemplified the manner in which that providence is concerned with individual members of our race. Let me ask you to think for a moment of the seed from which the Palmchrist sprung. It was not deposited in that place by chance, but the Divine choice was exercised in relation to it. It might have fallen on the west of the city, or on the north, or on the south. But antici-

pating the movements of Jonah, and knowing that
the prophet would build his booth on the east of the
city, the Lord caused the seed to fall precisely where
it would be of use to His servant. Nor is this all that
should be said on the subject. We must not merely
consider where, but when, the seed fell. There is a
coincidence of time as well as of place to be remarked.
The Palmchrist might have sprung up before Jonah
reached that spot, or after he had left it, and in either
case been useless to him. All this is very plain, and the
point to which it tends is at once apparent. As the
Divine providence was thus concerned with the individual man in the case of Jonah, so is that providence
concerned with the individual men and women among
ourselves. God knows beforehand what you and I
will do. He anticipates our movements, and prepares
the various things which enter into our condition and
experience. The most trivial circumstance, or what
may be considered such, does not transpire in connection with any of us by chance ; and whoso believes
this, will not doubt that there is a Divine providence
and preparation in respect of greater things. But you
ask me why I insist upon what is so plainly taught in
the Sermon on the Mount that we need be at no pains
to deduce it from the story of Jonah. I reply that
this part of that story is chiefly interesting as supplying an illustration of what is taught on the subject in
that great discourse of the Divine Master. Moreover,
the prophet's experience may fairly suggest to us that
as God takes this minute interest in the individual
members of our race, none of should be careless about
himself. Every man should well consider his own
conduct, and the manner in which he is influenced by

the circumstances which transpire in his personal
experience. He should take heed to himself, putting
away all undue apathy and frivolity, and conducting
himself as one who is conscious that his words and
works, thoughts and feelings, engage the attention of
his Maker, and are regarded in the Divine plans.

III.

There is no uncertainty about the purpose served
by this Palmchrist, for it is expressly said in the text
that " the Lord God prepared a gourd, and made it
to come up over Jonah, that it might be a shadow
over his head, to deliver him from his grief." But
did it answer the purpose thus set forth ? Certainly,
for " Jonah was exceeding glad of the gourd." Not
merely glad, but exceeding glad. The Hebraism
actually employed is that " Jonah rejoiced with great
joy." This exceeding gladness requires explanation ;
for there may seem, at first sight, some disproportion
between the prophet's joy and the circumstance that
occasioned it.

The exceeding gladness occasioned by the gourd
was partly owing to the manner in which it augmented
the prophet's physical comfort. As long as men are
in the body, their mood will be apt to be largely determined by their physical condition. There are circumstances in which a very trivial material blessing will
occasion great gladness to the person who receives it.
A man may be actually delighted to obtain a cup of
cold water on a very hot day. On the other hand, a
person may be rendered miserable by the continuance
of a little noise in his neighbourhood when he is
desirous of perfect silence. Exposed to the heat as

he was, and having only to wait till he should see what would become of the city, it was quite natural that Jonah should be " exceeding glad of the gourd," however indifferent to its presence he might ordinarily have been. Now the truth is that our personal comfort is largely dependent on the presence of various conditions, which are not apt to be keenly appreciated by us under ordinary circumstances. The smaller blessings which God bestows upon us daily are innumerable. If, however, we were removed from them for a time ; if we were deprived of our ordinary comforts, and limited to the bare necessities of life, the restoration of only one of those blessings or comforts would occasion us a degree of gladness that might seem very disproportioned to its value in the eyes of some chance witness of our joy. It would seem, therefore, that the value of the smaller blessings which God's providence usually secures to us is greater than we are apt to realise ; and that their enjoyment calls for a deeper gratitude on our part than we are prone to experience.

But this excessive gladness on Jonah's part in the shadow of the Palmchrist was doubtless partly attributable to the excessive grief which had preceded it. In the first verse it is said that the course of events " displeased Jonah exceedingly, and he was very grieved." Exceeding sadness, and exceeding gladness ! The narrative is, in this respect, in accordance with all that we know of human nature. When you observe that the tide is further out than usual, you are aware that it will presently be that much further in. When the pendulum swings far to the right, it will presently swing as far to the left. So it is with

the passions and energies of the human breast. The
man who is strong (or, as we say, strung) with excitement to-day, will be weak with exhaustion to-morrow.
The extreme of one emotion is apt to beget the extreme
of the opposite emotion. You remember how the
courage of the Apostle Peter, for example, gave way
to cowardice on a certain memorable occasion. Seeing his Master on the water, a courageous impulse
constrained the Apostle to cry, "Lord, if it be Thou,
bid me come to Thee on the water!" But he had
scarcely left the vessel when he cried through the
spray, "Lord, save me, or I perish!" Courage and
cowardice, grief and gladness, do thus displace each
other in the heart from time to time. It was a per-
fectly natural thing that exceeding sadness on Jonah's
part should be succeeded by the exceeding gladness
of which we read in the text. Now we ought to be
aware of this reactionary tendency in our nature.
We ought to consider well and carefully the ebb and
flow of feeling—the emotional oscillation—to which
we are liable; and it is because some worthy people do
not sufficiently consider it, or do not consider it with
sufficient intelligence, that they make certain serious
mistakes in relation to the cause and service of God.
They are always for holding special religious services,
and are never so happy as when they are arranging
and attending such services. But when these services
are over, and the emotional excitement they have
fostered has subsided, and the good people of whom I
speak resume their attendance on the ordinary services
in their own place of worship, you know how it is.
The ordinary services are pronounced cold and dull.
But really they are not dull. The dulness is in those

15

who complain of them ; and they are dull for the simple reason that they have been abnormally lively and excited, and have since experienced the inevitable reaction. The craving for constant religious excitement which they display is symptomatic of spiritual disease rather than of spiritual health; and the prescription applicable to their case is the one furnished by the Psalmist long ago, " Oh, rest in the Lord ! " It is such rest that is really reviving, whereas the excitement so craved by those of whom I speak is indubitably exhausting.

The principal reason of the prophet's gladness on account of the gourd, however, has yet to be given. Jonah could not fail to regard its growth in that place as evidence of God's concern for his comfort, and the conviction thus conveyed to his mind that God cared for him is quite enough to explain his exceeding gladness. His feeling must have been akin to that which Hagar had experienced long before, when God showed her a well of water, and thus enabled her to save her own life and that of her child. Her mistress might hate her, her master might allow her to wander about the world without assistance or protection ; but God cared for her, and all was well. Three times in the course of his eventful history must the prophet Elijah have felt a great gush of gladness in the realization of God's care for his comfort : once when the ravens brought him the first supply of food which reached him by their means, once when the widow of Zarephath gave him her last loaf and a draught of precious water with it, and once more when the angel called his attention to the cake and cruse in the wilderness. So with this other prophet, Jonah. The Palmchrist was welcome to him for its own sake, but still more welcome as a proof that he was the object of Divine care. A community will sometimes request one of its members to accept a sum of money as a mark of its esteem; and it will not improbably be remarked when the testimonial is presented or accepted, that it is not merely of value in itself, but is of greater value as an expression of goodwill on the part of those who have contributed it. Jonah's gourd had this kind of value, and the prophet's gladness was chiefly occasioned by his sense of that circumstance. Well, brethren, is there no similar reason for rejoicing on your part? Assuredly there is. You have not only the various comforts and advantages which are connected with your lot in life, but have the express assurance of the Lord Jesus that He to Whom the fall of a sparrow is not a matter of indifference, and to Whom ye are of more value than many sparrows, has numbered the very hairs of your head in His parental interest in your welfare.

Did I say that Jonah's principal reason for rejoicing in the gourd was the evidence it afforded him of God's care for his comfort? I was wrong. His chief reason for rejoicing was certainly the evidence it afforded that God approved of his conduct in remaining at that place in order to see what would become of the city. The prophet had neither remained in Nineveh nor hastened from its neighbourhood, but had taken up the position of a watchman at some little distance from it. Thus far he had acted appropriately, and secured the Divine approbation; and he himself was assured that such was the case by the providential growth of this gourd in the very place where he had erected his booth. Now there are many persons whose experience resembles that of Jonah in this particular. There is a proverb which says that "God helps those who help themselves;" and this witness is true. Jonah helped himself by building the booth, and God helped Jonah by causing the gourd to overshadow it. Among ourselves, a man may think himself called to a certain work, and set about it. If there be any mistake on his part in relation to the matter, it is better that he should fail than succeed in the task he has undertaken; and it is probable, therefore, that he will fail. But if there be no such mistake, it may be expected that God will help him in his work, and thus attest His approbation of his endeavour. Nor is this all; for when God co-operates with His people, He works more effectually than they do. Jonah builds a booth, but God prepares a gourd. Paul plants and Apollos waters, but God gives the increase. In this way the work in which God co-operates with His people is done effectually, however difficult it may be in itself. The Apostle who laboured more abundantly than all his colleagues said, "I can do all things through Christ which strengtheneth me;" and any man who is conscious of Christ's co-operation, and of his own consequent ability to do all that his duty demands, has good reason to rejoice, as Jonah did, with great joy.

XV.

THE WORM.

"But God prepared a worm when the morning rose the next day, and it smote the gourd that it withered."—JONAH iv. 7.

NOT long, then, was the prophet permitted to sit under the shadow of the Palmchrist. The gourd which had occasioned him such gladness was destroyed by the worm of which we read in the text; and again the question arises, Was there any miracle involved in its destruction? Some think there was, and others that there was not. Those who think that the preparation of the gourd was miraculous, think that its destruction was miraculous also; while those who see no miracle in the preparation see none in the destruction either. Our ideas in relation to this matter may be partly dependent on the view we take of the destructive agency employed in connection with it. This was "a worm," but what are we to understand by that? "Mother!" exclaims a little child. "Well?" is the mother's reply. "What are you doing with our window curtains?" inquires the child. "Taking them away." "Why, mother?" "Because the moth has got into them and spoilt them." The moth: not one tiny insect, but a host of these little creatures is indicated by the word thus employed. So here. The worm does not, one thinks, mean a solitary insect, but a swarm of such creatures, —the word being used collectively. At all events, it has been observed that such plants as Jonah's gourd are very frequently destroyed in that part of the world by the worms which feed upon them, and that their destruction is thus accomplished in the course of a very few hours. It was a harsh providence which thus destroyed the Palmchrist, but it was not therefore an unkind one. It was worth his while for the prophet to experience some physical discomfort as the condition of learning the lessons which we may, I trust, learn without such discomfort, if we closely attend to the account here given of the destroying worm. The line of remark to be adopted may be indicated by a single sentence relative to this worm. It was a swift, mean, foul destroyer; and these are the characteristics of the creature to which I have now to call your attention.

I.

This worm was a swift destroyer. Jonah was displeased because it appeared probable that Nineveh would not be speedily destroyed. But had he at all realized what manifold suffering was incident to such sudden destruction? He might do this the more readily, at least in some degree, if the gourd which had so greatly gladdened him were swiftly destroyed, and he himself thereby exposed to all that was trying in the climate of that region. So " God prepared a worm when the morning rose the next day, and it smote the gourd that it withered."

This work of destruction, then, took effect upon the next day. Let us dwell upon that circumstance for a little while. The next day! One day the prophet sitting under the shadow of the gourd with great delight, and the next day lamenting its destruction! How often has the experience of other human beings corresponded more or less closely with that of Jonah in respect of some swiftly-accomplished destruction! One day an army marches to meet the foe in all the pomp and circumstance of glorious war. Look at its waving banners and glittering accoutrements, and listen to the strains of martial music as it passes on its way. Ah, but the next day! Alas for the tarnished and damaged appointments which remain to it! Alas for the wounded, the dying, and the dead!

A ship sails from the port in which she has been laden for some Tarshish at the ends of the earth. As she clears the bar she presents a goodly spectacle to those who are watching her departure. Gracefully she glides beyond the range of their vision; but the next day that splendid vessel is nowhere to be seen upon the surface of the water, and but few of her seamen and passengers have escaped a watery grave.

A man sets out one day upon a long journey by rail, and leaves home in the enjoyment of perfect health; but the next day he is seen lying in pain and peril in one of the wards of a distant hospital, and all who look upon him know that he will never again be what he was before the occurrence of the accident which has occasioned the terrible change.

One day the beauty of some youthful maiden awakens the admiration of all who look upon her, and the next day it is known that her dress has caught fire and her face been permanently disfigured. One day a man is exulting in the possession of wealth he has acquired or inherited, and the next day his riches have taken to themselves wings and fled away. One day a woman is telling her children how thankful they should be that they have such a father as her husband is known to be, and the next day they are orphans and she herself is a widow.

These are the kind of changes which have been experienced in numberless instances, and which will be experienced as often in the future as they have been in the past. It is found by such experience that destructive agencies are apt to be swift in their action; and for this reason, among others, each one of us will do well to heed the caution contained in Holy Writ, "Boast not thyself of to-morrow, for thou knowest not what a day may bring forth."

But the note of time which is furnished by the text must be more closely scrutinized. It was not merely that the worm destroyed the gourd on the next day, but that it did so at the commencement of that day. It had been sufficiently trying had the plant been destroyed in the evening of the next day, or in the middle of that day. "But God prepared a worm when the morning rose the next day, and it smote the gourd that it withered." Unless Jonah was an early riser indeed, we may be sure that the morning rose before he did; so that the first thing he perceived upon opening his eyes was that the Palmchrist had perished.

There are those whose troubles begin early on some particular day, and there are those whose troubles begin early in life. Does it seem unkind on God's part to allow, and even to ordain, this ? People are only too prone to think so. Do you presume to think that it would be worthier of the Most High to allow young persons to escape the sorrowful experiences of life ? Does the Tempter suggest to you that God might so arrange matters as to apportion its disasters, disappointments, and manifold distresses to those only who are of riper years ? Let us consider the sinister suggestion for a moment.

God's erring children need to be chastised. Chastisement is designed and adapted to effect their improvement; and it is said that "whom the Lord loveth He scourgeth, and chasteneth every son whom He receiveth." It would seem to follow that the sooner the requisite chastisement is inflicted the better. The sooner the suffering incident to that chastisement has become a thing of the past, and its beneficial result a thing of the present, the better must it be for the sons and daughters of the Almighty. On this principle, and in this sense, "it is good for a man that he bear the yoke in his youth."

Or we may take another view of this matter. Sin is a disease, and the suffering which God ordains is of a medicinal character. If one of your own children were to exhibit symptoms of disease, and it were found necessary to administer medicine to the patient, would you not deem it desirable to administer it as soon as possible ? Then what unkindness can there be on the part of our Heavenly Father when He brings trouble on His children during their youth ? In the very circumstance that the trouble at which you are tempted to murmur comes upon them when the morning rises, there is reason to hope that by mid-day it will have departed from them, and left them the better prepared to discharge the duties devolving upon them.

II.

The meanness of the agency employed in the destruction of Jonah's gourd must be considered; and we shall fail to learn what this part of his history is designed to teach unless we do so. In the Sacred Scriptures a worm is the very emblem of what is mean, insignificant, and contemptible. Speaking of God, Bildad said, "The stars are not pure in His sight; how much less man that is a worm, and the son of man that is a worm!" What Bildad said of man in general, the Psalmist said of himself in particular: "I am a worm, and no man; a reproach of men and despised of the people." It is a characteristic of good men that they should be humbly conscious of their own insignificance and unworthiness, but God does not desire them to be discouraged by their lowly estimate of themselves; hence we find Him saying, "Fear not, thou worm Jacob; I will help thee." In all these passages the word employed is the same as the one rendered "worm"[1] in the text; and therefore it must be proper for us to think of the meanness of the agency by which the Palmchrist was destroyed.

Now of course God might have just as easily ordained the destruction of the gourd by a nobler agent as by this worm. A herd of cattle might have

[1] רִמָּה, *rimmah*, is the word rendered *worm* in many places, and once in one of the passages cited above, Job xxv. 6; where, however, the word used in the text and in other passages also occurs, viz., תּוֹלַעַת, *tolaath*, or תּוֹלֵעָה, *toleah*.

trampled it to the ground, a human being might have
cut it down, or it might have been blasted with fire
from heaven. But as He employed the mean agency
described in the text, we may ask why He did so.
Was it not, think you, to teach Jonah, and to teach
us all, that there is nobler work for God's servants to
be engaged in than that of destruction? The prophet
had desired the destruction of Nineveh, and yet had
reason to believe that his own preaching in its streets
had been the means of its deliverance. This distressed him; but God desired to show His servant
that his distress was inappropriate, and that he had
been called to nobler work than that. Let us pay
great attention to this, and to the truth in which we
are interested and to which it points. The Apostle
Paul urges us to covet earnestly the best gifts; but
why should we covet such gifts unless we aspire to
the noblest work that can be done in the service of
God? It is, indeed, precisely to this that we should
aspire. We should be anxious to co-operate with
God Himself in the edification of His Church and the
salvation of sinners.

1. It is a nobler work to construct or conserve
than to destroy; albeit it may not be easier. The
worm could destroy the gourd which overshadowed
the prophet, but he himself could not produce another
Palmchrist in its place. The best he could do, there
and then, was done when he had erected his booth;
but the gourd, which a worm could destroy, was the
workmanship of One greater than himself. It is comparatively easy to destroy. Time, toil, and tact are
required in order to the erection of a palace, the
painting of a great picture, the carving of a beautiful

statue from a block of marble, or the fashioning of a
rare and costly vase. But how easily may any of
these be destroyed! How easy to set the palace on
fire, to cut the picture in pieces, to shatter the statue
or the vase!

It is not only easy to destroy the works of man,
but also many of the works of God. There are things
which the mightiest and most skilful human beings
cannot produce, but which it is easy for very ordinary
men to destroy. All the husbandmen in the world
could not of themselves produce a crop of wheat, or
cause a single tree to grow; but how easy to destroy
the crop or the tree! There are, however, creatures
instinct with a higher kind of life than that which
pertains to vegetation; the fowl of the air, the fish of
the sea, the beast of the field and forest, as well as man
himself. God alone can create any of these, but how
easily do they destroy each other in many instances!

It is a nobler thing to build up the Church of
Christ than to disintegrate it; and this, my brethren,
is the work to which you and I are called in these
days. All who are familiar with the New Testament
are aware how Christians are directed to edify one
another, and instructed that charity edifieth. If we
are without charity, we are nothing; but if we possess
and exercise this grace, we shall contribute to the
edification of God's building. Anything on our part
which promotes the increase or unification or improvement of the Church is included in the work of
edification to which we are called.

2. It is a nobler work to save than to destroy, and
especially to co-operate with God in the salvation of
sinners. There is, however, an instinctive tendency

to destroy which is characteristic of human nature, and evinced in a thousand different ways. You know how the child, *e.g.*, will poke a hole in the drum which his father has given him, or pull a wretched fly to pieces for his own amusement. There is many a grown man, too, who is never so happy as when killing a number of birds or other game in a manner which will one day be regarded as shocking and barbarous in a high degree.

This destructive tendency is evinced more seriously by that fearful appetite for war which has been displayed by so many soldiers of fortune, and by the estimate of military glory which has commonly obtained among men. An eminent physician or philanthropist ought assuredly to be more highly honoured by his fellow men than an eminent soldier. If, indeed, the soldier be rather a deliverer than a destroyer, the force of this remark must be modified in its application to him. But as a rule such modification is unnecessary. You know how it is, and always has been. The princes and peoples of the earth have always lavished the highest honours in their gift upon successful military men. Napoleon was really a less noble person than Desgenettes, and yet the name of the former is infinitely better known than that of the latter. Think, however, of what is recorded concerning these two men. The warrior suggested to the physician that he should poison the sick soldiers who were unable to leave the hospital in Jaffa when the army abandoned that place. But Desgenettes replied that his business was to cure, not to kill; and all honour to his noble memory for having said so!

This destructive instinct has asserted itself most painfully in the persecution to which some devout men have resorted, under the impression that they were doing God service by the destruction of His enemies. There is reason to believe that many of these persecutors were by no means the selfish and worldly persons that some of them certainly were. They had a stern satisfaction in sentencing those whom they regarded as the foes of God to the block, the gallows, and the stake. But in some cases the persons thus destroyed were nobler than their destroyers; and even when the victims were indeed the foes of God, it would have been a better service to His cause had their salvation, rather than their destruction, been effected. Is not this the lesson taught by what is recorded of the two apostles who desired to destroy their Master's enemies with fire from heaven? Certain Samaritan villagers having refused to receive our Lord "because His face was as though He would go to Jerusalem," James and John said to Him, "Lord, wilt Thou that we command fire to come down from heaven and consume them, even as Elias did? But He turned and rebuked them, and said, Ye know not what manner of spirit ye are of; for the Son of Man is not come to destroy men's lives, but to save them." I suppose that Jonah's mood was akin to that which Christ rebuked in the two apostles. He was not for saving Nineveh, but destroying it. He did not perceive the many-sidedness of the truth he had himself confessed, "Salvation is of the Lord!" Hence God now teaches him that destruction may be effected by a worm; and that, as destruction is worm-like and

salvation God-like, it is for God's servants to aspire
rather to a work of deliverance than of destruction.
Do you say, however, that Elijah and Joshua were
divinely commissioned to destroy the foes of God?
It is true; but there are two things to be considered in connection with their commissions. One
is that the work of destruction in which they were
called to engage was not the noblest work they had
to do; and the other is that it was only a destructive
work in one of its aspects, being a work of deliverance in another.

Why, even a heathen potentate is said to have
grasped the truth on which I now dwell. The story
may be true or false, but it does certainly illustrate
the work of salvation in which God Himself is engaged,
and in which He calls upon His people to co-operate.
It having been told the monarch that a certain portion
of his dominions was in rebellion against him, and
that he would do well to march against his enemies
and destroy them all, he promised to do so. But
when he had subdued the rebels, he pardoned them,
loaded them with favours, and returned to his capital.
Being reminded that he had engaged to destroy all
his enemies, he replied that he had done so, and that
no enemies of his could now be found in the recently
rebellious province. His foes were not only destroyed,
but friends were found where they had been. It is
precisely thus that God loves to destroy His enemies;
and if there are men who continue to hate Him notwithstanding His clemency, it is because they are
destitute of faith in the testimony of the Scriptures,
which is to the effect that they owe allegiance to
Him, that they have deserved to be destroyed for

their disloyalty, that they are completely in His power, and that the reason why they are not yet destroyed is the grace and mercy in which He delights. If the enemies of the Most High believed this testimony, they would inevitably be transformed into His friends, and thus be saved by faith. He delights in the work of salvation, and calls upon us to co-operate with Himself therein.

It is the business of God's people to save their fellow men from physical evil. If any of their neighbours are destitute of food or raiment, home or help, it is the duty of Christians to do all that may be possible to deliver them from this destitution. If there is any work to which we are certainly and clearly called, it is this; and I could easily confirm this assertion by numerous quotations from the Scriptures. It will be enough, however, to remind you at present of two of our Saviour's parables, viz., the Good Samaritan and the Sheep and the Goats, from which portions of Holy Writ it plainly appears that those who refuse to rescue their fellow men from the physical evils which afflict them, when it is in their power to do so, have no right to be regarded as disciples of the Saviour, however they may profess to be such.

It is the business of God's people, moreover, to co-operate with Him in saving their fellow men from intellectual evil, *i.e.*, from ignorance, and especially from ignorance of the character and will of God Himself. Now it is true that many faithful servants of the Most High are themselves uneducated persons in the ordinary sense of the expression. But it is also true that they have severally some knowledge of the most important matters, and are able to unite for the purpose of promoting a knowledge of those matters among themselves and others by the agency of those who are apt to teach the truth concerning them. This is the honourable work in which Christ's people have been engaged for ages and generations, and in which all who profess and call themselves Christians among ourselves are under obligation to take part.

But, after all, it is the chief concern of God's people to co-operate with Him in saving their fellow men from spiritual evil. They are instrumental, by His grace, in effecting the conversion of sinners, and what a noble work is that! No wonder that some devoted disciples of the Lord Jesus have hastened to the ends of the earth in order to engage in it where they thought it was most needed. It is, however, by no means necessary to go so far in search of such employment. There are myriads of unconverted men and women in our own country, and there are many of our brethren who are labouring to effect their conversion with a diligence and devotion which will not be fully recognised until the great day of the Lord has come.

It must be remembered that the work of saving men from spiritual evil not only includes the conversion of sinners, but also the sanctification of those who are converted, and the restoration of those who have wandered from the right way. Be it ours, then, brethren, to keep the nature of our high vocation well in mind. There be those who resemble the worm that destroyed the prophet's gourd, besliming and besmearing institutions and forms of life which, but for

16

them, would have blessed and adorned the world;
crawling hither and thither with disastrous and destructive consequences to everything with which they
come in contact. Let us refuse to resemble them in
any degree. Let us not crawl and creep about the
world, but remain upright; exuding no moral slime,
but exerting an influence for good on all persons and
institutions with which we are connected; doing
nothing which has a tendency to destroy, but co-
operating with God in the work of saving our fellow
men!

III.

The worm mentioned in the text was not merely
a swift and mean destroyer, but a foul one. The
mention of such a creature in the Scriptures is often
associated with the idea of corruption. In the account
of the manna supplied to the Israelites in the wilderness, *e.g.*, we read that, when it was preserved
until the morning in opposition to the Divine decree
respecting it, "it bred worms and stank." Thus,
too, in a poetic and triumphant anticipation of the
death and burial of the king of Babylon, the Jews
are represented as saying: "The worm is spread
under thee, and the worms cover thee." The Book
of the prophet Isaiah concludes with the prediction:
"They shall go forth, and look upon the carcases
of the men that have transgressed against Me: for
their worm shall not die, neither shall their fire be
quenched; and they shall be an abhorring unto all
flesh." The worm that feeds upon corpses is surely
the very emblem of corruption, and as such our
Saviour employed it when, in speaking of the doom
of sinners, He made mention of a place "where their

worm dieth not, and the fire is not quenched." We
must not fail, therefore, to remark the foulness of the
agency by which the Palmchrist was destroyed, especially as it would seem that God intended the prophet
himself to consider that circumstance.

We have already seen that Jonah desired the destruction of Nineveh in order to the deliverance of
Israel. If Nineveh were not itself destroyed, he was
afraid that Israel would be destroyed by its arms.
We know that what the prophet feared actually came
to pass, but it would not have done so could Israel
have been reclaimed from corruption. The lesson
which the Lord evidently desired the prophet to learn
was that corruption destroys. Nineveh was to have
been destroyed by reason of its corruption; but as
its people had repented, its destruction was to be
averted. It did not, however, follow that Israel was
to be destroyed because Nineveh was spared. If the
repentance of the Ninevites exempted them from
destruction, much more might Jonah hope that the
repentance of his own countrymen would do as much
for them. The prophet would doubtless return to
them resolved upon doing all that might be in his
power to effect their reformation. He could do
nothing better than call upon them to forsake the
corruptions which were, like so many worms, making
their prosperity to wither. We may be sure that
Jonah was a sufficiently apt scholar to learn the
lesson thus taught, and a sufficiently faithful servant
of the Most High to act in accordance with it. But
this lesson is for ourselves, as surely as it was for the
prophet; and I want to proclaim as we approach the
close of the present lecture, and to proclaim it as

emphatically as possible, that to be purified is to be
saved, whereas corruption must issue in destruction.
Rotten houses, rotten trees, rotten races, and rotten
churches are doomed to destruction in the nature of
things. Corrupt persons, also, are thus doomed;
and therefore I entreat you to beware of corrupting
agencies and influences of all kinds.

Beware, *e.g.*, of corrupt creeds. There are many
such creeds abroad, and in these days there is a
spurious charity in relation to those who hold them
which ought to be denounced. It is of unspeakable
importance that men should believe the truth, and
not any lie which may impudently claim to be such.
" We are saved by faith," and faith is merely our
appropriation of the truth. If a man is so deluded
as to reject the truth, and surrender his life to the
influence of a lie, the corrupt creed he thus adopts
will destroy him. You don't see that, perhaps. I
will ask you then to consider the case of a man who
arrives at nightfall where the road on which he has
been walking branches off in two different directions.
One of these branch roads is all that it should be,
whereas the other has a terrible gap in it by reason of
a certain bridge having broken down with the pressure
of a flood in the stream it had previously spanned.
He has been told beforehand of these two roads, but
the testimony he has received respecting them has
been conflicting. He has been truly told that the
right-hand road is the path of safety, and falsely told
that it is the path which leads to destruction. You
see at once that he will be delivered or destroyed
according as he believes the truth or the falsehood he
has heard on the subject. If he believe the truth,

his faith will save him ; whereas if he believe the
falsehood, his superstition will destroy him. A sound
creed saves, and a corrupt one destroys.

Beware also of corrupt customs. There are many
such customs in connection with the business and
pleasure to which men and women are addicted, and
it is difficult to adopt an independent course. But
such a course must be adopted by those who desire
to escape " the corruption that is in the world through
lust." One of our Lord's Apostles says, " Be not
conformed to this world, but be ye transformed ; "
and another, " Love not the world, neither the things
that are in the world." These inspired counsels
require to be repeated very frequently and in all
directions among those who claim to be Christians,
and the repetition should be loud and solemn. Worldliness is only another name for corruption, and
corruption destroys.

Beware, moreover, of corrupt companionship. It
was an inspired sage who penned the caution, " My
son, if sinners entice thee, consent thou not." A
young man may be sometimes observed to conduct
himself in a way that is full of promise, but after a
while it is apparent that the promise is not to be
fulfilled. The bud is blighted, and cannot bloom.
You seek an explanation from those who know more
about the youth than you do, and they attribute his
deterioration to the companions he has chosen. Those
companions are said to be clever enough to have
acquired a complete ascendancy over him, and have
led him astray. Young men and young women,
beware of such companions ! Ye also, who are older,
should beware.

Beware, finally, of the corrupt cravings which consciously arise in your own hearts. Do not yield to them, but resolutely resist and repress them. Do they promise you all manner of enjoyment if you will but gratify them? The enjoyment will at best be brief, and destruction will follow. Are they too strong for you? Then seek the aid of One Who is omnipotent; and be well assured that, by His grace, you shall come off more than conqueror, and obtain by the discipline of conflict a spiritual power which shall enable you to render good service to His blessed cause.

XVI.

THE EAST WIND.

" And it came to pass, when the sun did arise, that God prepared a vehement east wind; and the sun beat upon the head of Jonah, that he fainted, and wished in himself to die, and said, It is better for me to die than to live."—JONAH iv. 8.

SOME of you, my brethren, may be disposed to think that the east wind is not a very suitable subject for meditation on such an occasion as the present. But of this you will be able to judge better at the close of my discourse than its commencement. I may remind you at the outset that the winds are said in the Scriptures to be God's messengers, and that He is said to ride upon the wings of the wind. It is also said that the operation of His Spirit resembles that of the wind: "The wind bloweth where it listeth, and thou hearest the sound thereof, but canst not tell whence it cometh nor whither it goeth: so is every one that is born of the Spirit." Thus spoke Christ to Nicodemus; and we are told by the Evangelist that the descent of the Holy Ghost on the great day of Pentecost was signalised by a sound which suddenly came from heaven, and resembled that of "a rushing mighty wind." It would seem, therefore, that there is no want of dignity or interest in the subject to which attention is now directed;

and you will observe that the particular wind mentioned in the text was one which God " prepared," as He had prepared the great fish, the gourd, and the worm. Its action involved no miracle, but was a providential arrangement which concerned a particular person, viz., Jonah; and the prophet's experience in connection with it, however unpleasant to him, may be considered with advantage by ourselves. "It is an ill wind that blows no one any good;" and the wind described in the text has, so to speak, continued to waft certain messages westward for ages and generations in which we have all reason to be interested. The various points of the description must obtain our particular regard. It was an east wind, a vehement east wind, and a wind that exposed the prophet to the scorching influence of the sun.

I.

It was an east wind which God prepared. There is nothing genial about an east wind, and the injurious effects it is apt to produce are adverted to in the familiar couplet,—

> " When the wind is in the east,
> 'Tis neither good for man nor beast."

Persons who are afflicted with various pulmonary and rheumatic diseases usually find the symptoms of those diseases much aggravated during the prevalence of east winds. I have somewhere read of two eminent judges who were spending some leisure time together in the Scottish Highlands, and were heard by an old shepherd to complain of the bitter east wind that was then blowing. " There is no good in an east

wind," said one. " None at all," said the other ;
and they continued to disparage that wind till they
were interrupted by the shepherd. He assured them
in his broad northern dialect, which I must not
imitate here and now, that there was a great deal of
good in the wind of which they complained ; and in
reply to their questions on the subject, he went on to
say that "it dries the soil, refreshes the ewes, and
blows by the will of God." I do not know to what
extent the learned judges were consoled by the shepherd's address ; but I suspect that he would not have
expressed himself in any such terms had he been as
delicate as they, or been engaged in some other kind
of business. It is true that the east wind blows by
the will of God, but it is not the less injurious on
that account. The earthquake that suddenly destroys
a large city occurs by the will of God, and so does the
tempest that destroys a large vessel. Men should be
submissive to the Divine will; but they are not
expected to rejoice in their exposure to tempests,
earthquakes, and injurious winds, or in any other
dangerous and destructive providential arrangement.
Good men will indeed rejoice that God has the control of all such things ; and that it will ultimately be
well with all who love Him, notwithstanding their
existence and operation ; but they need not affect to
find comfort in the things themselves. At all events,
we find the east wind associated with the idea of
destruction in the Bible itself. One feature in one of
Pharaoh's dreams that Joseph interpreted was the
spectacle of " seven ears, withered, thin, and blasted
with the east wind ; " and there are other allusions
in Scripture to this blasting property of that

wind. Its principal peculiarity is its power to produce drought. Even in this country, as the shepherd said, it dries the soil; but in the regions with which Jonah was concerned, it not only dries the soil, but the fruits of the earth, the plants which produce them, and the bodies of human beings. By putting a stop to perspiration, it occasions much distress to those who are exposed to it; and, to give you an idea of its moisture-exhausting property, I may mention that it has been known to suck out of the leathern bottles of the district a third of the water with which they were filled in the course of a single morning.

To this east wind, then, Jonah was exposed. Being himself on the eastern side of Nineveh, the force of the wind was not broken by the intervention of the city, as it would have been had he been on its opposite side. But however great the prophet's physical discomfort may have been, the distress occasioned him by this wind was chiefly of another nature. The wind was blowing from himself towards Nineveh, and from the longitude of that city to that of his own country; and I cannot doubt that Jonah regarded it as illustrative of the destructive force which would pass from Assyria to the land of Israel. If you think this idea too fanciful, let me ask you to observe the terms in which another Hebrew prophet, who lived after Jonah's time, predicted the invasion and conquest of his country by the Assyrians. Speaking of Ephraim, which was the leading tribe in the kingdom of Israel, and of Samaria, which was its capital, Hosea says: "Though he be fruitful among his brethren, an east wind shall come, the wind of the Lord shall come up from the wilderness, and his spring shall become dry, and his fountain shall be dried up: he shall spoil the treasure of all pleasant vessels. Samaria shall become desolate, for she hath rebelled against her God: they shall fall by the sword: their infants shall be dashed in pieces, and their women with child shall be ripped up." If the prophet Hosea thus represented the Assyrian invasion of Israel as a destructive east wind, is it not probable that the same idea was in the mind of Jonah when actually exposed to such a wind in the neighbourhood of the Assyrian capital? This probability is increased by the circumstance, that as Hosea likened the Assyrian invasion of Ephraim to the operation of a destructive east wind, so did Ezekiel liken the Chaldean invasion of Judah to the same thing. Speaking of Jerusalem under the figure of a vine, the prophet demands, " Shall it not utterly wither when the east wind toucheth it? " and presently adds, " She was plucked up in fury, she was cast down to the ground, and the east wind dried up her fruit." I quote these remarks of later prophets in justice to the memory of Jonah, lest any one reading the account which is given of him in the text should persist in regarding him as a peevish, ill-conditioned, and impatient person, who was put out of sorts and rendered profanely discontented by such a trifle as the blowing of an east wind.

If, then, the Hebrew prophets, men like Jonah, Hosea, and Ezekiel,[1] had the notion that the east wind is illustrative of those providential dispensations which occasion distress and disaster to the professed people of God, why should not we adopt the notion?

[1] Ezek. xvii. 10, and xix. 12. Hosea xiii. 15, 16.

The Church is God's garden, and we desire it to be as fruitful as possible. Does that garden require rain? Then remember that when the land of Israel in Elijah's time had been without rain for more than three years, and the prophet prayed that rain might fall, it was a west wind that brought that blessing in answer to his prayer. An east wind brings drought and barrenness and destruction, but a west wind moisture and fertility and blessing. Is there at this moment less fragrance and fertility in God's garden than there should be? At the call of its Proprietor a healthy influence will be exerted in relation to it, and we may conceive of Him as saying in the language of the sacred Canticle, "Awake, O north wind; and come, thou south! blow upon My garden, that the spices thereof may flow out!" A west wind, a north wind, or a south wind by all means; but who would pray for an east wind in order to the prosperity of God's garden? Nevertheless it may be found in the long run that even an east wind, though trying while it lasted, has contributed something to that prosperity. There are certain influences which are injurious to the Church at present, but which must yet be included among the things which "work together for good to them that love God," seeing that "all things" are said to do that. And it should not be forgotten that the resurrection which took place in Ezekiel's vision was occasioned in part by a wind from the east. The invocation which the prophet was prompted to utter had a certain complete and majestic scope and symmetry of its own: "Thus saith the Lord God, Come from the four winds, O breath, and breathe upon these slain, that they may live." The wind, then, should be welcome, come whence it may, if only it vitalise the Israel of God.

II.

It was not only an east wind, but a vehement east wind, which God is said to have prepared to play a part in connection with the experience of the prophet Jonah. The word rendered "vehement"[1] occurs in no other passage of Scripture, and there has been some doubt among the learned with respect to its precise meaning. The marginal reading, "silent," is by no means a happy one. It would, perhaps, be more correct to render "deafening" than "silent." If regard be had to the root of the word, it should be translated "cutting." With us, however, a cutting east wind is apt to be a cold wind, as it is also on the transatlantic shore in corresponding latitudes. A poet of our own time represents a youth, whose spirit had been deeply stirred by a train of circumstances in which he was interested, as pacing the sands of the New England shore, with his head bared to the east wind, "cooling his heated brow and the fire and fever within him," and saying,

" Welcome, O wind of the east, from the caves of the misty Atlantic !
Blowing o'er fields of dulse and measureless meadows of sea-grass,
Blowing o'er rocky wastes and the gardens and grottoes of ocean !
Lay thy cold, moist hand on my burning forehead, and wrap me
Close in thy garments of mist, to allay the fever within me ! "[2]

There is no doubt, however, that the wind described in the text, whether "cutting" or not, was a hot wind; and on the whole we shall probably be unable to exchange the expression employed in our version for a better representative of the original. If the

[1] חֲרִישִׁ   [2] Longfellow.

sound of the Hebrew word be at all suggestive of its meaning, it was a rushing wind: *Charishi !* But a rushing wind is a vehement wind, and a vehement east wind is by no means an infrequent thing in those regions of the earth with which the prophet Jonah had to do.

It is a terrible thing for travellers to encounter this vehement east wind in the desert. There it appears to be generated, and its course across the waste is indicated by the clouds and columns of sand which go whirling and careering before it. At this signal of its approach the cattle will scamper away at their hardest, and men cast themselves prone to the ground, to allow it to pass over them as harmlessly as possible.

This vehement east wind is a terrible thing also in the pasturages of that part of the world, as it will wrench the tents from the soil to which they are fastened, and inflict injury and death on those beneath them at the time. The last of the messengers who came to Job with the evil tidings recorded in his history, is reported to have said to the patriarch, " Thy sons and thy daughters were eating and drinking wine in their eldest brother's house : and, behold, there came a great wind from the wilderness, and smote the four corners of the house, and it fell upon the young men, and they are dead ; and I only am escaped alone to tell thee."

This vehement east wind is, moreover, a terrible thing at sea. We have seen that the ships of Tarshish were the largest and best appointed vessels of ancient times ; but the Psalmist nevertheless had occasion to pen the sentence, " Thou breakest the

ships of Tarshish with an east wind." It is not improbable that " the great wind " which the Lord sent
out into the sea after Jonah had embarked in one of
those ships of Tarshish was an east wind; and there
is evidence that the tempestuous wind which occasioned the shipwreck of the Apostle Paul and his
fellow-voyagers was from the east.

In such an exposed place as that which Jonah
occupied on the east side of Nineveh, this vehement
east wind is indeed a terrible thing. It dries the
palate of the person assailed by it, makes his tongue
rattle like a piece of dry leather in his mouth, and
tortures him with thirst. Yet it did not merely
occasion Jonah a certain amount of physical discomfort, but conveyed reproof and consolation to the
prophet at the same time. At least, one thinks so.

It was certainly adapted to convey some timely
reproof to Jonah. Was there not a certain corre-
spondence, of which he could scarcely fail to be conscious, between his own mood at the time and that
parching eastern blast? Was he not himself at that
very time an incarnation of that evil wind? Did it
not express and illustrate the temper with which he
was even then scowling down on Nineveh, and must
not some reproof have found its way to his heart as
he perceived that circumstance? Sooner or later, the
contrite consciousness of his own unamiable and
unworthy mood was sure to come home to him as on
the wings of this vehement east wind.

But this wind was even more adapted to convey
consolation to the prophet than reproof. Did he not
remember, think you, that such another wind had
played an important part in connection with the

deliverance of Israel from the bondage of Egypt?
He had read, as we have, that "Moses stretched
forth his rod over the land of Egypt, and the Lord
brought an east wind upon the land all that day, and
all that night; and when it was morning, the east
wind brought the locusts. And the locusts went up
over all the land of Egypt, and rested in all the
coasts of Egypt: very grievous were they; before
them there were no such locusts as they, neither after
them shall be such. For they covered the face of
the whole earth, so that the land was darkened; and
they did eat every herb of the land, and all the fruit
of the trees which the hail had left: and there
remained not any green thing in the trees, or in the
herbs of the field, through all the land of Egypt."
The east wind brought the locusts, but the west
wind took them away again, and as Pharaoh and his
people were not destroyed by this visitation, they
continued to oppress the people of God. Then Moses
stretched forth his hand again. He had previously
stretched forth his rod over the land of Egypt: now
"Moses stretched out his hand over the sea; and
the Lord caused the sea to go back by a strong east
wind all that night, and made the sea dry land, and
the waters were divided." We need not pursue the
history; but if Jonah thought of it as he found
himself exposed to the vehement east wind described
in the text, he would be consoled by the conviction
that it was as easy for the Lord to save His people
from the Assyrians as it had been for Him to save
their fathers from the Egyptians. Let us likewise
be cheered by the consideration that He who brought
the locusts into Egypt and divided the Red Sea by

means of a strong east wind, is still able to wield all
the forces of the universe, and is disposed to exercise
His power in the interests of His people.

III.

It remains to be considered that this east wind was
not only itself very trying to the prophet, but that it
exposed him to the action of the sun. It was intended
to do so, for it was prepared when the sun did arise.
There were still some withered remnants of the gourd
at that time, and even some shrivelled relics of the
booth; and during a calm, sultry day these might
have continued to afford the person cowering beneath
them some little shelter from the sun. But "it came
to pass, when the sun did arise, that God prepared a
vehement east wind; and the sun beat upon the head
of Jonah, that he fainted, and wished in himself to
die." The flimsy remains of both gourd and booth
were gone in a moment with the rush of that mighty
wind, and then the position of the prophet became a
sufficiently serious one. The natives of that country
seek the shade as much as possible during the day
because of the intolerable heat and glare from the
great luminary; and even the Arabs then keep under
their tents, performing their journeys at night. But
Jonah had no tent, no booth, no gourd, no shade or
shelter of any kind, and was so extremely miserable
that he said, "It is better for me to die than to live!"
As you see, there are four particulars in this part of
the narrative before us which claim our attention.

1. The first is that " the sun beat upon the head of
Jonah." It was a comparatively small matter that
the gourd was smitten, but it was far otherwise when

17

the man who had found shelter beneath it was smitten also. The Palmchrist was to the prophet what the frame is to the picture, the casket to the jewel, the lamp to the light, and the shell to the nut. The destruction of the less precious thing would be of little consequence but for the circumstance that its destruction endangers what is of far more value than itself. As we contemplate the condition of Jonah under that burning Oriental sun, we may be reminded of the reasons we have for gratitude to God respecting our own condition and prospects.

We should be thankful for the physical shelter we enjoy from sun and wind and the other adverse influences to which we might be exposed but for the good providence of our Father in heaven. The extremes of heat and cold, drought and wet, would soon undermine the health of even the strongest among us but for the shelter of our homes. It is obvious to remark, therefore, that our gratitude is due to that Divine Being, without Whose sanction those homes could not have been established or maintained.

But there is greater reason than this for gratitude on our part to Him in the circumstance that we enjoy, by His grace, such spiritual shelter as is essential to our welfare. In His interpretation of His own Parable of the Sower, our Blessed Lord likens the tribulation or persecution which is brought upon some of His disciples by their confession of the truth to the destructive heat of the scorching sun. It is happily true that very few, if any, of those who declare their attachment to Christ among ourselves are called upon to experience such tribulation and persecution because of the Word as others have en-

dured before them. The Lord is pleased to shelter
His people in these days, and in this land, from the
deadly heat which destroyed so many of His people
in former times from the face of the earth. There is
some tribulation and persecution because of the Word
even now, but it is not much in comparison with that
which our fathers endured; and, such as it is, it is
more than compensated for by the circumstance that
" God is our refuge and strength, a very present help
in trouble."

Nor is this all. We have seen that a shelter from
the scorching sun is enjoyed in God's providence and
grace. Let me remind you that such shelter is to be
one of our privileges in glory: " The sun shall not
smite thee by day," is an Old Testament promise;
but it acquires the principal interest which belongs
to it from a passage in the New Testament. In
describing the blessedness of the redeemed, one of
the Elders said to the writer of the Apocalypse,
" Neither shall the sun light on them, nor any heat."
Once in heaven, the saints will have no further
experience of trouble; and, in anticipation of the
perfect blessedness which is there to be enjoyed,
should we not be deeply and devoutly thankful here?

2. The next particular in the narrative is that
Jonah fainted. The prophet swooned away; and it
was at once an indication and a mitigation of his
distress that he thus became unconscious. It is impressive evidence of the Divine benevolence that we
are constituted in such a way that extreme suffering
has a tendency to find relief for itself. Martyrs at
the stake, *e.g.*, have behaved in a manner which
plainly showed that the pain occasioned by the fire

had, to a certain extent, effected its own cure by deadening the nerves in the very act of torturing them. The case of Jonah was not thus extreme, but still it exemplified the same merciful law; and we have all reason to rejoice that such a law is in constant operation.

The only other remark which occurs to me just now in relation to the prophet's swoon is that such a swoon was not nearly so bad a thing as the fainting in spirit which is also attributed to him, and of which I shall have to speak presently. Even good men are apt to lose heart with regard to the work in which they are called to engage in the service of their Lord. They are discouraged by its inherent difficulty, or by the opposition it provokes, or by the contempt it excites, or by the manner in which their associates abandon it entirely to them; and they are thus tempted to relinquish it altogether. Is there any way in which such persons can be prevented from fainting outright in this spiritual sense? Yes. If they will duly consider the reflex influence of the work which is attended with so much discouragement upon their own moral nature, and take heed also to what is recorded concerning their Divine Exemplar, there will be no such fainting on their part. Let me rehearse to you certain apostolic expressions, experimental and hortatory, and you will see that I have warrant for saying this: " For which cause we faint not; but though our outward man perish, yet the inward man is renewed day by day. For our light affliction, which is but for a moment, worketh for us a far more exceeding and eternal weight of glory; while we look not at the things which are seen, but

at the things which are not seen : for the things which
are seen are temporal ; but the things which are not
seen are eternal." "For consider Him that endured
such contradiction of sinners against Himself, lest ye
be wearied and faint in your minds."

3. The prophet was not in such a good position as
we may occupy with regard to the encouraging truths
to which attention is thus directed by New Testament
penmen, and he did apparently faint in the more
serious sense of the word. He "wished in himself to
die." He had already prayed for death, but does not
venture to repeat the prayer in so many words. After
all, however, what is prayer ? "Prayer is the soul's
sincere desire, uttered or unexpressed;" and as Jonah
"wished in himself to die," he did virtually pray for
death the second time. It is impossible not to be
reminded by this part of the narrative of what is
recorded in other Scriptures concerning two other
illustrious servants of the Most High, viz., the
Prophet Elijah and the Apostle Paul.

Persecuted by Jezebel, and deeming himself the
only surviving servant of Jehovah, "Elijah went a
day's journey into the wilderness, and came and sat
down under a juniper tree ; and he requested for himself that he might die ; and said, It is enough ; now,
O Lord, take away my life ; for I am not better than
my fathers." Writing to his friends in Philippi, the
Apostle said : "Christ shall be magnified in my body,
whether by life or by death. For to me to live is
Christ, and to die is gain. But if I live in the flesh,
this is the fruit of my labour : yet what I shall choose
I wot not. For I am in a strait betwixt two, having
a desire to depart, and to be with Christ, which is far

better : nevertheless, to abide in the flesh is more needful for you."

Now it is evident that in wishing to die, Jonah felt more like Elijah than Paul. The feeling of the Apostle was a combination of faith and hope and love and joy unspeakable. The feeling of the two prophets was one of disappointment and despondency ; and when the case of either of them is closely considered, a very curious, and yet not uncommon, feature may be detected in it. Jonah, like Elijah, and like many a man in subsequent times, had enough self-importance about him to regard the cause of God as dependent upon his own personal experience. There are many in these days who think that because *they* are not prospering, the cause of God is not prospering. It is by no means unnatural that a man's personal experience should affect his idea of the condition of the entire Church ; and Jonah, in all probability, regarded his own case as typifying that of God's cause ; and, thus regarding it, "wished in himself to die."

4. We need not greatly wonder, then, that, under these circumstances, Jonah repeated his former remark, " It is better for me to die than to live." We know that he was mistaken. It was better for the prophet to live than to die at that time, if only because he was not then in a frame of mind which fitted him for death. He was not able to say, as Simeon said afterwards, " Lord, now lettest Thou Thy servant depart in peace, for mine eyes have seen Thy salvation." Jonah would by no means have departed in peace, had that been the hour of his departure. He would have departed in anxiety and

disappointment rather than in peace. Before he could chant his *Nunc Dimittis*, he would find more work in the service of God. The truth is that Jonah was not the best judge as to whether it was better for him to live or die at that time, and that none of us is called upon to decide as to the best time for his own departure from the present world. All that we know is that, in proportion to the fidelity with which we have consecrated our life to God, will be the advantage we shall acquire in connection with death. As long as we are permitted to remain here, it is better for us to live than to die ; better for ourselves, better for the Church to which we belong, better for the world in which we live ; but it will be better still for us to depart, and to be with Christ, when the appointed time of our departure arrives.

XVII.

JEHOVAH'S APPEAL TO JONAH.

" And God said to Jonah, Doest thou well to be angry for the gourd ? And he said, I do well to be angry, even unto death. Then said the Lord, Thou hast had pity on the gourd, for the which thou hast not laboured, neither madest it grow ; which came up in a night, and perished in a night : and should not I spare Nineveh, that great city, wherein are more than sixscore thousand persons that cannot discern between their right hand and their left hand ; and also much cattle ? "—JONAH iv. 9-11.

PERHAPS there never was a more pathetic appeal addressed to a human being by the Most High than the one recorded in this passage, and all that Jonah had recently experienced was adapted to render him the more susceptible to it.   His mission to Nineveh had been attended with manifold discomfort and distress.   In the ship, in the sea, in the fish, in the city, in the booth, and in his present exposed position, his experience had been abundantly illustrative of his name.   He was Jonah; a Dove, a Mourner, as well as a Messenger of the Most High. His distress was occasioned in part by various circumstances which have been commented upon in previous lectures of this course ; but I suppose it was chiefly occasioned by the action of his own conscience.   He was too good a man for his conscience to permit him

to be at ease when he did wrong, or when he allowed
unworthy feelings to take possession of his breast.
But might not his conscience have slumbered, as did
that of David after his atrocious treatment of Uriah
the Hittite? No. There were too many appeals
directly addressed to it for that. When the captain
came to him with the cry which aroused him from
his physical slumber in the storm, "What meanest
thou, O sleeper? Arise! call upon thy God; if so be
that God will think upon us, that we perish not," we
may be sure that the prophet's conscience was aroused
at the same time. When the crew clustered and
clamoured around him, while the storm raged and the
foam flew and the wind raved and the ship rose
and fell like a cork upon the angry water, there was
no chance of his conscience subsiding into torpor.
Think again of the pointed questions put to him by
the sailors: "Tell us, we pray thee, for whose cause
this evil is upon us? What is thine occupation? and
whence comest thou? What is thy country? and
of what people art thou? . . . Why hast thou done
this? . . . What shall we do unto thee, that the sea
may be calm unto us?" Such questions thus put
must have been so many stabs to such a man, and
yet they cannot have occasioned him such compunc-
tion as those recorded in the text. It is the Lord
who now appeals to him with a power and pathos of
which even we are sensible at this distance of time.
The appeal is a double one. It relates to the feeling
of Jonah respecting the gourd and the forbearance
of Jehovah in relation to Nineveh. It is a question
of propriety; of what was becoming on the part of
the prophet, and on that of the Most High: "Doest

thou well to be grieved for the gourd? . . . and should
not I spare Nineveh?"

I.

The first branch of this Divine appeal relates to
Jonah's then mood. "God said to Jonah, Doest
thou well to be grieved for the gourd?"

1. Observe the point of this appeal. It makes
mention of the gourd; but, before the gourd had
sprung up, a similar appeal had been addressed to the
prophet. No sooner did Jonah perceive that Nineveh
was to be spared than he abandoned himself to the
distress which that perception excited within his
breast. "Then said the Lord, Doest Thou well to
be grieved?" To this question the prophet made no
reply, but proceeded to build his booth, his grief
giving place to gladness as he saw it shaded presently
by the Palmchrist. But the Palmchrist withered,
and another revulsion of feeling occurred in him; and
then the question was not merely what it had been
previously, "Doest thou well to be grieved?" but,
"Doest thou well to be grieved for the gourd?"
You perceive the point. To be grieved for the gourd
was to be grieved for himself. The gourd had been
unconscious of its own usefulness while it lasted, and
of its own destruction as it perished. Grief, therefore, would have been wasted for the gourd, except
for its connection with the prophet himself. It had
been so serviceable to Jonah, however, and its destruction had occasioned him such distress of mind
as well as bodily discomfort, that it was proper for
him to consider how far that distress was becoming
on his part. So "God said to Jonah, Doest thou
well to be grieved for the gourd?"

2. Now remark the compliment involved in this
Divine appeal. God made Jonah judge in his own
case. The sailors had previously done so. They had
said to him, " What shall we do unto thee, that the
sea may be calm unto us ? " But the same compliment is worth more or less according as it is paid
by one party or another ; and by so much as God is
greater than man was the compliment involved in
this appeal superior to the one conveyed by that
of the sailors. " God said to Jonah, Doest thou
well to be grieved for the gourd ? " He might have
addressed His servant in very different terms. He
might have said to him, " Thy present frame of mind
is not to be justified. Thy grief is selfish and excessive. Repent, or I will smite thee with the rod
of Mine anger." But no. The Lord uttered no
reproof and pronounced no sentence. He simply
invited Jonah to pronounce sentence in his own case
with regard to the moral character of the feeling
which then had possession of his breast. I take this
to be evidence that God thought well of Jonah on
the whole, however He might regard some things in
his character and conduct as blameworthy. Nor was
the case of the prophet peculiar in this respect. God
honours all who honour Him in various ways ; and
one way in which He does so is by inviting them to
sit in judgment upon themselves. The compliment
thus conveyed consists in the circumstance that their
capability of thus judging is acknowledged, and their
judicial integrity confided in. To one God says,
" Doest thou well to be grieved at the loss of money
thou hast just sustained ? " To another, " Doest
thou well to transact such and such a business in such

and such a manner?" To another, "Doest thou well to treat this or that neighbour so contemptuously?" To yet another, "Doest thou well to spend thy time thus carelessly on the Lord's Day?" There are hundreds of pointed questions of this kind which the Holy Spirit is continually putting to the consciences of Christ's people, and I assert that they are greatly honoured thereby. I assert, moreover, that such appeals are adapted to deepen the devotion of those to whom they are addressed. If men be treated like dogs, it is no great wonder that they behave like dogs; whereas if they are treated with the respect due to their manhood, they are thereby encouraged to act in a manner which becomes it. God wants His children to behave themselves as such, honourably; and therefore honours them in the way of which I speak and otherwise. The effect is that they respect themselves, and reverence Him, and act accordingly.

3. The response of the prophet to this appeal must not be overlooked. "I do well to be grieved, even unto death." I suppose that this response has been generally regarded as a mere outburst of passion and presumption upon Jonah's part. But was it merely that? Was there nothing in it worthy of so good a man? What about the candour which characterizes it? There are some persons among the professed servants of God who are sadly wanting in this respect. You know how such persons are apt to address the Most High: "O Lord, we are altogether depraved; our best righteousnesses are as filthy rags; our repentance needs to be repented of; we are unworthy of the very least of all the favours Thou hast bestowed

upon us; and, if Thou hadst been swift to mark
iniquity, we had long since been swept away from
the land of the living and the place of hope." Well,
and is not this all true? Yes, it is true; but *they*
are not true who thus express themselves. They
would, indeed, be more truthful if they employed less
truthful language. It would be far better for them to
tell the Most High just what they really feel, instead
of describing themselves as feeling as they ought
to feel. There are doubtless some men who use the
language to which I have called attention with perfect
sincerity, but they are not the persons I have in view.
I speak of those who adopt or imitate the contrite
confessions of better men than themselves, but do
so either with downright hypocrisy or without any
realization of the feelings they sincerely desire to
experience. You may tell me that they cannot feel
as they ought and want to feel before God. Then let
them do as Jonah did. He was unable at the time
to which the text refers to cherish a becoming frame
of mind, but he did not simulate the feeling of which
he was destitute, or disingenuously deny that he was
moved by an opposite feeling. He simply spoke as
he felt when he said, "I do well to be grieved, even
unto death." He said, in effect, that he was not
only deeply distressed by the position in which he
then found himself, but that his distress was justi-
fiable and appropriate. Suppose he had returned a
less candid answer to the Divine appeal. Suppose
he had said, "I do ill to be thus grieved, and I know
well that I should rather rejoice in all the dispensations of Thy providence." He would not have
deceived God by so disingenuous an answer, and he

would have deeply displeased Him. It was better
for the prophet to speak sincerely as he did; and it
will be better for us also to do so as often as we
address the Divine Being. If men approach Him,
or respond to Him, in sincerity and in truth, they
may be full of faults, but they will not be cast out
of His sight; and communion with Him will itself
suffice to correct all their faults in good time.

These remarks have no relation to those descrip-
tions and invocations which we address to the Most
High from time to time in language prepared beforehand for our use. It is certain that many of our
hymns, *e.g.*, are expressive of an exalted piety to
which but few of us have attained; but they ought
not to be disused on that account. It is well understood, or should be, that they are, and are intended
to be, rather descriptive of the feelings we ought to
possess than of those which actually operate within
us. A congregation unites in singing the paraphrastic
verse,—

> " As pants the hart for cooling streams
>   When heated in the chase;
>   So pants my soul, O God, for Thee,
>   And Thy refreshing grace."

It is quite possible that this language expresses the
actual feeling of a few persons among the singers.
But how about the rest? Are we to say that they
must either refrain from singing or incur the charge
of hypocrisy? Not so. To them also the utterance
of this language may be a means of grace; for it not
only shows them how others have felt and they ought
to feel, but is adapted to awaken in themselves that
very longing after God and His Grace of which it

makes such pathetic mention. So is it with other
hymns. If they are sung thoughtlessly, so much the
worse for those who sing them. But if they are sung
solemnly by those who feel, in the very process of
singing, that they express a more exalted piety than
their own, there is neither wrong nor harm in it; for,
on the one hand, there is no intention to deceive;
and, on the other, it is understood that the language
employed is expressive of what should be, and may
be, rather than of what really is.

The prophet Jonah, however, was not one of a
congregation; nor was he invited to recite any form
of devout words prepared for his use beforehand. He
was called upon to reply to a plain question; and
his answer was bound to be at least a candid one,
however unsatisfactory it might be in some other
respects. " God said to Jonah, Doest thou well to
be grieved for the gourd ? And he said, do well to
be grieved, even unto death."

II.

The other branch of this appeal on God's part to
the prophet relates to the propriety of the Divine
procedure with respect to Nineveh : " Then said the
Lord, Thou hast had pity on the gourd . . . and
should not I spare Nineveh ? " There is a correspond-
ence, as a glance at the margin will show, between
the words rendered " pity " and " spare." We may
either read, " Thou hast had pity on the gourd ; and
should not I have pity on Nineveh ? " or " Thou hast
spared the gourd, and should not I spare Nineveh ? "
But on this we need not insist. The thing to observe
at the outset is that God did not contradict the

prophet, but accepted his account of his own mood
as correct.   Also He made Jonah's response to the
appeal concerning himself the ground of a more
important appeal.   It was of some consequence that
the prophet should conduct himself in a becoming
manner, but it was of infinitely greater consequence
that God should do so.   Jonah betraying no consciousness of anything inappropriate on his own part,
the Lord took no measures to convict him of impropriety, but said to him in effect, "If I do not complain
of thee, how canst thou complain of Me?   I do not
complain of thee for deploring the destruction of the
gourd : then why shouldst thou complain of Me for
preventing the destruction of this great city?"   There
is a double contrast presented in this branch of the
appeal, viz., the contrast between Jonah and Jehovah,
and the contrast between the gourd and the city :
"Thou hast had pity on the gourd, and should not I
spare Nineveh?"   Thou, I—the gourd, Nineveh.

1. Let us dwell for a little while on the contrast
thus presented between Jonah and Jehovah.   "Thou
hast had pity, and should not I pity?"   Men are apt
to want their own way, and yet to be displeased with
their Creator for doing as He pleases.   It was thus
with Jonah.   He was displeased because God's will
was at variance with his own, and was yet accomplished.   But if it was becoming on the prophet's
part to pity the Palmchrist, how much more becoming
was it on God's part to pity populous Nineveh!   God
wanted Jonah to be impressed with the propriety of
the Divine procedure, as He wants us all to be impressed with it; and the train of thought thus
suggested is that, if we feel that certain things are

becoming on our own part, so much the more
should we feel that certain things which corre-
spond with them are becoming on that of the Most
High.

It is a becoming thing for the owner of property to
do as he pleases with it.   There are, indeed, certain
obvious qualifications to this proposition which must
be taken into account, but it is broadly expressive of
the truth.   The owner of property may sell it, exchange it for something else, give it away, or destroy
it as he pleases, if his procedure respecting it does
not interfere with the rights of other owners.   Then
why should any one murmur when God does as He
pleases with that which belongs to Himself?   The
gourd was His property, and so was Nineveh.   He
had a right to spare either or both of them, or to
destroy either or both of them ; and who was Jonah,
that he should complain because God destroyed the
plant and spared the city?   The prophet, however,
is by no means the only person who has complained
of God for doing as He pleases with His own.   He
deprives a man of health or wealth, or of some one
who is near and dear to him, and the man murmurs.
But God asks, " Is it not lawful for Me to do what I
will with Mine own ? " and what can any man reply
to such a demand?   You call some things *yours*,
brethren.   Well, they are yours ; *i.e.*, they belong to
you in distinction from any fellow-creatures, but they
belong to God more truly than to yourselves.   You
would have no right, if you had the power, to keep
them when God desires to take them from you ; and
when He deprives you of them, you do wrong to
repine.   But He is the absolute Owner of the universe,

18

and it becomes Him to deal with His possessions precisely as He pleases.

It is becoming on the part of a physician to occasion pain to his patients when he knows that it will be of adequate advantage to them. Then why should any one complain when God afflicts certain of the children of men? Are they not morally diseased? Is He not a more competent Healer than the most skilful and experienced human physician that ever practised? When we see a fellow-man suffering, and at the same time hear him complain that God allows him to be distressed as he is, it might not be amiss to address to him the enquiry, " Wilt thou be made whole?" It might also be suggested to him that, inasmuch as it is becoming in an earthly physician to occasion pain to his patients for their advantage, it cannot be unbecoming in the Divine Physician to adopt precisely the same course.

It is considered an appropriate arrangement when a tutor decides on the order in which his pupils betake themselves to the several studies in which they are expected to engage. It is not for them, but for him, to do this. Then why should any of us complain because certain things in which we are interested are not yet made clear to us by the Divine Teacher? What the Lord Jesus said to His disciples while He was yet with them is what the Most High virtually says to all of us: "I have many things to say unto you, but ye cannot bear them now." It is our wisdom to lay to heart what God has actually revealed and explained to us, awaiting in faith and patience the time when He shall fulfil in the experience of each of us that gracious promise, "What I do thou knowest not now, but thou shalt know here-after."

It is well for parents to withhold some things from their children for the present, which may ultimately be entrusted to them with advantage. " Mother! whose watch is that ? " " Yours, my boy." " Mine! well then, mother, let me have it; let me wear it; let me carry it about! " But the mother intimates to her eager child that he is not to be entrusted with the watch as yet, but must wait till he is older. Is that becoming on the mother's part? Then why should any one complain of our Father in heaven for reserving some things for the future use and enjoyment of His children which they desire to receive at present? God's plan is, school first, and then home; education, discipline, preparation, and then the inheritance.

It becomes a man to choose his own companions, friends, guests and intimates. No one has any right or reason to complain that he is not invited to his house and table, or chosen for his companion. Then why should people complain, as many do, when it is intimated to them that God has chosen certain persons to be His companions, to share His home, and to participate in those exalted pleasures which are only possible in His presence? The very word "election " has scared many persons away from the places of worship they once attended, and there are many preachers who are apparently afraid to pronounce it in their discourses. There is a chosen people of God, however, and the Divine choice in relation to them has been no less appropriate than the other resolutions of the Most High. The perverse disposi-tion to complain of such a choice being exercised on

His part will be dissipated as soon as its subjects come to understand and believe that He invites them, and you, and me, and all who become acquainted with the Gospel, to have fellowship with those whom He is even now preparing for the inheritance of the saints in light.

It is becoming in a magistrate to administer justice without respect of persons. If a person were convicted before a judge of some crime laid to his charge, it would become that judge to punish the criminal, even though a connection of his own. Then what reason had Jonah to murmur, even in spirit, when it appeared probable that his own countrymen would be punished by the Supreme Ruler of nations for their confirmed rebellion against Him? It is true that they were descended from men who had been friends of God; but Abraham himself had asked the question to which but one answer can be given, "Shall not the Judge of all the earth do right?" As surely as God is the Supreme and Righteous Ruler of the world, so surely will He punish those who transgress that law to which we are all subject, either in their own persons, or in the Person of that Divine Substitute of Whom we read in the Gospel of His grace.

2. But let us pass on to the other contrast presented in this appeal. You see how the gourd is contrasted with the city: "Thou hast had pity on the gourd, and should not I spare Nineveh?" Jehovah had already destroyed the gourd which Jonah would have spared; but He purposed to spare Nineveh, and the language He addressed to the prophet vindicated the propriety of His saving the city rather than the plant.

(1) The labour which had been expended on the

city was one reason why it became God to spare it.
No such labour had been expended on the Palmchrist.   Jonah had not laboured for it, nor had any
other person ; but how many had laboured to make
Nineveh what it was !—how long they had laboured,
and how hard ! The houses of "that great city"
must have cost much toil, and the walls around it
more.   Much of the work had doubtless been done
by successive generations of its citizens, but the major
part had probably been done by prisoners and captives and slaves.   Fires had roared and anvils rung ;
pick and spade, axe and saw, crane and hod, had
been busily employed ; barrows, ladders, pulleys,
levers, had been in requisition ; the painter, the sculp-
tor, the decorator, and the architect had furnished
their respective contributions : the result being that
Nineveh was the greatest city in the world.   And
now it appears that God attaches a certain value to
all such labour, for He represented the labour which
had been thus lavished on Nineveh as one reason why
it would become Him to spare that great city.

I suppose that certain persons, who are not compelled by the circumstances of their lot in life to
labour themselves, are apt to look with scorn on
those who are under obligation to do so.   I suppose,
too, that there are others whose condition is such as
to require them to labour for their livelihood, and who
yet contrive to evade their obligations in this respect,
and to live by their wits, as we say.   I suppose, moreover, that many of those who perceive that they must
labour, and who do labour accordingly, are yet sometimes in heaviness of spirit on this account.   Let
such persons know that, if only the work they do is

good and honest in itself, God attaches a value to it
which is not to be measured by its market price.   If
God despises any work which men do, it is either
such as is bad in itself or such as is done badly; the
work which they refrain from doing with all their
might; the work which is unworthy of themselves
and of the wages they receive for it.   But hard and
honest work He values; and the twenty, thirty, forty,
or fifty shillings a week which men get for such
work is not destined to be the whole of their reward.
When all other pay-days have come and gone, a day
shall dawn whereon God will say to many a workman
who has eschewed mere " eye service " like that of
the " men-pleasers," " Well done, good and faithful
servant; enter thou into the joy of thy Lord."

(2) The growth of Nineveh was another reason
why it became God to spare that great city.   Jonah
had not made the gourd to grow.   He had no power
to do so.   All the men in the world are unable to
make a plant grow.   But cities grow as well as
plants; grow in size, power, beauty, wealth, and
prosperity; and men have some power in relation
to such growth as theirs.   It is delegated power, of
course.   It is not power which renders men independent of their Maker in respect of this matter.
" Except the Lord build the house, they labour in
vain that build it: except the Lord keep the city, the
watchman waketh but in vain."   But, as a matter
of fact, the Lord is apt to keep the city which grows
into importance by means of the enterprise and
courage, sagacity and diligence, patience and perse-
verance of its inhabitants.   The wickedness of the
Ninevites had come up before God, but not their

wickedness alone. There were certain mental and moral qualities exercised in the great city to which He is never indifferent. The circumstance that their exercise is conducive to prosperity in the nature of things, is proof enough of that. That that exercise had ensured the growth of Nineveh was a circumstance to which Almighty God Himself was not indifferent.

3. The antiquity of Nineveh rendered it the more becoming on God's part to spare it. The gourd came up in a night, and perished in a night. The poetic expression employed is that it was the son of a night; but of how many nights and days and years and generations was Nineveh the offspring? From the time of Nimrod to that of Jonah it had lasted; and it transcends the power of fancy to imagine the extent and seriousness of the trouble which would surely result from the destruction of such a long-established city. A mighty tree which has been growing for a hundred years cannot be uprooted without a great disturbance of the soil in all directions. A great mercantile establishment cannot be overthrown at the close of a long career of appropriate enterprise without involving many persons in its ruin. But there must have been many such establishments in that great city of which I am speaking. The fall of Nineveh would have been felt to the ends of the earth. The crash connected with its overthrow would have resounded to distant Tarshish. It is pleasant to know that God was as much influenced by this consideration as He was aware of its pertinence. He is, happily, not indifferent to earthly institutions, or to those whose welfare is affected by them, but re-

members how interdependent men are. He never
forgets, however we may forget, that none of us
liveth unto himself, or dieth unto himself, but that
distant lands are affected by what is done here or
there for good or evil, as the case may be.

4. The commodiousness and magnitude of Nineveh
is the last of the reasons assigned in the text for its
being a becoming thing on God's part to spare that
great city. The gourd had sheltered the prophet
from the sun while it lasted, but he was only one
man; whereas there were in Nineveh " more than
six score thousand persons that could not discern
between their right hand and their left hand, and
much cattle." This last reason for sparing the city,
therefore, is really two reasons, having respect to
the children and the cattle contained in it.

*Nineveh afforded shelter to one hundred and twenty
thousand children,* and it would become God to spare
it on *their* account. There were four hundred and
eighty thousand older persons in the city, and it was
on their account that the Lord had sent His servant
to cry against Nineveh, for their wickedness had
come up before Him. But He says nothing of these
seniors and their depravity here. He only speaks of
those who were too young to be responsible for their
own conduct or that of their elders.

God cares for children, and men should take heed
therefore not to treat them unkindly or unjustly.
Woe to those who neglect to make provision for the
physical well-being of the children entrusted to their
care! to those who mislead them by false teaching!
to those who set them an injurious example! to those
who conduct themselves in relation to them as though

Christ had never said, "Suffer little children to come unto Me," and, "Feed My lambs!"

God cares for children, and bereaved parents may therefore be comforted. The little ones removed from your caresses are enfolded in a stronger and more tender parental embrace than your own. They are taken from their earthly home to the better one prepared for them by their Father in heaven. Take to your bereaved heart the consolation which David had in thinking of the child he was not allowed to keep. "I shall go to him, but he shall not return to me," said the inspired mourner; and I would have you reflect that, if that child of sin and shame thus went to God, there is no reason for any anguished father or grief-stricken mother to think with despair of any little child who has been called away from its earthly home before acquiring the capacity to distinguish between the right hand and the left.

God cares for children, and this may assure us that anxiety is needless on our part with respect to those children of heathen parents who die in their infancy. Nineveh was a heathen city, but God had so tender a feeling for the children within its walls as to spare the city for their sake. Where, then, is the man whose heart does not leap to the conclusion that the children of heathen parents who have died in infancy have reaped the benefit of that redemption which Christ effected when He poured out His soul unto death? It was doubtless that the interest of little children in His redemptive work might be rendered the more apparent that He Himself became a little child.

But it was not of the children only that God was

thinking when He resolved to spare the great city in which they dwelt. *It afforded shelter for "much cattle,"* and *that* circumstance rendered it becoming that He should do so. A city which was sixty miles in circumference could easily accommodate "much cattle." It contained extensive pasturages within its walls. From those pasturages, as God spoke to His servant, the mighty cry of the fasting beasts may have ascended again and again; and Jonah would thus be the more emphatically assured that their cry was heeded by the Lord as well as by himself. The cry of the cattle was an *Amen* to the prayer of their penitent masters, and gave some added force and pathos to that prayer. Knowing as He did of the painful and untimely death that would be endured by those poor brutes in the event of the destruction of the city, the Lord was the more disposed to spare it on their account.

Doth God take care for oxen? Yes, and for sheep, and for swine, and for fish, and for birds; "for not a sparrow falleth to the ground without your Father." "His tender mercies are over all His works," and there can be no doubt that He is much displeased with those who inflict needless suffering on the dumb creatures He has placed in subjection to men. They are not so dumb but that they can cry mightily unto Him in a language He can understand; and He will as certainly avenge them on those who subject them to needless torture as He Himself is just and merciful. There are some sportsmen who will find hereafter that the victims of their cruelty have not perished unnoticed by the Universal Judge. There are some unworthy men of science who will find that the vivisection in which they delight cannot be practised with impunity to themselves. There are some men of business who will discover that it was bad policy on their part to allow their cattle to be overworked. It may be worth while for all of us to remember that "blessed are the merciful, for they shall obtain mercy;" that "the merciful man is merciful to his beast;" and that

> " He prayeth best who loveth best
> All things both great and small;
> For the good God who loveth us,
> He made and loveth all."

Jonah made no response to this Divine appeal. It was, in truth, unanswerable. It vindicated the propriety of God's conduct in sparing Nineveh most fully and triumphantly. Jonah could not afterwards dispute that the Lord had acted appropriately in the matter, but might he not have acknowledged that such was the case? He did. He returned to his own country, and wrote this Book which bears his name, in order to testify that all which God had done was worthy of Himself. They, brethren, are but purblind readers of the Book who fail to perceive, however, that it not only magnifies the Name of the Lord as its author intended it to do, but also reflects great honour upon himself. The prophet has by no means flattered himself. He has not attempted even to excuse the perversity he displayed in relation to the mission entrusted to him. Nevertheless, while the world or the Bible endures, the name of Jonah, the son of Amittai, shall be cherished as that of one who cared for his country so much as to run the risk of rejection from the Divine service and favour in his erring but ardent zeal for its welfare ; and cared for the Divine glory so much as to record his own disobedience, disgrace, and discomfiture in his endeavour to promote it. Whatever the prophet had been at the time to which his Book refers, he was a highly sanctified man when he addressed himself to its composition. When we have attained to the lowly and devout disposition which it proves to have characterized Jonah, we shall occupy a higher spiritual level than the majority of God's people do at present. Meanwhile, let us do justice to the prophet's memory, and be thankful for the example he exhibited and the Scripture he has written for our learning !

[1] See Rom. ix. 3. The Prophet Jonah and the Apostle Paul were alike capable of the utmost self-sacrifice on behalf of their compatriots ; but neither the self-sacrifice practised by the Prophet, nor that which was contemplated by the Apostle, was required ; nor could such self-sacrifice have any redemptive efficacy, as the latter knew very well. It was the prerogative of One greater than Jonah or Paul to redeem the true Israel by the sacrifice of Himself; and " Christ hath redeemed us from the curse of the law, being made a curse for us " (Gal. iii. 13).

XVIII.

CHRIST'S REFERENCE TO JONAH.

"Then certain of the Scribes and of the Pharisees answered, saying, Master, we would see a sign from Thee. But He answered and said unto them, An evil and adulterous generation seeketh after a sign; and there shall no sign be given to it, but the sign of the prophet Jonas: for as Jonas was three days and three nights in the whale's belly; so shall the Son of man be three days and three nights in the heart of the earth. The men of Nineveh shall rise in judgment with this generation, and shall condemn it: because they repented at the preaching of Jonas; and, behold, a greater than Jonas is here."—MATTHEW xii. 38-41.

THE Old Testament account of Jonah derives much of its interest and importance from this reference to it on the part of our Blessed Lord. It is, therefore, not to be expected that this series of discourses should be concluded without an attempt on the part of the preacher to secure the attention of his hearers to the remarkable passage now before us. It is true that there has been some occasion to glance at it already, but such glancing is not enough. It ought to be well considered, and due consideration will not be wanting on the part of those who perceive that our Divine Lord evidently reflected while here with much interest on the story of Jonah. There be those who refuse to admit its veracity, and affect to regard it as ridiculous; but Christ repeatedly referred to it in terms which indicated His own acceptance of its historic accuracy. At the commencement of the sixteenth chapter of this Gospel we have an account of a very similar conversation to the one recorded in the text. Here the Scribes and Pharisees are represented as asking a sign from the Lord Jesus, and there the Pharisees and Sadducees are represented as asking the same thing. Here and there our Saviour is recorded to have replied that no sign should be given but that of the prophet Jonah. The remarks to which your attention, brethren, is now invited will relate to the Request and the Reply recorded in this passage of Holy Writ.

I.

You see what manner of request it was which was thus addressed to our Lord. "Master, we would see a sign from Thee."

1. The persons who presented this request were certain of the Scribes and Pharisees. The Scribes were in reputation for their learning, and the Pharisees for their piety ; but the learning of the Scribes did not make them wise unto salvation, and the piety of the Pharisees was pretended. Both Scribes and Pharisees, however, had great influence with the people, and might have done a vast amount of good among them by simply teaching them the truth. But they were like corrupt trees, and their doctrine was corrupt. Christ Himself had just said to them : " O generation of vipers, how can ye, being evil, speak good things? for out of the abundance of the heart the mouth speaketh." This is a very solemn consideration for ourselves. It is important that we should know that even men who, like the Scribes,

have a large acquaintance with the Scriptures; and
men who, like the Pharisees, profess intense devotion
to the Divine service, will exert an evil influence on
those around them, if destitute of genuine piety.
The Scribes and Pharisees taught some truth, no
doubt, but that truth made the error they mingled
with it more mischievous than it would otherwise
have been. The increasing popularity of our Lord
excited their jealousy; and, under the influence of
this passion, they sought to entangle Him in His
talk, to ruin Him in the estimation of the people,
to bring upon Him the vengeance of the Roman
authorities, and to sweep Him by any means from
their own path and presence. It was by their persistent efforts that He was at length condemned to
that cruel death which He actually endured upon the
Cross. On His part, He exposed and denounced
these men in language which is positively startling by
reason of its indignant vehemence and severity. It
was not, however, intemperate language. It was not
in any way disproportioned to the condition of things
which called for it. It was not indicative of any loss
of self-command on His part. It was simply the
language that He deemed suitable to the case of such
men, although it would not be right for us to adopt it
in addressing such. Christ had a power to read the
hearts of men which we do not possess, and did not
affect any of that spurious charity which is so common
in these days. Courtesy is all very well in its own
place, but it is not a proper substitute for faithfulness.
True charity will rebuke rather than flatter the men
whom it perceives to be making great pretensions to
piety without sustaining those pretensions in practice.

He who warns others, and, if necessary, rebukes and exposes them, is not necessarily their foe. "Faithful are the wounds of a friend, but the kisses of an enemy are deceitful."

2. The purport of this request is worthy of remark. "Master, we would see a sign from Thee." Many of the people were at this time disposed to regard Jesus of Nazareth as the long-promised Messiah. Some of them had just raised the question respecting Him, "Is not this the Son of David?" The Pharisees had discountenanced this idea, and our Lord then solemnly warned them of the danger they incurred by doing so. Upon this some of them, in conjunction with certain Scribes, addressed to Him the request now under consideration. In itself there was nothing unreasonable. It was not in the nature of things possible that men should believe in the Messiahship of our Lord until they had received some "sign" of that Messiahship. Nor is it possible for human beings now to exercise the faith in Christ to which they are exhorted in the Gospel, unless they have some kind of evidence that He is worthy of their confidence. It is of little use for preachers to urge and entreat their hearers to believe in Christ unless they also show them, or unless they already know, where some evidence of His trustworthiness can be found. The evidence may be historical, philosophical, experimental, or that which is supplied by the consistent conduct of Christ's professed disciples; but there must be evidence of some kind. Hence, it is not enough for the Christian minister to preach that Christ is divine, that His death was a sacrifice for sin, that He makes successful intercession for all

who come unto God by Him, and that He justly claims the homage of our hearts and lives. These are indeed glorious truths. They cannot be too frequently proclaimed. They cannot be too strongly insisted upon. But it is desirable that they should be not only preached, but proved; and the preacher should be ready to point to the proper evidence that they are worthy of acceptance. But is not the discharge of this duty somewhat difficult? Certainly. There are, indeed, some persons who are never weary of extolling and demanding "the simple Gospel," as they phrase it; and the effect of their language on the subject may be to occasion the unreflective among their auditors to suppose that the ministry of the Gospel is itself a simple matter. But is the Gospel so very simple? Is it not rather profound? Is it not an account of the deep things of God? It may seem a simple thing enough to say, "Come to Christ, and be saved." But to give an adequate account of Christ, to show how men may come to Him, and to persuade them to do so, are not such simple things as some who are themselves but simple persons may suppose. There was, then, upon the face of it something reasonable in this request of the Pharisees and Scribes, "Master, we would see a sign from Thee."

3. But beneath its apparent reasonableness, our Lord had no difficulty in detecting its perverseness. It was a virtual falsehood. It implied that they had seen no sign from Him, whereas He had given them many an one. His miracles were so many wonders and signs. They were signs of His Messiahship, and as such He Himself directed attention to them. We

19

read at the commencement of the foregoing chapter
that "when John had heard in the prison the works
of Christ, he sent two of his disciples, and said unto
Him, Art Thou He that should come, or do we look for
another? Jesus answered and said unto them, Go
and show John again those things which ye do hear
and see : the blind receive their sight and the lame
walk, the lepers are cleansed and the deaf hear, the
dead are raised up and the poor have the gospel
preached to them." One of the signs of His Messiahship had just been given by our Lord when the Scribes
and Pharisees came to Him with this request. "Then
was brought unto Him one possessed with a devil,
blind and dumb; and He healed him, insomuch that
the blind and dumb both spake and saw." The
miracle could not be denied, and could not be explained away; and it suggested to those who witnessed
it precisely what it was intended to suggest, viz., the
Messiahship of the Person who performed it. "All
the people were amazed, and said, Is not this the Son
of David?" But the Pharisees, annoyed at this
result, perversely professed to see in it a sign of
His employment in the service of the devil; and said,
"This fellow doth not cast out devils, but by Beelze-
bub the prince of the devils." Our Lord condescended
to reason with these men in relation to the absurd
account they had given of His conduct, and then
added certain words of solemn warning as to the issue
of such perversity as they displayed. He was interrupted in a manner which showed that some of His
hearers were not beneficially impressed by His
admonition. In impudent disparagement of the sign
He had just both furnished and vindicated, "certain

of the Scribes and of the Pharisees answered, saying, Master, we would see a sign from Thee."

Is there no such perversity as this apparent in our own time? Christ has furnished us with ample evidence that He is able and willing to save and sanctify all who seek His grace, and that He is actually engaged in the work of salvation and sanctification. We have some evidence of this in the Bible, and more in the experience of His people. But this is not enough for some people. They must have additional signs that He is thus engaged, and these signs must not be mere symbols,[1] but instinct with miraculous power. They must be "mighty works" as well as "signs;" and when any one presents himself to such persons as a preacher and teacher of religious truth, about the first thing they say to him is what the Scribes and Pharisees said to our Blessed Lord, "Master, we would see a sign from thee."

Nor will a single sign suffice. There must be at least four signs exhibited before such persons are satisfied, and these may each be denoted by a single word, viz., christening, confirmation, consecration, and censer-swinging. Christening is regarded as a sign that the person subjected to it is there and then and thus regenerated by the grace of God. Confirmation is regarded as a sign that the Holy Ghost is

---

[1] σημεῖον, *semeion*, a sign which is at once an illustration and an attestation. The ordinances of Baptism and the Lord's Supper are signs in a certain sense. They are illustrative of the truths we are taught to associate with them. But they are not attestations of those truths, and therefore they are not "signs" in the peculiar sense which belongs to the expression as used in the text and other parts of the New Testament.

then and there and thus conveyed to the person who
receives the imposition of hands.   The consecration
of the eucharistic elements is regarded as a sign that
they are there and then and thus transformed into
the flesh and blood of the Lord Himself.   Censer-
swinging, or incense-burning, is regarded as a sign
that the prayers of saints, and especially of priests,
are there and then and thus conveyed upwards to
God's throne with a power which results in the communication of His blessing to all on whose behalf
they are presented.

There are doubtless many who attend the places
where these rites are performed who regard then in
no such way.   Of these, some attend merely from
custom, or curiosity, or a relish for the companionship
of those who are near and dear to them, or some other
non-religious motive.   Others regard the rites of which
I speak as so many ancient ceremonies which distinguish the Church to which they belong from other
Churches ; or as having, indeed, a certain archæolo-
gical and æsthetic value, but as entirely destitute of
any spiritual vitality or power to impart it.   Such
persons, happily, constitute a large and influential
class.   They neither object to ecclesiastical symbolism nor rely upon it.   They can distinguish accurately
between the ordinances of Christian Baptism and the
Lord's Supper on the one hand, and the histrionical
performances of a pretended priesthood on the other.
But there are others, alas ! who regard the " signs "
of which I speak as so many " powers," and as such
rely upon them for their own salvation and that of the
Church at large ; and I say that this demand for
additional signs to those which our Lord has furnished

in the miracles of Scripture, and the manifest renewal of our nature in the persons of His disciples, is a perversity akin to that of the Scribes and Pharisees who said to Him in the days of His flesh, " Master, we would see a sign from Thee."

But, brethren, when the votaries of superstition " require a sign," as when their rationalistic neighbours " seek after wisdom," " we preach Christ crucified," and call attention to Him as " Christ the Power of God and the Wisdom of God."

II.

The reply which the Lord Jesus gave to this request of the Scribes and Pharisees was a sufficiently remarkable one. " He answered and said unto them " the things which are recorded in the remainder of the text, giving utterance to the rebuke and the prediction to which our attention is now to be directed.

1. The rebuke addressed to these men was, indeed, a terrible one. " An evil and adulterous generation seeketh after a sign." The stigma thus affixed to the Scribes and Pharisees is to be regarded as literally justified by their conduct. Christ did not merely represent them as in a general way estranged from God and unfaithful to Him, but as addicted to the gross sensuality to which His language points. Sufficient evidence of this may be found in a remarkable narrative related in the Fourth Gospel.[1] Ritualistic religion is quite compatible with gross and habitual moral delinquency; and in the case of these particular men, the guilt which Christ attributed to

---

[1] John viii. 1-11.

them was aggravated by various circumstances of which we are reminded by the passage before us.

It was aggravated, *e.g.*, by their knowledge of Scripture. The scribes were professed students and teachers of Divine truth, and there is no doubt that they were intimately acquainted with the letter of God's Word. Now it will be admitted, that while guilt attaches to all sin, the sinner who is better acquainted with Divine law than his fellow-sinner is the more guilty of the two. On this principle did Christ declare that the servant who knew his lord's will, and did it not, shall be beaten with many stripes; whereas the servant who did things worthy of stripes, without such knowledge, shall be beaten with few stripes. It is a principle we can all appreciate ; and, in view of it, I would urge you, brethren, not only to acquire as extensive an acquaintance with the Scriptures as possible, but also to remember that increased knowledge of God involves a larger responsibility in relation to His service. The Bible contains ample instruction as to what you should do in order to please God; "and if ye know these things, happy are ye if ye do them."

The guilt of the Scribes and Pharisees mentioned in the text was aggravated also by their saintly professions. The word " pharisee " has much the same meaning as our word " puritan," and the Pharisees of our Lord's time made great professions of piety which were not sustained by their practice. He Himself, distinctly, repeatedly, and indignantly accused the members of their order generally of horrible hypocrisy. He likened them to " whited sepulchres, which indeed appear beautiful outward, but are within

full of dead men's bones and of all uncleanness."
Now, no one is likely to dispute that the guilt of a
sinner in other respects is aggravated by his hypocrisy. The man who lives in sin is sufficiently guilty
under any circumstances; but the man who lives in
sin, and yet labours to convince his fellow-men that
he is a very saintly person, is immensely the more
guilty on that account. What, then, shall I say to
any one who is conscious that, notwithstanding his
profession of devotion to God, he is addicted to some
vicious practice which brings him carnal pleasure or
pecuniary profit? Shall I urge him to relinquish
his profession of piety or his practice of vice? The
latter, certainly; and would God that I might prevail
upon him to do so without delay!

The guilt of these men was aggravated, moreover,
by the manner in which they hardened themselves
against the appeals which came to them in the words
and works of the Lord Jesus. He was greater than
Jonah, or than any of the Old Testament prophets,
and yet they refused to repent at His call, or to profit
in any way by the ministry which He exercised under
their very eyes. But great as their religious advantages were, they were not so great as our own; for if
they had the ministry of Christ in the flesh, we have
the ministry of Christ in the spirit. But, of course,
none of us will be any the better for that, but must
be very much the worse, if, notwithstanding his privileges, his life is habitually evil and impure.

2. The Saviour's reply to the request of the Scribes
and Pharisees contains a prediction as well as a
reproach, and the prediction has two branches. One
of them relates to the present dispensation, and the

other to the judgment which is to follow it : one to the sign of the prophet Jonah, and the other to the judicial function of the men of Nineveh.

(1) The former branch of this prediction relates to the sign of the prophet Jonah in connection with the present dispensation of things. " An evil and adulterous generation seeketh after a sign ; and there shall no sign be given to it but the sign of the prophet Jonas : for as Jonas was three days and three nights in the whale's belly, so shall the Son of man be three days and three nights in the heart of the earth." We are in a position to understand this prediction better than the men who heard it fall from the lips of the Lord Jesus, inasmuch as it is now in course of fulfilment. Its meaning would seem to be something like this : As Jonah was a sign to the Ninevites and to his fellow-countrymen who knew of his mission to them, so would Christ be a sign to the nations and to His own countrymen who knew of His mission to them. Jonah preached to the Gentiles, as represented by the people of the greatest Gentile city of his time ; and Christ also would preach to the Gentiles. As Jonah had addressed himself to his own people before his typical burial and resurrection, and to the Gentiles afterwards : so Christ's ante-resurrection ministry was exercised among the Israelites, and His post-resurrection ministry was to be among the nations at large. I have only to remind you, as we arrive at this point, that Christ did undergo the interment here predicted, and that He is engaged in preaching to the nations even now. The Church, which is His body, and which is animated by His Spirit, has long been committed to that work of

calling the nations to repentance, which has already
been attended with such blessed results, and is destined to be crowned with complete success. This
ministry of the risen Christ is the sign of the prophet
Jonah ; and if any one ask of what it is significant,
the answer may be readily given.

The ministry of the risen Christ is a sign that all
He said of Himself before His death was true and
faithful. And what did He say? " I, if I be lifted
up from the earth, will draw all men unto Me. I am
the way, the truth, and the life: no man cometh
unto the Father but by Me. Him that cometh unto
Me I will in no wise cast out. I am the Bread of
Life. If any man thirst, let Him come unto Me and
drink. It is expedient for you that I go away ; for
if I go not away, the Comforter will not come unto
you; but if I depart, I will send Him unto you. I
and My Father are one." These were some of the
things our Lord said of Himself. Moreover, He
showed His disciples "how that He must go unto
Jerusalem, and suffer many things of the elders and
chief priests and scribes, and be killed, and be raised
again the third day." Nevertheless He added that
" the Son of man shall come in the glory of His
Father, with His angels, and then He shall reward
every man according to his works." What if the
Person who said all this of Himself had not been
raised again on the third day ? Or what if it could
not have been proved even that He had been raised
on that day ? He must have been regarded as an
impostor or as a mistaken enthusiast. But He arose
from the dead, " showed Himself alive after His
passion by many infallible proofs," ascended to heaven

in His own Person, returned to earth in the Person of His Spirit, employed the instrumentality of His disciples in the work of calling the nations to repentance, and has made it impossible for those who candidly and carefully consider the facts of the case to doubt that He is the Faithful and True Witness; and that those who confide in His invitations and promises will be saved by His means.

The ministry of the risen Christ is a sign that He desires all classes and conditions of men to profit by His death. As the sign of the prophet Jonas it is exhibited to the Gentiles as well as to the Israelites, and no member of the human race is excluded from the offer of mercy which accompanies Christ's call to repentance. If you are not saved, it is not because He is unable or unwilling to save you, but merely because you reject His offer of salvation.

The ministry of the risen Christ is a sign that men are in so deplorable a condition that they will never seek Him until He has sought and found them. The physician may remain at home to receive such patients as come to consult him, but what about those victims of disease who are much too weak to approach him? If he is to do *them* any good, it is clear that he must go after them; and thus it is with the Physician of souls. After the process of healing has fairly commenced, those who are spiritually diseased may come to Him from time to time as they realise their need of His further help; but in the first instance He must go after them.

The ministry of the risen Christ is a sign of the peculiar power that belongs to His Gospel. As the resources of the universe are at His disposal, we may be certain that He will employ the best means for the accomplishment of the work in which He is engaged. I need not inform you that this is the Gospel, which is declared by an Apostle to be "the power of God unto salvation to every one that believeth." Other things have been tried here and there, but nothing has been found, as nothing can be found, which is so well adapted to save men from all that debases and embitters their condition as the Gospel of the grace of God.

The ministry of the risen Christ is a sign that He still requires the co-operation of His people. "He hath committed unto us the word of reconciliation," and His Gospel is to be proclaimed and otherwise made known by our instrumentality. He might have adopted another plan. He might have commissioned angels to proclaim His grace; as, indeed, an angel did once preach the glad tidings of His advent to the shepherds in the field. It was to men, however, not to angels, that He said as He was about to withdraw His visible Presence from the earth, "Go ye into all the world, and preach My gospel to every creature!" Those who have themselves embraced His Gospel are under obligation to make it known to others. The ministry to which all Christians are called is that of co-operation with Christ Himself in this work of disseminating His truth. Among the young or their elders, to individuals or assemblies, directly and personally or otherwise, you are bound to make the Gospel known.

Finally, the ministry of the risen Christ in the world is a sign of the success which attends His ministry in heaven. He is here in spirit, and there in person; and every sinner rescued from destruction by His earthly ministry is a living proof of the power He has with God on high. If you are a regenerate person, *e.g.*, there is evidence in that circumstance that Christ has made successful intercession on your behalf at God's right hand. If you are not, alas! regenerate, that does but show that you have not yet entrusted your cause to the Great Advocate above. If you will only do so, He will undertake it, will charge you nothing for His services, and will be certain to succeed.

(2) It remains to consider the other branch of the prediction uttered by our Lord in His reply to those who sought a sign from Him. " The men of Nineveh shall rise in judgment with this generation,[1] and shall condemn it : because they repented at the preaching of Jonas ; and, behold, a greater than Jonas is here ! " The Ninevites who repented at Jonah's preaching shall hereafter condemn the Jews who refused to repent at the call of the risen Christ. The circumstance that the Ninevites repented at the preaching of Jonah, leaves the Jewish contemporaries of our Lord without excuse, inasmuch as He was so much more than Jonah ;[2]—so much more than Jonah that, if He had exercised His ministry in Tyre and Sidon, Sodom and Gomorrah, as He did actually exercise it in Bethsaida and Chorazin, Capernaum and Jerusalem, the people of those wicked places would have re-

---

[1] γενεά, *genea* here means race, not time. The *generation* with which the Ninevites are to rise in judgment and are to condemn, consists not of our Lord's contemporaries, but of the nation to which He belonged.

[2] Πλεῖον Ἰωνᾶ ὧδε. There is more than Jonas here.

pented as did the Ninevites in Jonah's time. Alas for those countrymen of Christ, who heard His Gospel from His own lips before His resurrection, and from those of His Apostles afterwards, but still rejected it and Him! Alas for them, but not for them only. Alas for many among ourselves! The risen Jonah went among the Ninevites, and they repented at his preaching; but there are many among ourselves who do not repent, although a greater than Jonah, the risen Christ Himself, is here. I shall not labour to prove the two glorious truths that Christ is greater than Jonah and that Christ is here, but shall conclude with an enumeration of some particulars in which Christ is greater than Jonah, and which are pertinent to the subject that has occupied us so long.

Christ is greater than Jonah in respect of His resurrection. The preaching of Jonah was rendered effective by the resurrection he had experienced; but the resurrection of the Lord was superior to that of the prophet, inasmuch as it was real, final, and attested by many miracles. We have not been eye-witnesses of those miracles, indeed, but have a record of them in the New Testament which the utmost efforts of mockers and sceptics have failed to discredit.

Christ is greater than Jonah in respect of the purport of His preaching. Whereas the prophet did but threaten the Ninevites with destruction, the Lord Jesus invites, and even entreats, all sinful human beings to accept His salvation, as well as warns them of the consequences of rejecting His grace.

Christ is greater than Jonah in respect of His affection for all kinds of men. Jonah desired the deliverance of the Israelites and the destruction of the Ninevites; but Christ desires the salvation of all men.

Christ is greater than Jonah in respect of His more persistent proclamation of the Word of God. When the prophet had passed through Nineveh, and had rehearsed the message entrusted to him in its streets on the one occasion of which we read, his part in relation to that great city and its people was played out; but Christ has been calling men to repentance for ages. He is calling them still. He is calling you at this moment by my voice; and how often has He called you before! Repent, then, I beseech you. Repent while you are yet called to repentance, lest you also be condemned by the men of Nineveh in the judgment to come! "Repent, for the kingdom of heaven is at hand," and "a greater than Jonah is here!"

1981-82 TITLES

0102	Blaikie, W. G.	Heroes of Israel	19.50
0103	Bush, George	Genesis (2 vol.)	29.95
0202	Bush, George	Exodus	22.50
0302	Bush, George	Leviticus	10.50
0401	Bush, George	Numbers	17.75
0501	Cumming, John	The Book of Deuteronomy	16.00
0602	Bush, George	Joshua & Judges (2 vol. in 1)	17.95
2101	MacDonald, James M.	The Book of Ecclesiastes	15.50
2201	Durham, James	An Exposition on the Song of Solomon	17.25
2302	Alexander, Joseph	Isaiah (2 vol.)	29.95
3001	Cripps, Richard S.	A Commentary on the Book of Amos	13.50
3201	Burns, Samuel C.	The Prophet Jonah	11.25
4001	Morison, James	The Gospel According to Matthew	24.95
4102	Morison, James	The Gospel According to Mark	21.00
4403	Stier, Rudolf E.	Words of the Apostles	18.75
4502	Moule, H. C. G.	The Epistle to the Romans	16.25
4802	Brown, John	An Exposition of the Epistle of Paul to the Galatians	16.00
5102	Westcott, F. B.	The Epistle to the Colossians	7.50
5103	Eadie, John	Colossians	10.50
6201	Lias, John J.	The First Epistle of John	15.75
8602	Shedd, W. G. T.	Theological Essays (2 vol. in 1)	26.00
8603	McIntosh, Hugh	Is Christ Infallible and the Bible True?	27.00
9507	Denney, James	The Death of Christ	12.50
9508	Farrar, F. W.	The Life of Christ	24.95
9509	Dalman, Gustav H.	The Words of Christ	13.50
9510	Andrews & Gifford	Man and the Incarnation & The Incarnation (2 vol. in 1)	15.00
9511	Baron, David	Types, Psalms and Prophecies	14.00
9512	Stier, Rudolf E.	Words of the Risen Christ	8.25
9803	Gilpin, Richard	Biblical Demonology: A Treatise on Satan's Temptations	20.00
9804	Andrews, S. J.	Christianity and Anti-Christianity in Their Final Conflict	15.00

TITLES CURRENTLY AVAILABLE

0101	Delitzsch, Franz	A New Commentary on Genesis (2 vol.)	27.75
0201	Murphy, James G.	Commentary on the Book of Exodus	12.75
0301	Kellogg, Samuel H.	The Book of Leviticus	19.00
0901	Blaikie, William G.	The First Book of Samuel	13.50
1001	Blaikie, William G.	The Second Book of Samuel	13.50
1101	Farrar, F. W.	The First Book of Kings	16.75
1201	Farrar, F. W.	The Second Book of Kings	16.75
1701	Raleigh, Alexander	The Book of Esther	9.00
1801	Gibson, Edgar	The Book of Job	9.75
1802	Green, William H.	The Argument of the Book of Job Unfolded	10.75
1901	Dickson, David	A Commentary on the Psalms (2 vol.)	29.25
1902	MacLaren, Alexander	The Psalms (3 vol.)	43.50
2001	Wardlaw, Ralph	Book of Proverbs (2 vol.)	29.95
2301	Kelly, William	An Exposition of the Book of Isaiah	13.25
2401	Orelli, Hans C. von	The Prophecies of Jeremiah	13.50
2601	Fairbairn, Patrick	An Exposition of Ezekiel	16.50
2701	Pusey, Edward B.	Daniel the Prophet	19.50
2702	Tatford, Frederick	Daniel and His Prophecy	8.25
3801	Wright, Charles H. H.	Zechariah and His Prophecies	21.95
4101	Alexander, Joseph	Commentary on the Gospel of Mark	15.25
4201	Kelly, William	The Gospel of Luke	16.95
4301	Brown, John	The Intercessory Prayer of Our Lord Jesus Christ	10.50
4302	Hengstenberg, E. W.	Commentary on the Gospel of John (2 vol.)	34.95
4401	Alexander, Joseph	Commentary on the Acts of the Apostles (2 vol. in 1)	27.50
4402	Gloag, Paton J.	A Critical and Exegetical Commentary on Acts (2 vol.)	27.50
4501	Shedd, W. G. T.	Critical and Doctrinal Commentary on Romans	15.75
4601	Brown, John	The Resurrection of Life	13.25
4602	Edwards, Thomas C.	A Commentary on the First Epistle to the Corinthians	16.25
4801	Ramsay, William	Historical Commentary on the Epistle to the Galatians	15.75
4901	Westcott, Brooke, F.	St. Paul's Epistle to the Ephesians	9.75
5001	Johnstone, Robert	Lectures on the Book of Philippians	16.50
5401	Liddon, H. P.	The First Epistle to Timothy	6.00
5601	Taylor, Thomas	An Exposition of Titus	17.50
5801	Delitzsch, Franz	Commentary on the Epistle to the Hebrews (2 vol.)	29.95
5802	Bruce, A. B.	The Epistle to the Hebrews	15.00
5901	Johnstone, Robert	Lectures on the Epistle of James	14.00
5902	Mayor, Joseph B.	The Epistle of St. James	19.25
6501	Manton, Thomas	An Exposition of the Epistle of Jude	12.00
6601	Trench, Richard C.	Commentary on the Epistles to the Seven Churches	8.50
7001	Orelli, Hans C. von	The Twelve Minor Prophets	13.50
7002	Alford, Dean Henry	The Book of Genesis and Part of the Book of Exodus	11.50
7003	Marbury, Edward	Obadiah and Habakkuk	21.50
7004	Adeney, Walter	The Books of Ezra and Nehemiah	11.50
7101	Mayor, Joseph B.	The Epistle of St. Jude & The Second Epistle of Peter	15.25
7102	Lillie, John	Lectures on the First and Second Epistle of Peter	18.25
7103	Hort, F. J. A. & A. F.	Expository and Exegetical Studies	29.50
7104	Milligan, George	St. Paul's Epistles to the Thessalonians	10.50
7105	Stanley, Arthur P.	Epistles of Paul to the Corinthians	20.95
7106	Moule, H. C. G.	Colossian and Philemon Studies	10.50
7107	Fairbairn, Patrick	The Pastoral Epistles	14.95
8001	Fairweather, William	Background of the Gospels	15.00
8002	Fairweather, William	Background of the Epistles	14.50
8003	Zahn, Theodor	Introduction to the New Testament (3 vol.)	48.00
8004	Bernard, Thomas	The Progress of Doctrine in the New Testament	9.00
8401	Blaikie, William G.	David, King of Israel	14.50
8402	Farrar, F. W.	The Life and Work of St. Paul (2 vol.)	43.95
8601	Shedd, W. G. T.	Dogmatic Theology (4 vol.)	49.50
8701	Shedd, W. G. T.	History of Christian Doctrine (2 vol.)	30.25
8702	Oehler, Gustav	Theology of the Old Testament	20.00
8703	Kurtz, John Henry	Sacrificial Worship of the Old Testament	15.00
8901	Fawcett, John	Christ Precious to those that Believe	9.25
9401	Neal, Daniel	History of the Puritans (3 vol.)	54.95
9402	Warns, Johannes	Baptism	11.50
9501	Schilder, Klass	The Trilogy (3 vol.)	48.00
9502	Liddon, H. P. & Orr, J.	The Birth of Christ	13.95
9503	Bruce, A. B.	The Parables of Christ	12.50
9504	Bruce, A. B.	The Miracles of Christ	17.25
9505	Milligan, William	The Ascension of Christ	12.50
9506	Moule, H. C. & Orr, J.	The Resurrection of Christ	16.95
9801	Liddon, H. P.	The Divinity of our Lord	20.25
9802	Pink, Arthur W.	The Antichrist	10.50
9803	Shedd, W. G. T.	The Doctrine of Endless Punishment	8.25